CHATHAM COLLEGE LIBRARY

Spencer

The Evolution of
an Urban School System

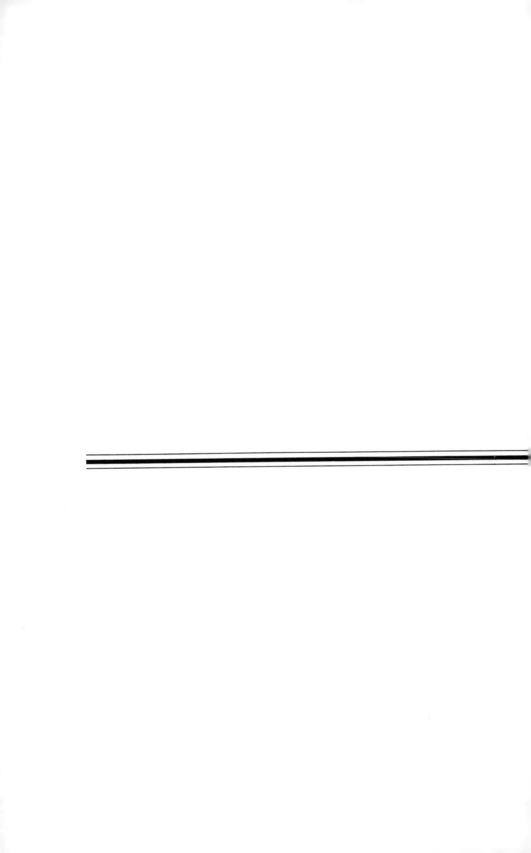

The Evolution of
an Urban School System

New York City, 1750 - 1850

Carl F. Kaestle

Harvard University Press, Cambridge, Massachusetts, 1973

370.193
K118

© Copyright 1973 by the President and Fellows of Harvard College
All rights reserved
Library of Congress Catalog Card Number 72-93950
SBN 674-27175-0
Printed in the United States of America

*To My Mother
and the Memory of
My Father*

PREFACE

This book is not an omnibus history of education in New York City from 1750 to 1850. It is an attempt to explain when, why, and how the schools became organized into a system. The focus is therefore on institutions of formal instruction, and the discussion includes informal educational settings only in relation to schooling. Because it begins in the late colonial period, when schools were not responsible for the whole education of the child, this study seeks to find out what the schools did not do, as well as what they did do.

As a graduate student at Harvard, I was in Professor Bernard Bailyn's seminar, where he once told us that the basic task of any historian is to explain how we got from "A" to "B." The chronological span of this book grew out of that simple piece of advice. The central, transforming, institutional development in the history of American education was the creation of a common, uniform school system in the nineteenth century. However, the historians who have studied this development have not generally explained how we got from "A" to "B," that is, from a society without systematic schooling to a society with organized, universal schooling, because they started in the middle of the story rather than at the beginning. As Bailyn pointed out in his own very important book, *Education in the Forming of American Society,* earlier historians of education did not pay much attention to colonial society, precisely because it *had* no free, obligatory, "public" schools, and these historians were seeking in the past the prototypes of the institutions they knew in the present.[1] Bailyn's essay, in contrast, sketched a fundamental shift in colonial education, from a reliance on informal agencies like the family, the church, and apprenticeship, to a predominant reliance on deliberate schooling. This study of New York City continues, in a sense, the story of that shift. It traces, in an urban setting, a further stage in the transformation: the consolidation of schools into a single, articulated, hierarchical system which was amenable to uniform policy decisions. It seeks to identify the forces that led to this systematization.

Among the many purposes of education in society, four of the most essential are the transmission of literacy, occupational skills, cultural traditions, and moral attitudes. When people feel that informal institutions are failing to perform any of these four functions adequately, their concern to expand formal instruction increases. For example, the desire for an informed public can create pressure for wide literacy training. Also, as the occupational structure becomes more complex, schools may deal more directly with occupational training, becoming the arbiter between the economy and the future worker. Third, as immigration and consolidation bring together a culturally diverse population, public leaders strive to create a unifying culture through schooling. Fourth, as these same cultural differences strain consensus about behavior, and economic stratification increases crime and indigence, the pressure for explicit moral instruction increases. Once these processes have begun, another factor enters the picture. Increases in the mere numbers of schools and children have qualitative effects on the process of schooling, independent of social concerns.

Each of these forces has played a role in the creation of the American public school system, but the first two were weaker than has been believed traditionally. Literacy training for political participation and occupational training for particular jobs were not prominent in the minds of those who created New York City's school system. As this study will show, that system grew out of an attempt to provide free elementary schooling for poor children, and the intent was moral and cultural. It was an institutional response to the threat of social fragmentation arising from population growth,

---

1. Bernard Bailyn, *Education in the Forming of American Society; Needs and Opportunities for Study* (Chapel Hill, University of North Carolina Press, 1960).

poverty, and immigration, forces which were felt earliest and most intensely in our Eastern coastal cities. In New York City, the effect of these forces is particularly clear, for two reasons. First, the potential pressures for schooling were relatively weak in eighteenth-century New York, resulting in discontinuous, nonregulated educational arrangements; second, in contrast, the city's preeminent growth in the nineteenth century created severe social pressures, resulting in the development of a fully articulated school system which displayed by 1850 many of the characteristics we associate today with urban school bureaucracies.

The first two chapters of this study describe the role of schools in late colonial New York and at the turn of the eighteenth century. The remaining four chapters assess the socioeconomic, moral, cultural, and bureaucratic developments which influenced the systematization of schooling in the period 1800 to 1850. These later chapters are thus organized around substantive themes rather than a chronological narrative. The events in the educational history of early New York are, however, reiterated in a few appropriate places, in the hope that occasional repetition will avoid confusion.

My research on this subject took me to a great number of archives, municipal bureaus, and churches in New York City, where I received valuable assistance from the custodians of the city's recorded past. All deserve my thanks; a few require special mention. I am grateful to James Katsaros, administrator of the New York Municipal Archives, for shepherding me through the maze of the city's repositories. At the New-York Historical Society, where I did the bulk of the work, Arthur Breton, the Society's former archivist, provided expert advice and service far beyond my expectations, as well as sponsoring luncheon sessions among researchers which made my days there all the more enjoyable.

In the writing of the work, and in my general education as a historian, two men stand out. Lawrence Cremin of Teachers College, Columbia University, first interested me in the history of education and has been a friend and an inspiration ever since. He has read and commented generously on various drafts of this book. My greatest debt is to Bernard Bailyn of Harvard, who directed this study as a doctoral dissertation. In everything, from his lectures and published work, to his constant probing of my own ideas, to his indispensable editorial advice, he has made the writing of this book, and my graduate education in general, as delightful as it was demanding. My friend Robert Church, of Northwestern University, read the entire manuscript and has discussed my ideas at various stages, to my benefit; and Theodore Sizer, formerly the Dean of the Harvard Graduate School of Education, made valuable suggestions as a reader of the dissertation.

Thanks are also due to the Manuscript Division, The New York Public Library, Astor, Lenox and Tilden Foundations; the Municipal Archives and Records Center of the City of New York; the New-York Historical Society; Harvard University Archives; the Columbiana Collection and the DeWitt Clinton Papers, Columbia University; and the Teachers College Press, Columbia University, for permission to use or quote from unpublished materials.

Portions of Chapter Two of the present work appeared in the *History of Education Quarterly* (Winter 1972) and are used here with the editors' kind permission.

A year as a Visiting Fellow at the Shelby Cullom Davis Center for Historical Studies at Princeton University provided both the time and the resources for revising the manuscript. I am happy to record here my earnest gratitude to the Davis Center and its director, Lawrence Stone. Members of the Davis Center Seminar also read and criticized parts of the manuscript. Mrs. Dorothy D. White typed the final draft with superb accuracy and good cheer. Meanwhile, my wife, Elizabeth MacKenzie Kaestle, has buoyed me, bolstered me, fed me, and loved me, as well as performing countless tasks having to do with the study itself over the past four years. My debt to my parents, whose broad tolerance and constant encouragement have been a blessing, is recorded in the dedication.

C. F. K.

Princeton
May 1972

CONTENTS

TABLES

The Evolution of
an Urban School System

ABBREVIATIONS

Advertiser	*New York Daily Advertiser*
Amer. Mag.	*American Magazine*
Argus	*The Argus, & Greenleaf's New Daily Advertiser*
A.I.C.P.	New York Association for Improving the Condition of the Poor
CU	Columbia University
Diary	*The Diary, or, Loudon's Register*
FSS	The Free School Society of the City of New York
Gaz.	*New York Gazette or Weekly Mercury*
NYHS	New-York Historical Society
N.Y. Mag.	*New York Magazine, or, Literary Repository*
NYMA	New York Municipal Archives
NYPL	New York Public Library
NYSL	New York State Library, Albany
Merc.	*New York Mercury*
M.C.C.	*Minutes of the Common Council of the City of New York, 1784–1831,* ed., Arthur E. Peterson, 21 vols. (New York, 1917, 1930)
PSS	Public School Society of the City of New York

CHAPTER ONE

Schooling in
Late Colonial
New York City,
1750–1785

During the long course of the colonial period, education had become increasingly more self-conscious and deliberate, which led to more emphasis on schooling.[1] However, the process of schooling was still informal and discontinuous. There was no hierarchy of schooling levels, and there were no explicit connections among schools at the same level. The schools of colonial New York City had not arisen from public legislation. Schooling was not amenable to public policy-making, except for the rudimentary requirement that apprentices receive some instruction. Schools did not have a monopoly on the skills they taught. Although the adequacy of the family and the church was sometimes questioned, they still bore the primary responsibility for moral education. Many children could learn the three R's at home, accounting could be learned in the counting house, and navigation at sea. Each man decided how much, when, and what kind of schooling he needed or could afford for his children.

MODES OF ELEMENTARY INSTRUCTION

Most children, it seems, learned to read at home in the eighteenth century. Families combined religious and literary education by the

1. Bernard Bailyn, *Education in the Forming of American Society; Needs and Opportunities for Study* (Chapel Hill, University of North Carolina Press, 1960), pp. 21–22; Lawrence A. Cremin, *American Education: The Colonial Experience, 1607–1783* (New York, Harper and Row, 1970), pp. 544–546, and *passim.*

fireside. John Pintard recalled, "My uncle had in his family a copy of Beausobre's French Bible—every page of which contained a picture of the Bible History. Brought up in the strictest manner, he would allow us to read no Book but the Bible."[2] Stephen Allen, born in 1767, was the son of a carpenter. His father died, and at the age of seven Stephen was sent to live with an uncle, James Giles, a New York schoolmaster. Stephen later recalled that Giles "would frequently insist on my reading to him. And although I barely knew how to read at that early age, much less comprehend what I read, I nevertheless received some benefit from the operation."[3] Both of these boys had received classroom instruction by the time they were ten, Pintard in a Long Island grammar school, and the less affluent Allen in the day schools of New York; but their first instruction was at home, much earlier.

Other children first learned to read in inexpensive reading schools, like the "dame" schools common in England.[4] Denominational charity schools also offered instruction in the three R's. The Anglican, Dutch, and Jewish congregations hired teachers to give rudimentary education, both religious and literary, to the children of the poor of their congregations. A "common education," as it was then conceived, could be acquired in about three years, after which charity school boys were to be apprenticed and girls usually put out to service.[5] It seems that no more than 130 children of the poor were being instructed in charity schools in any given year during the period, although the white child population (ages 0

2. John Pintard, Reminiscences, Box 3, Pintard Papers, NYHS, p. 97.

3. Stephen Allen, Memoirs, 1767–1852, typescript, ed. John C. Travis (New York, 1927), at NYHS.

4. Because there was no reason to advertise such small neighborhood schools in the newspapers, they are not very visible historically. In the suburb of Greenwich Lady Warren established a neighborhood school, and in the city Mrs. Ann Rogers found young girls to teach without advertising in the papers. These schools may have been typical of many. I. N. Phelps Stokes, *Iconography of Manhattan Island,* 6 vols. (New York, R. H. Dodd, 1895–1928, dates refer to his "Chronology"), general heading for 1740; Philip L. White, *The Beekmans of New York in Politics and Commerce, 1647–1877* (New York, NYHS, 1956), p. 482. On English dame schools, see M. G. Jones, *The Charity School Movement* (Cambridge, Cambridge University Press, 1938), p. 33.

5. William H. Kilpatrick, *The Dutch Schools of New Netherland and Colonial New York* (Washington, United States Bureau of Education, Bulletin No. 12, 1912), p. 158.

to 16) increased from about 5700 to 8000.[6] Thus, it may be conjectured, the potential white enrollment for common education from all income groups in any year (the common education cohort) would be approximately ³⁄₁₆ of the white population under sixteen years old. In 1771, then, if every white child was to receive a three-year elementary education, about 1400 children would have received instruction that year, either at home or at school. The charity schools were then enrolling about 130 children, or 9 percent of that cohort. If New York had had only a small class of poor children, then, the charity schools, along with the evening schools for apprentices, would have served well those who could not pay for instruction. Actually, as contemporary accounts attest, there was probably a more substantial lower group whose budgets were consumed by necessities more critical than schooling.[7]

The number of teachers in colonial New York reflects the fact that education and schooling were not synonymous. The highest number of paid schoolmasters identified in any given year before the Revolution is about twenty-five, and some of those were engaged in teaching higher subjects. They could account for only a fraction of the instruction in the three R's.[8] Yet the evidence is fragmentary;

6. William W. Kemp, *The Support of Schools in Colonial New York by the Society for the Propagation of the Gospel in Foreign Parts* (New York, Teachers College Contributions to Education, No. 56, 1913), p. 106 (cited hereafter as *SPG*); Henry W. Dunshee, *History of the School of the Reformed Protestant Dutch Church in the City of New York, 1633–1883* (New York, 2nd ed., 1883), pp. xv, 46–47, 50; David and Tamar de Sola Pool, *An Old Truth in the New World; Portrait of Shearith Israel, 1654–1954* (New York, Columbia University Press, 1955), p. 212. The white population under 16 was 5710 in 1749, 7499 in 1771, and 8620 in 1786. Evarts B. Greene and Virginia D. Harrington, *American Population before the Federal Census of 1790* (New York, Columbia University Press, 1932), pp. 100, 102, 104. There were also 1016 black children in 1749, most of whom were slaves. Negro education was entirely segregated throughout the period covered by this study and thus requires separate attention beyond the scope of the subject treated here.

7. Jackson T. Main, *The Social Structure of Revolutionary America* (Princeton, Princeton University Press, 1965), pp. 158, 278–279.

8. A list of teachers was developed from the following sources: Robert F. Seybolt, "New York Colonial Schoolmasters," in Thomas Finegan, *Free Schools* . . . (Albany, *Annual Report of the University of the State of New York for 1919*, vol. I, 1921), pp. 653–669; Seybolt, "The Evening Schools of Colonial New York," *ibid.*, pp. 630–652; Seybolt, *Apprenticeship and Apprenticeship Education in Colonial New England and New York* (New York, Teachers College Contributions to Education, No. 85, 1917); Carl Bridenbaugh, *Cities in Revolt: Urban Life in America, 1743–1776* (New York, Alfred Knopf, 1955); Dunshee, *Dutch Church;* Kemp, *SPG;* Kilpatrick, *Dutch*

many teachers are probably lost to history.[9] It is clear from extant receipt books that tuition charges, at eight to ten shillings per quarter, were low enough to be within the means of many workers of the middling sort. For example, eight shillings was a day's wages for a ship's carpenter in 1758.[10] Furthermore, if the home instruction described by Pintard and Allen was general practice, the literacy rate would not depend on the schools.

Although the literacy rate in colonial New York is unknown, the fact that over 80 percent of those leaving wills could sign their names suggests, indirectly at least, that literacy was quite general

Schools; Burgher Right and Freeman Lists for Colonial New York City (NYHS, *Collections,* vol. 18, 1885); Henry B. Weiss, "The Writing Masters & Ink Manufacturers of New York City, 1737–1820," NYPL *Bulletin* 56 (August 1952), 382–391; Oscar T. Barck, Jr., *New York City During the War for Independence* (New York, Columbia University Press, 1931); Stokes, *Iconography; Abstracts of Wills on File in the Surrogate's Office, City of New York,* 17 vols. (NYHS, *Collections* 25–41, 1892–1908), cited hereafter as *Wills;* also, MS family records and selected newspapers. See Cremin, *Colonial Experience,* pp. 537–540.

9. Some masters advertised only when they opened their school or moved to a new location; others, known by word of mouth, never advertised at all. Isaac Skilman opened a school in 1767 that went unrecorded but for Beekman's account book. White, *Beekmans of New York,* p. 480. Nicholas Bayard paid Jane and Blanche Beau between £50 and £60 a year each for his daughters' board at a school that never advertised. Nicholas Bayard, Receipt Book, 1762–1772, NYHS. From these examples it seems probable that there were many more teachers and schools than we shall ever know about.

10. John Avery's school at Huntington, 1763–1779, 7 s. per quarter tuition. Avery, Ledgers, NYHS. Stephen Bayard's tuition, 1770, £6-14, or £1-13-6 per quarter, probably private, with Stephen Voorhees. Nicholas Bayard, Receipt Book, 1762–1772, NYHS. Schooling for three Beekman boys with Thomas Johnson, 1764–65, £1-11-0 per quarter each; schooling for three Beekman boys with Isaac Skilman, 1767, £12-14-0 for six months, i.e., about £2-2-0 per quarter each; Catharine Beekman, private tutoring by James Lesley, 1771, £3-1-6 for nine months, or £1-0-6 per quarter. White, *Beekmans of New York,* pp. 481–483. Shearith Israel school, paying students at 8 s. per quarter in 1733. Pool, *Shearith Israel,* p. 212. John Van Beverhoudt, Jr., schooling with Richard Smith, 1751, 10 s. per quarter. Van Beverhoudt Family Papers, bills and receipts, 1750–1764, NYHS. These few examples suggest that tuition for public day school was often available at 10 s. per quarter during this period, although it could cost as much as £2. A few suggestive, though very sketchy, examples of wages are: ship carpenters in New York, 1758, 8 s. per day; journeyman tailors, Philadelphia, 1771, 4 s. per day. Carl Bridenbaugh, *The Colonial Craftsman* (New York, New York University Press, 1950), pp. 145, 146. Mariners, average, £2-8 per month; carpenters 2/6 to 4 s. per day. Main, *Social Structure,* pp. 74–77. Further information on colonial wages is given in Bureau of Labor Statistics, *History of Wages in the United States from Colonial Times to 1928* (Washington, United States Bureau of Labor, rev. ed., 1934).

in the middle reaches of society and above.[11] The best generalization possible is that New York, like other American towns of the Revolutionary period, had a high literacy rate relative to other places in the world, and that literacy did not depend primarily upon schools.

The reason it is difficult to estimate who schooled whom, for how long, in late colonial New York City is that schooling was haphazard, and arrangements were often temporary. Students came and went, enrolled in schools and changed their minds. They went to different schoolmasters for different subjects and quit school often to change masters, to work, or to travel. In 1767 a teacher announced lessons in both the morning and the evening in order to "suit some of both Sexes, who attend other Places of Education at different Periods, for other purposes." Stephen Allen's mother entered him in three different schools in 1777–78 because he didn't get along with the masters.[12] People in all ranks of society gained their education in a patchwork, rather than a pattern, of teachers and experiences.

THE TEACHING TRADE

Schooling was bought in an open market, and the teachers, like the students, were unregulated and transient. Competing schoolmasters offered to teach anything from the ABC's to astronomy, at all times of the day, to students of widely varying ages. Schoolteaching was more a trade than a profession; indeed, it was even less organized than most trades, for there were no standard qualifications or preparation. Many schoolmasters taught intermittently or part-time, combining it with a more reliable means of livelihood. Thomas Carroll advertised that he would teach both evening and day classes, but added that if unsuccessful he would "accept of any employment in the writing Way, settling Merchants Accounts, drawing Plans etc., or of a decent Place in the Country." Carroll was not the only one to combine teaching with writing; a man with a fair hand had a saleable skill in a town busy with legal and commercial matters. Another teacher, Henry Peckwell, announced that "gentlemen of the law, merchants and others, that have writing to put out, may be assured of its being executed with

11. Cremin, *Colonial Experience,* p. 540; see also *ibid.,* pp. 546–549.
12. *Gaz.,* April 16, 1767, in Seybolt, "Evening Schools," p. 636; Allen, Letters, pp. 21–23.

the utmost care and dispatch."[13] Peckwell and John Hutchins, another schoolmaster, witnessed so many wills, especially those of men in lower status occupations, that it seems probable they were called in to write them.[14] Schoolmasters acted as neighborhood clerks, adding to their income with copying and transcribing tasks. There were other occupational combinations. Among New York's teachers were found an engraver, a jeweller, a flax-dresser, an almanac writer, and several ministers.[15]

There was no hierarchy or upward mobility in the teaching occupation, and most teachers advertised only for a year or two. The transience of teachers, their dual occupations, and the lack of hierarchical promotion in the trade further illumine the role of schooling in colonial society. Teaching was only part of a man's life, as schooling was for the child. Teaching was not a very permanent, nor a very specialized, occupational category. Parents and apprentices' masters increasingly chose to pay for schooling rather than teach the children themselves, but it was still a service that almost any literate member of the community could provide if he had a mind to. In colonial New York there was little concept of the teacher as an expert pedagogue or the school as a unique place to learn.

Not only the teachers were transient; the school as an institution had little stability throughout the late colonial period. Indeed, a "school" in most cases was simply a person who taught, and when he stopped, the "school" stopped. The only collective efforts in schooling in this period were the three denominational charity schools and King's College. Efforts to establish continuing schools with group sponsorship generally failed for lack of sustained interest. The last effort to operate a town grammar school had ended in 1738.[16] Wealthy New Yorkers seemed content for the most part to send their boys away from the city to prepare for college.[17] And

13. *Merc.,* May 6, 1765 (for Carroll), April 22, 1771 (for Peckwell).

14. For Peckwell, see *Wills,* VI, 106, 307, VII, 56, 304; for Hutchins, IV, 413, VI, 147, 266, 414, VII, 33, 433, VIII, 12, 17.

15. Weiss, "Writing Masters," p. 386; Dunshee, *Dutch Church,* p. 62; Barck, *New York in the Revolution,* p. 166; *Wills,* IX, 299; Stokes, *Iconography,* July 8, 1762.

16. David M. Schneider, *The History of Public Welfare in New York State, 1609–1866* (Chicago, University of Chicago Press, 1938), p. 78.

17. For examples, see Pintard, Reminiscences, p. 43, and John Avery, Ledgers, 1766–1775, NYHS.

as for schools offering rudiments and nonacademic specialties like bookkeeping and navigation, the lack of public effort does not indicate a lack of schools so much as a lack of controversy about them. The little independent pay schools have been overlooked historically because they were transient, unorganized, and uncontroversial. They were uncontroversial because common schooling in colonial New York City had a tenuous relationship both with job training and with the inculcation of community values. New Yorkers' collective inattention to schooling is not sufficiently explained by saying that a laudable Dutch tradition of municipal schooling was superseded by an English laissez-faire tradition, or by noting the bustling, commercial nature of New York City, implying that New Yorkers were somehow more venal than their neighbors in Boston or Philadelphia.[18] The reasons for the lack of systematic public effort in schooling in late colonial New York will be found by examining the relationship of schooling to occupations and to cultural assimilation.

OCCUPATIONAL TRAINING AND THE COMMON MAN

In the twentieth century, schools have become largely responsible for the occupational choices and at least some of the occupational training of youths in our complex economy. The eighteenth century differed in two ways: the choices were fewer and schools had less to do with preparation for work. This was especially true of the poor. Until the Revolution the Anglican churchwardens were overseers of the poor in New York and had the power to bind out as apprentices any children dependent on the public purse. The indentures were sometimes annulled if a child was maltreated, but not if he simply preferred a different calling. These children, therefore, had little choice.[19] All youths, however, faced a simpler occupational structure than today. A survey of 297 trade indentures

18. Kilpatrick, *Dutch Schools,* p. 159; Bridenbaugh, *Cities in Revolt,* p. 174; Louis B. Wright, *The Cultural Life of the American Colonies, 1607–1763* (New York, Harper, 1957), pp. 106–107; Van Wyck Brooks, *The World of Washington Irving* (New York, E. P. Dutton & Co., 1944), p. 36; T. E. V. Smith, *The City of New York in the Year of Washington's Inauguration* (New York, 1889), p. 189.
19. Schneider, *Public Welfare,* pp. 76–77; Seybolt, *Apprenticeship,* pp. 74, 80–82.

from the early eighteenth century reveals only 44 different trades, including merchant, lawyer, and surgeon. The 1786 *New York Directory* lists 133 different callings. In contrast, the United States Employment Service listed 22,028 American occupational designations in 1955.[20]

Not only were there fewer occupations to choose from in eighteenth-century New York City, but social and economic factors restricted choices further. The working-class boy was often restricted from occupations that required expensive training and equipment. Some apprenticeships required a fee; other trades required expensive tools when the boy finished his training. Those requiring little equipment, such as cordwaining and coopering, tended to pay less.[21] Wills in which fathers leave tools to their sons suggest the advantages of apprenticing in one's own family and following the father's trade. Abraham Fincher, a joiner, gave his son all his carpentry tools, a large Bible, and his wearing apparel; Benjamin Jarvis left his boy James all the tools of the hatter's trade; and Joseph Liddell, a pewterer, gave his son his brass molds and pewtering tools. The wealthy William Walton provided that his slaves be freed after his wife's death, with £14 a year for maintenance and £25 when of age "to purchase tools to enable them to carry on a trade."[22]

Apprenticeship was the basic mechanism for career training; schooling, if any, was a preliminary for literacy and a supplement in fields like accounting. A boy's occupational choice depended upon a number of factors: his father's trade, income, or acquaintances, the availability of work (more shoemakers were needed than coachmakers), and his own initiative. Few jobs had prerequisites in terms of formal schooling. In everything from milling flour to

---

20. Samuel McKee, *Labor in Colonial New York, 1664–1776* (New York, Columbia University Press, 1935), pp. 83–85; David Franks, *New York Directory for 1786 . . .* (New York, 1786); *Dictionary of Occupational Titles; Supplement* (Washington, United States Employment Service, 1955), p. xi. In counting the occupations for 1786, current census practice was followed: duplicate titles, like druggist and apothecary, counted as one, but special subgroups, like carpenter and ship's carpenter, counted as two. The 1786 figure is low, however, for there were obvious subdivisions not specified. The only mariners listed were captains; only six types of merchant were specified. Nevertheless, the contrast is clear.

21. Main, *Social Structure,* p. 80.

22. *Wills,* IV, 369 (1751); V, 125 (1756); IV, 467–468 (1754); VII, 180 (1768); see also VI, 375–376, carpenter's tools; VI, 414, sadler's tools; VIII, 375–376, cordwainer's tools, and VII, 316–317, printer's tools.

doctoring, entrance to occupations depended upon apprenticeship. The way to occupational success for the ordinary man was not through the schoolhouse door, but in the workshop of a skilled craftsman.

Of the institutions that educated New York's children, then, apprenticeship, and thus in many cases the family, played the major role in occupational choice and training. This, rather than the supplementary schooling that indentures customarily guaranteed, is the educational significance of apprenticeship. Training in the three R's may have been helpful for some, but a boy could not learn much at evening school three months a year if reading and writing did not also have a functional role in his daily activity.[23] The emphasis placed on literary training by historians of colonial apprenticeship overlooks not only the main educational task of apprenticeship—job training—but also its noneducational tasks, which were economic and custodial. Apprenticeship provided cheap child labor in a production system which valued man hours highly. It also served as a means of social control in an era before the schools had established their monopoly on children's time.

The New York Common Council's references to apprentices usually dealt with this custodial function. The statute of 1737 forbidding tavernkeepers from serving apprentices was reenacted in 1745 and 1773. In 1748 the Council passed an ordinance against "the firing of leather guns pistols pop guns squibs crackers & all sorts of fire works," by "Servant Apprentice or any other person."[24] Though boys would be boys when released from their duties, the sunrise to sunset working hours for apprentices served an important custodial function and kept the drinking, gaming, and fireworks to a tolerable level. Discipline could be harsh, and apprentices, who

23. If an apprentice attended one quarter of evening school sessions, the usual provision, and if he could stay awake, he would receive about 120 hours of elementary education in a year (3 months × 4 weeks × 5 days × 2 hours), and he would have 9 months in which to forget what he learned. Elementary schools today, in contrast, give about 700 hours of academic instruction (175 days × 4 hours), and teachers still worry about the two-and-a-half month forgetting process in the summer. Robert Seybolt overlooked such distinctions when he declared that apprenticeship "took care of the entire problem of public elementary education during the colonial period." Seybolt, *Apprenticeship*, pp. 104–105, and *passim*.

24. McKee, *Labor*, pp. 67–68; *Minutes of the Common Council of the City of New York, 1675–1776* (New York, Dodd, Mead and Company, 1905), V, 239.

usually worked over sixty hours a week without pay, hardly had
a lucrative contract, but this was the accepted arrangement, and
some masters showed affection for their apprentices and helped
them get started. There is evidence of kindness as well as severity
in the treatment of apprentices. Kept well or kept ill, however,
apprentices were kept busy.

Schoolmasters who offered accounting, foreign languages, navigation, and surveying tried to strengthen the tenuous connection
between schooling and occupational success. Their advertisements
emphasize two main claims: practical instruction and expertise from
Europe. These men tried to persuade the public that, unlike teachers of the three R's, they had skills that were directly useful and
were available from no one else. Nathan Hutchins offered field
work. "Young gentlemen inclined to learn surveying," he advertised, "will be instructed in the Practick as well as the Theoretical
Part, he being provided with Chain and Compass, and has obtained
Liberty of exercising his Scholars on a convenient Tract of Land
not far distant." John Philipse offered to teach French "in the Most
Modern and Expeditious Method; and according to Mr. Paillaret's
System, who had the Honour of teaching the Royal Family."
George Robinson offered to teach bookkeeping "as used in London,
either in the wholesale or retail way," and John Lewis explained
that "what is called a new method of Navigation, is an excellent
method of Trigonometry here particularly applied to Navigation."[25]

These attempts to be practical and up-to-date show the effect
of provincial New Yorkers' emulation of European developments.
Commerce looked to London; so did schoolmasters, claiming sole
knowledge of the latest accounting and navigation methods used
there. The same phenomenon applied to ornamental skills. Polite
society looked to the Continent as well as to London; so did dancing, fencing, and language masters, who claimed credentials from
mentors across the Atlantic. Vogue was a force for changes in the
eighteenth-century curriculum, for not only did the commercial and
shipping activities of New York City prompt masters to offer new
subjects, but the effort to keep up with European models created
an expectation of constant change in methods as well, an appeal
to innovation rather than tradition.

25. Seybolt, "Evening Schools," pp. 643, 644; Stokes, *Iconography,* January
30, 1750.

By the time of the Revolution many seem to have thought the new subjects important. Thus Ezekiel Archer, an innkeeper, provided that his children were "to be brought up to Learning, and in particular my son Ezekiel, to navigation, and accounts, as merchants accounts."[26] Nevertheless, if a young man was "designed" for commerce, he could learn on the job. Joseph Watts, sending young Jack Franks back to his uncle's firm in Philadelphia after some practical experience in New York, reported, "He can write very prettily, his Skill in Bookkeeping I apprehend not to be as great, as he has been little conversant in that Branch of the Compting House, however, as he understands figures well enough, the defect is easily remedyd."[27]

Even if a boy could learn accounting outside the counting house, he still had to get inside, and family undoubtedly played a large role in determining the desirable places in commerce, as in law. Mrs. Peter DeLancey displays the range of concerns involved in training and placing one's sons in business, even in a prominent family. In June 1755, she wrote to her father, Cadwallader Colden,

> I wish Stephen was with a good Merchant but we [have] been so unlucky that those, that Mr. DeLancey has [s]poke to, could not take him. I believe he will do better at that busyness than any other. Chambers is learning [him] bookkeeping, with his other studies.

To her mother she wrote the next year,

> Stephen . . . is going to live with Mr. Beverly Robinson to learn the Merchants busyness . . . Peter is also to go to toun soon, & both of them would have been there before now, could we have got lodging for them to our liking . . . neither are we neglectfull of my Fathers favourite John, I think I told you I had wrote my self to Mr. Nickolls about taking him, & that he had not refus'd, but say'd as he had three Clarks then whose time would not be out till the fall, it would be best for John to continue at his learning till then.[28]

26. *Wills*, VIII, 153 (1773).
27. John Watts to Moses Franks, November 23, 1763, in *The Letter Book of John Watts, 1762–1765* (NYHS, *Collections* 61, 1928), p. 201.
28. Elizabeth DeLancey to Colden, September 2, 1750, in *Letters and Papers of Cadwallader Colden* (NYHS, *Collections* 68, 1935), IX, 75; Elizabeth DeLancey to Mrs. Cadwallader Colden, June 24, 1775, in *ibid.*, pp. 155–156.

If the DeLanceys had problems like these, the commoner's son would hardly be able to compete for a good place in business.

In the Revolutionary period there was a gradual trend in American cities toward a tighter class structure and less opportunity for occupational mobility.[29] Although New York City was an expanding commercial center, and some teachers emphasized accounting and navigation, the newcomers to business tended to be those with connections, money, or both.[30] It was not just acquaintances that mattered in the business world, but, just as with the craftsman and his tools, a stake was important. John McAdam came as a youth from Ireland in 1770, was staked by his uncle, and made a fortune as an auctioneer in the occupied "Tory Haven." The ninety-six dollars Thomas Eddy brought with him to New York in 1777 allowed him to get a start. He was able to rent a room where "some respectable merchants" boarded and begin retailing small quantities of items from auctions at the coffeehouse.[31] Opportunity was abundant for those with resources, less so for those without.

Nor was there a general expectation of mobility. Wills display a sense of appropriateness, of limitations on a boy's choices. Men of various ranks had a strong concept of station and thought that educational patterns should conform to their level. Harmanus Rutgers, a wealthy brewer, instructed his daughter-in-law to give her children an education "suited to their condition." John Waddell, merchant, left money for his son to be educated "after a creditable and Genteel manner." Similarly, though, a ship joiner, Josiah Bagley, willed that his children should be educated "in a manner suitable to my condition in life."[32] In general, the "manner suitable" to the condition of the ordinary colonial New Yorker was some training in the three R's, with occupational training reserved almost entirely for the apprenticeship process. Those who rose in occupational status might achieve it through schooling, but it was

29. Main, *Social Structure*, pp. 286–287.

30. Virginia Harrington, *The New York Merchant on the Eve of the Revolution* (New York, Columbia University, Studies in History, Economics and Public Law, No. 404, 1935), p. 16.

31. Robert H. Spiro, Jr., "John Loudon McAdam in Revolutionary New York," NYHS *Quarterly* 40 (1956), 29–54; Samuel L. Knapp, *Life of Thomas Eddy* (London, 1836), p. 33.

32. *Wills*, IV, 445, VI, 155, VII, 230.

not characteristic, and other factors, especially financial resources and personal connections, were usually prerequisite.

OCCUPATIONAL TRAINING AND THE ELITE

For the wealthy, occupational choices were also restricted. Acceptable callings included the military, the ministry, medicine, commerce, and the law. The military, a fairly common avenue for younger sons in England, was limited in the colonies because there was no standing army. Military careers before the outbreak of the war consisted either of sporadic colonial officership, such as Washington's, or of British service. Only three men of the fifty King's College graduates whose careers are given in Fuld's *Alumni* were full-time military officers. The ministry was also thinner in opportunities than in the mother country, for there were few fashionable cosmopolitan pulpits and no hierarchy to generate sinecures. Of the same fifty King's graduates, ten became ministers, two of whom were also members of the King's College faculty.[33] The structure of the medical profession in pre-Revolutionary New York also differed from that of England; it included no elite group of "physicians," but rather required all to act as general "surgion-apothecaries," as Richard Shryock has explained. Formal medical training blossomed in the 1760's, especially at Philadelphia, but the profession offered relatively few prestigious positions compared to law or commerce. King's College began its medical program in 1767 but admitted only seventeen students in the ten years before the Revolution. For many, then, the choice boiled down to two occupations. John Watts, a partisan of the business world, wrote, "I have some young folks growing up who must be taught some Business, the Law or Commerce seems to be the only alternative with us & such Numbers infest the first that the latter I think upon the whole is become full as Creditable."[34]

Collegiate training was the same for all and thus played little role in occupational selection, although it gave some future profes-

33. Leonhard F. Fuld, *King's College Alumni* (New York, 1913).
34. Richard Shryock, *Medicine and Society in America, 1660–1860* (New York, New York University Press, 1960), pp. 4–7; The Matricula, or Register of Admissions & Graduations . . . , Columbiana Collection, King's College Room, Low Library, CU; Watts to Gedney Clarke, July 23, 1765, in *Letter Book of John Watts*, p. 361.

sionals requisite language training. The degree itself seemed of little importance. Of the 155 students who entered King's College in the Classes of 1758 to 1775, 99 graduated. Of the 9 who entered the first class in 1754, for example, 5 men graduated in 1758, one went into the army after two years, another "to merchandize," and another went simply "to England" after three years. Others of later classes left for business, law, medicine, or just "indifference." One went "to privateering," another "to nothing."[35] William Livingston and some other prominent lawyers in town attempted to require the B.A. for the practice of law but succeeded only in getting a longer required apprenticeship for nongraduates. Among doctors in America as a whole, J. M. Toner estimated that at the time of the Revolution only 200 of 3500 doctors had degrees and another 200 had had some formal medical education.[36]

Those who went to England for medicine or law were the exceptions, and crusty old John Watts declared that London "beyond doubt is the worst School for Youth of any of his Majestys Dominions, Ignorance, Vanity, Dress & Dissipation being the reigning Characteristics of their insipid Lives."[37] Most New Yorkers, even those with money enough, seemed to agree that English education was expensive and hazardous. From 1750 to 1780 only eleven young New Yorkers went to the Inns of Court, and a few others to Oxford and Cambridge.[38] Some few more went to Glasgow or Edinburgh for medical education. Even in the colonies only nearby Princeton attracted many New Yorkers. As Beverly McAnear has pointed out, college choice depended more on proximity and cost than on quality or denomination. It is not surprising. James Beekman paid £741 just to send his three sons to Princeton. No New York residents are reported from 1750 to 1780 in the matricula of Harvard, nor in the alumni of William and Mary College. The College of Philadelphia received three New Yorkers, and Living-

35. King's College Matricula. 206 students matriculated at King's altogether, but the four-year course of all those entering between 1773 and 1777 was interrupted by the Revolution; they were eliminated from this comparison.

36. Milton M. Klein, "The Rise of the New York Bar: The Legal Career of William Livingston," *William and Mary Quarterly* 15 (1958), 337, 357; the Toner estimate, made in 1874, is reported in Shryock, *Medicine and Society,* p. 9.

37. Watts to Moses Franks, November 24, 1763, in *Letter Book of John Watts,* p. 200.

38. Edward A. Jones, *American Members of the Inns of Court* (London, The Saint Catherine Press, 1924).

ston's alma mater, Yale, attracted two in the same period.[39] New Yorkers bound for college seemed content with the choice of Presbyterian Princeton or Anglican King's.

Despite the historical importance of the intellectual training of leaders, and the correspondingly large role the college has played in educational historiography, the actual numbers who attended were, of course, very few. A count of available records yields evidence of about 150 New Yorkers who attended college in the whole period, 1750–1776. If, allowing for records missing, colleges not checked, or residences not given, it is assumed that 200 attended college for some time during the period, they would equal about 6 percent of all the college age men.[40]

College attendance, although suitable to young men of a certain station, was not really required and, like other schooling, was not functionally related to occupational choice or training except for

39. Samuel D. Alexander, *Princeton College During the 18th Century* (New York, 1872), *passim;* Beverly McAnear, "The Selection of an Alma Mater by Pre-Revolutionary Students," *Pennsylvania Magazine of History and Biography* (1949), p. 440; White, *Beekmans of New York,* p. 481; A List of Students Who Entered Harvard College, 1725–1828, Archives, Harvard College Library; *The History of the College of William and Mary (Including the General Catalog)* . . . (Richmond, 1874); University of Pennsylvania, *Biographical Catalogue of the Matriculates of the College.. . . 1749–1893* (Philadelphia, 1894); Franklin B. Dexter, *Biographical Sketches of the Graduates of Yale College* . . . (New York, H. Holt and Company, 1885–1912).

40. Fuld, *King's College Alumni,* gives enough information to determine the place of boyhood residence for thirty-four alumni. Twenty of these were New Yorkers. If this percentage (59%) held for all matriculates (204 by 1776), 120 New Yorkers attended King's, 1754 to 1776. Two New Yorkers attended Yale, none attended Harvard or William and Mary. Three attended Philadelphia College (although two of these, the DeLanceys, are counted among those attending the Inns), and seventeen or more went to New Jersey. Ten New Yorkers went to the Inns of Court, 1750–1775. Two Livingston brothers who attended Cambridge are counted among the ten who attended the Inns. The published Cambridge and Oxford matricula are alphabetical for a period of over 150 years and thus a search on the basis of geographical origins is impractical. The number of college age boys was calculated as follows: roughly $\frac{5}{16}$ of the white boys age 0–15 in 1749 turned 16 from 1750 to 1755 ($\frac{5}{16} \times 2346 = 733$); in 1756 there were 2260 white males under sixteen, all of whom would turn sixteen (or die) by 1771, the date of the next census. At that time there were 3720 white males under sixteen, of whom about $\frac{1}{16}$ would turn sixteen by the beginning of the Revolution (= 930). All white males turning sixteen from 1750 to 1776, then, were $733 + 2260 + 930 = 3923$. Since these figures ignore mortality among the youth, it should be rounded to at most 3500 for purposes of this speculation. The hypothetical 200 college students make up 5.7 percent of these 3500 college-age youths. Census figures are from Greene and Harrington, *American Population,* pp. 100–102.

ministers and, to a lesser degree, for lawyers. College, like the rest of the elite pattern of education—tutors, boarding schools, travel, and literary clubs—related more to general social leadership than to specific occupational roles. It was in men's social, rather than their economic, relations that schooling had a more formative influence, and thus New Yorkers' concept of public education was forged in social terms.

THE CONCEPT OF PUBLIC EDUCATION

Long before New Yorkers dreamed of public schools in the modern sense, they had a distinct concept of the relation of education to the public interest. There was a dichotomy between public and private education in late colonial New York, but it does not correspond directly to later episodes under that heading. The term "public" education underwent a change in connotation in the nineteenth century which has somewhat obscured the importance of the word in the English-colonial context. The word had two related meanings, both inherited from Renaissance England. Education could be public in setting, meaning simply in a classroom as opposed to individual lessons, and it could be public in intent, directed toward the public good, as contrasted to selfish pleasure or gain.

These meanings combined to give to England's elite grammar schools the name "public." Nor were these concepts new in the sixteenth century, for Renaissance educators appealed often to antiquity. Quintilian, discussing "the Comparative Merits of Private and Public Instruction," recommended that "the future orator, whose life is to be spent in great assemblies and in the blaze of public life, become accustomed from his earliest years to face men unabashed and not grow pale by living in solitude." Sir Humphrey Gilbert, alluding to Plato and Licurgus, argued in 1570 that "the educacion of children should not altogether be under the puissance of their fathers, but under the publique power and aucthority, becawse the publique have therein more Interests then their parentes." Richard Mulcaster summed up this English persuasion in 1581: "How can education be private? it abuseth the name as it abuseth the thing . . . Whatsoever inconveniences do grow in common schooles . . . yet the private is much worse, & hatcheth more ills . . . To knit up this question therefore of private & publicke education, I do take publicke to be simply better, as being more upon the stage, where faultes be more seene and so sooner amended."[41]

Both sides of the argument about the public setting were heard in New York in the 1750's. Cadwallader Colden felt that despite the disadvantages of isolation, a private education was best. Accordingly his children received all their instruction at Coldengham, his estate, and his son David said he "never so much as saw any publick School or University." Even among those who thought the group experience of college desirable, there were yet some who feared the full "blaze of public life" which Quintilian had recommended. However, when newspaper writers argued that the proposed New York college should be located in the country, William Smith, more cosmopolitan in outlook, retorted: "To say the Temptations are fewer in a Village than in a City, however spacious, is saying no more to the Purpose, than that a Man (if the Comparison may be allow'd) should rather quench his Thirst in a Brook than a River, when there is more than enough in either . . . But further, the Knowledge of Languages, Philosophy and Mathematicks, is but a small Part of the Education of such as are design'd to be useful in Society: Those ought to know Men and the World."[42]

Thus "public" education carried both its Renaissance meanings in provincial New York. In its sense of a group setting, William Clajon proposed to open a French "public School" in the Consistory of the French Church in 1766, and Peter Sparling announced "a Public School . . . where the Public may depend upon having their Children taught after a most concrete Method, applicable to Business; in Reading, Writing Arithmetic &c." The "Liberal Arts Academy" proposed for Harlem was called a public school, as were the charity schools of Trinity Church and Shearith Israel.[43]

41. William M. Smail, ed., *Quintilian on Education* (Oxford, Clarendon Press, 1938), pp. 21–26; Sir Humphrey Gilbert, *Queen Elizabeth's Academy*, ed. F. J. Furnivall (London, Early English Text Society, extra series, VIII, 1869), pp. 10–11; Richard Mulcaster, *Positions* . . . (London, 1581), p. 186.

42. Brooke Hindle, "The Coldens of Coldengham," NYHS *Quarterly* 45 (1961), 239; "Z." in *New York Evening Post*, May 18, 1747; William Smith, *Some Thoughts on Education* . . . (New York, 1752), p. 7.

43. Stokes, *Iconography*, May 19, 1766; *ibid.*, May 14, 1767; *Gaz.*, June 11, 1770; Kemp, *SPG*, p. 109; Pool, *Shearith Israel*, p. 213.

New Yorkers were concerned about public education in the normative sense, too. Public education meant an experience that would impress on young men their public responsibilities and give them the abilities to act as public figures, as Smith's arguments for an urban college demonstrate. In this sense, New York's wealthy had always had patterns of public education open to them. Boys could be sent to the City's "public" schoolmasters or to boarding schools with their peers, and on to the colleges of neighboring colonies. Some few went "back home" in preference to the colonial institutions, but by 1750 many felt that neither of these alternatives would do. "I have often wondered," said Smith, "that this Province should have been near a whole Century, in the Hands of a civilized and enlightened People; and yet, not one public Seminary of Learning planted in it." Livingston saw "numberless Advantages that will naturally result from a publick Seminary of Learning," among which were "a surprizing Alteration in the Behaviour of our young Gentry" with respect to religion, as well as a reduction in drunkenness and an increase in the supply of wise and candid politicians.[44]

Many saw schooling as a means of promoting social responsibility for society's elites, but the moral education of the great majority was not a public responsibility. What the common man's children learned from his parents, their church, and the moralisms in his schoolbooks about conduct in society—about sobriety, industry, and authority—had to suffice.

CULTURAL DIVERSITY AND MORAL EDUCATION

There is no evidence that New York's leading citizens saw common schooling as a means of moral education for the great majority of children in society. Since the evidence is negative, the reasons for the lack of connection between public morality and common schooling will have to be sought deductively rather than inductively.

American history suggests that people look to schooling as a mechanism for conformity when the cultural hegemony of some group is threatened. In seventeenth-century New England the

44. Smith, *Some Thoughts,* p. 2; [William Livingston], *Some Serious Thoughts on the Design of Erecting a College in the Province of New York,* . . . (New York, 1749), pp. 3–6.

hegemony was Puritan, and the threat was largely from within, a fear of "Creolean degeneracy" in the succeeding generations. In nineteenth-century New York City the threat was from without, or at least it was convenient for native New Yorkers to think of it that way. They feared the increasing crime, vice, and poverty of the expanding city, and they associated it with immigrants, especially Catholic immigrants. This threat helped unify the native Protestants into an interdenominational bloc that could exercise hegemony in economic and cultural affairs. In both cases the dominant group tried to develop a school system to transmit their values.

In late colonial New York there was neither a cultural threat nor a cultural hegemony. The group that later became the dominant city leaders, native Protestants, were divided in the eighteenth century. This was apparent in the controversy over the founding of King's College, which raged from 1753 to 1755. Anglican churchmen, long anxious to establish a colonial college of their own to contend with dissenting Yale and Harvard, proposed that the New York college seek a royal charter, employ an Anglican president, and maintain Anglican services. William Livingston and his faction argued vigorously for a legislatively controlled, nondenominational college instead. Through an alliance with the conservative Dutch and the approval of Lieutenant Governor Delancey, the Anglicans were able to secure their charter and give King's College a denominational cast. The Livingston supporters, for their part, were strong enough to block the legislative aid the Anglicans sought. The college was launched, but the battle was a stalemate.[45]

Instead of dominant and threatening cultural groups, provincial New York had several balanced but shifting factions, each of which had leaders from respectable old New York families. These groups aligned themselves differently on different cultural, political, and educational issues. Since the factions could not agree on the religious complexion of a college for their future leaders, they could hardly

45. The best account of the King's College controversy is found in Milton M. Klein, The American Whig: William Livingston of New York, unpub. diss., Columbia University, 1954, with whose kind permission I draw upon and cite his unpublished material; see also Klein, ed. *The Independent Reflector* . . . (Cambridge, Harvard University Press, 1963), pp. 32–45; Beverly McAnear, "American Imprints Concerning King's College," *Papers of the Bibliographical Society of America* 44 (1950), 301–339; Richard Hofstadter and Walter Metzger, *The Development of Academic Freedom in the United States* (New York, Columbia University Press, 1955), pp. 187–191.

have pictured a single system of lower schools in the city to train all of their children. Lacking this consensus on moral education, common schooling did not become a public issue.

Huguenot, Dutch, Anglican, Presbyterian, Deist—each arranged his child's moral and doctrinal education to his liking, not only at home and at church as in later periods but also in school. This latitude extended for cultural traditions and language as well as religious and moral education. The Huguenots maintained their language not only by the fireside but in distinctive schools. New Rochelle had fashionable French schools to which some New York boys were sent, and the French Church had a school for a while.[46] The Dutch and Jewish schools helped conserve the traditions of their groups. Instruction in foreign languages was not seen as a threat. This contrasts with the short-lived experiment in German language schools by the Public School Society in the 1840's, which was meant as a lure to assimilate those whose differences were seen as undesirable.[47] Nor was the conformist urge lacking in colonial times, under certain circumstances, as Franklin's desire to Anglicize the Germans in Pennsylvania shows.

In provincial New York City, however, the pressure to Anglicize the Dutch services and school was internal. "Now their language and customs begin pretty much to wear out," observed Dr. Alexander Hamilton in 1744, "and would very soon die were it not for a parcel of Dutch domines here who, in the education of their children, endeavor to preserve the Dutch customs as much as possible."[48] But these conservatives could not maintain a hold on their children. The generation gap was exacerbated by the reform demands of the evangelical wing of the church. Although the conservatives, loyal to Amsterdam and the mother tongue, remained in control in New York, by the 1760's many younger people were leaving the church. A petition in favor of English services lamented in 1762 that "there is scarce a principal family in this Citty and even of our own Church whose children clearly understand the Dutch Language by means of which we have Daily the mortifica-

46. On New Rochelle and the Huguenots, see Wright, *Cultural Life,* p. 56, and Dexter, *Biographical Sketches,* II, 289.

47. Public School Society, Minutes of the Executive Committee, 1836–1841, NYHS, December 7, 1837. See Chap. Five, below.

48. Alexander Hamilton, *Itinerarium* . . . , quoted in Kilpatrick, *Dutch Schools,* p. 153.

tion to see the offspring of the wealthiest members . . . leave our Divine worship." A counterpetition by the pro-Dutch faction in 1767 complained that "the Dutch School is not taken care of by the rulers to the total ruin of the Dutch education." The school trustees replied that the master was well paid to take thirty poor children, but that thirty who wished to be taught solely in Dutch had not appeared.[49] The conservatives bowed to this reality. English sermons were introduced in 1764, and the school became bilingual upon a change of masters in 1773.[50]

The Jewish congregation quietly underwent a similar evolution. Shearith Israel had been founded by Sephardic Jews and, in its first school, Spanish as well as Hebrew and English were taught. Although the Sephardic ritual was maintained, the Spanish and Portuguese Jews were actually a minority of the congregation by the eighteenth century, and Spanish was dropped in the school with the appointment of New Yorker Abraham Abrahams as reader and teacher in 1762. Furthermore, as Hyman Grinstein suggests, "the printing of Isaac Pinto's English translation of the prayer book in New York in 1761 and 1766 indicates that even at that early date many Jews were unfamiliar with Hebrew."[51]

The pressure to conform in language or religion came from self-interest, not societal regulation. The lack of regulation resulted in diversity which troubled some men. An unsympathetic Dutch minister said in 1741, "Because there is here perfect freedom of conscience for all, except Papists, a spirit of confusion is ever blazing up more and more. Everybody may do what seems right in his own eyes, so long as he does not disturb the public peace."[52] Similarly, since society as a whole did not organize schools, moral and social education were not governed by collective decisions.

49. Proceedings of the Consistory of the Dutch Church of the City of New York in regard to the Petitions of their Congregation for Calling an English Preacher and the Disputes arising therefrom—1762, NYHS, p. 47; Kilpatrick, *Dutch Schools,* pp. 156–157.

50. F. T. Corwin, ed., *Ecclesiastical Records of the State of New York* (Albany, J. B. Lyon, 1905), VI, 3891; Thomas J. Wertenbaker, *The Founding of American Civilization: The Middle Colonies* (New York, Scribner's Sons, 1938), p. 111; Kilpatrick, *Dutch Schools,* p. 157.

51. Pool, *Shearith Israel,* pp. 212–214; Hyman B. Grinstein, *The Rise of the Jewish Community of New York, 1654–1860* (Philadelphia, Jewish Publication Society of America, 1945), p. 226.

52. John W. Pratt, *Religion, Politics and Diversity; the Church-State Theme in New York History* (Ithaca, Cornell University Press, 1967), p. 64.

When the English conquered New Netherland, they had created a situation unique in English colonization: they had to deal with a subject European majority. They needed the goodwill of the Dutch, who had fully developed cultural and economic institutions. English governors could hardly plan to "assimilate" the majority Dutch population. A nominal Anglican establishment, continually controversial, was imposed on the four southern counties, and attempts to license teachers continued sporadically until the time of the stormy authoritarian Governor Cornbury early in the eighteenth century. After Cornbury, however, such efforts waned. Teacher licensing disappeared; it had never been very clear who should approve teachers anyway.[53] The Dutch maintained their Dutch school and Dutch sermons, but Dutch culture proved no threat. Although the use of the Dutch language declined, what happened was more an amalgamation than an assimilation. Commercial cooperation, a policy of tolerance by English rulers, and the ready adaptability of the Dutch all tended to minimize Dutch-English differences. The development of internal religious rifts among both English and Dutch denominations during the Great Awakening also blurred lines. Finally, the Dutch, English, and French groups in colonial New York all included a broad range of educational backgrounds and economic status, acquired in Europe or the New World. There were no strong economic grievances between national groups. No immigrant threat was imagined, no connection between disruption and nationality made. Under such conditions there was little talk of schools for assimilation. There was no talk of a "system."

Common education, then, was not "neglected" in provincial New York. It just took place in informal and unregulated settings. The average colonial New Yorker had more educational resources of his own than his mid-nineteenth-century counterpart. The transmission of skills, language, and traditions was not as problematic as it was to become after immigration brought waves of unskilled foreign laborers to the city. Independent schools offered elementary schooling at rates that at least craftsmen, perhaps even laborers,

---

53. On early teacher licensing, see Daniel G. Pratt, *Annals of Public Education in the State of New York* (Albany, 1872), pp. 19, 90–94, 144, 147; *Minutes of the Common Council*, I, 24, II, 291; E. B. O'Callaghan, ed., *Documents Relative to the Colonial History of the State of New York* (Albany, 1861), III, 372.

could afford. Religious and cultural differences were not seen as a liability to advancement or as a threat to public morality. Moral education was thus left to diverse institutions and parental initiative.

SCHOOLING AND THE REVOLUTIONARY WAR IN NEW YORK CITY

This unregulated, provincial mode of education survived the Revolution. The war is no watershed in the city's educational history, and even the disruptions of the British occupation seem not to have affected the process of schooling very much. The war's effects on New York's population, on the other hand, were drastic indeed, and the physical disruption of the town was severe. There was a massive population turnover when the Patriots evacuated in 1776 and again when the Loyalists evacuated in 1783.[54] In occupied New York formerly wealthy refugees were on relief, while privateers, tavern keepers, and provisioners grew rich. Two fires left over one-sixth of the city "a mass of black, unsightly rubbish," further complicating severe housing problems.[55] Private as well as public buildings were appropriated for barracks and hospitals. The Dutch and Hebrew charity schools were disbanded, and the British used King's College as a hospital. College classes continued for some time at the home of Leonard Lispenard, but "almost all the apparatus and a large portion of the books belonging to the College, were wholly lost." The two Trinity Charity School buildings were lost in the first fire, but the school continued to operate in a private house until the death of the master in May 1777, whereupon the boys were sent to two private schoolmasters. In April 1778, the school was reopened under a new master, Amos Bull, but church officials claimed it was "the only one that has survived the general wreck occasioned by this detestable Rebellion."[56]

54. On wartime population estimates, see Greene and Harrington, *American Population,* p. 104; Thomas J. Wertenbaker, *Father Knickerbocker Rebels; New York City During the Revolution* (New York, Scribner's Sons, 1948), pp. 98, 103, 214; David M. Ellis et al., *A History of New York State* (Ithaca, Cornell University Press, rev. ed., 1967), p. 118.
55. Ellis, *History of New York State,* p. 108; William Dunlap, *History of the American Theater* (New York, 1832), I, 79.
56. John H. Van Amringe, "King's College and Columbia College," in *A History of Columbia University, 1754–1904* (New York, Columbia University Press, 1904), p. 51; Kemp, *SPG,* pp. 118–119.

Historians have emphasized these disruptive effects of the war. Thomas Boese, overlooking Trinity's effort, stated flatly that all schools were closed during the war. Alan Nevins said, "The war struck a disastrous blow at education all over the Union . . . Charity schools were usually the first to close, but private and even town schools soon followed them. In New York City the schools almost went out of existence when the British took possession."[57] This is an incorrect picture of schooling during the occupation of New York. Those who could afford boarding costs could send their children out of the city, as they had before the war. Inside the city there was a great turnover of teachers, as with the population in general, but there was no shortage of schoolmasters. A search of available sources yielded the names of eighteen teachers in the city in 1770 (excluding King's College faculty), twenty-five in 1774, and seventeen in 1777.[58] Although most of the teachers were new, rapid turnover was a normal characteristic of the colonial teaching occupation. The widow Allen was not wealthy, but she had no trouble in finding three different masters for her son Stephen.[59]

Schooling was more difficult where Loyalists and Patriots were in active contention. Pintard recalled, "Westchester County, during the Revolutionary War, lay between the lines and the inhabitants were deprived for eight years of all worship, & their children grew up without schools."[60] But Revolutionary New York City, once Howe entered, experienced neither military nor political strife. Despite the fires, the hardships of the refugees, and the usual problems accompanying occupying armies, New York settled down into a routine that was peaceful and, for many, even gay. People were not all rich or poor; there was a large middle group. Many prospered despite high inflation; some speculators prospered because of it.[61] There is thus no reason to conclude that education, which had been largely informal and noninstitutional, declined during,

---

57. Thomas Boese, *Public Education in the City of New York . . .* (New York, 1869), p. 20; Alan Nevins, *The American States During and After the Revolution, 1775–1789* (New York, The Macmillan Company, 1924), p. 466.

58. Sources are given in n. 8 above.

59. Allen, Letters, p. 23.

60. John Pintard to his daughter, November 22, 1819, in *Letters from John Pintard* (NYHS, *Collections* 1937–1940), I, 247.

61. Wertenbaker, *Father Knickerbocker*, pp. 198, 205, 217.

or after, the occupation. Such a conclusion would overlook not only the educational functions of the family, the church, and apprenticeship, but also the large amount of schooling given by independent masters. Their work is less visible after two centuries, but was more significant at the time than the few record-keeping schools that closed.

Schooling arrangements were the same before, during, and after the Revolution in New York City. The typical teacher held more than one job, often advertised expertise from England or Europe, and rarely stayed in teaching more than ten years. The typical school was held in quarters rented where the master lived. The typical pupil learned to read first at home or from a neighbor, went to day school for a few years, then moved on either to another sort of school, or a trade. Many, of course, missed the classroom altogether, but it does not seem that any were excluded a priori except those among the poor who could not get into a charity school.

The careers of two boys for whom a substantial amount of consecutive data survives will serve to illustrate typical educational patterns. Stephen Allen, mentioned above, learned to read at home from his uncle, studied the three R's in a series of private classrooms for a few years, and then became an apprentice to a sailmaker in occupied New York. He continued to read in his spare time, and considered this self-education an important element in his later success.

> My education was very limited, having left school before I was twelve years old. I could read and write indifferently, and had learned a few of the rules in Arithmetic, but possessed no knowledge of grammar, and was wretchedly deficient in my spelling. I was nevertheless very fond of reading, and would readily part with any of my possessions in order to obtain a book . . . it is to this reading that I owe the little erudition I possess, and, at the same time, the ability of conveying my thoughts to others in a plain garb, by means of writing.[62]

Wealthier boys got more schooling, but in the same wandering, sporadic manner. William Dunlap was born in Perth Amboy in 1766. He was first taught from picture books by a kindly man

---

62. Allen, *Letters*, p. 45.

in the neighborhood, then learned letters from a nearby schoolmistress, and

> was then turned over to Master M'Norton and learned to spell, perhaps read—commenced more regular instruction with an English gentleman; read 'Anson's Voyage,' and had the mysteries of grammar put in my hand; but they went no further.

In 1755 his father moved to Piscataway, where young William read some on his own and had lessons from his father, but mostly he swam and fished. "The Declaration of Independence caused a sensation which I distinctly remember, but my sports and rambles had more interest for *me*." When the British plundered Piscataway, Dunlap's family moved to New York.

> In New York I was sent to Latin School, and Mr. Leslie heard me say the grammar by rote; but I was removed from him, I know not why, and attended an English school, where, with a good old Quaker, I might have acquired a common education, but another and a final interruption to my school instruction occurred.

In a game with friends, a piece of wood blinded William's right eye, which ended "all further regular schooling," and he turned to art. His education was not finished, however; the last phase illustrates what the system offered to the fashionable young men who did not go to college. Dunlap planned a trip to London in 1784.

> The education which prepared me for entering the labyrinth of London, alone and unguided, at the age of 18, ought to be before the reader. The winter previous to my voyage I had attended evening school for French, and gained a superficial knowledge of the language; and, from the dancing school of William Hulett, who, with his sons, accomplished several generations of New Yorkers, I carried the reputation of one learned in that valuable mystery—it was more than my French master could say for my grammar. Another branch of my education will throw light on my fitness for self-government in London, I had been introduced to the billiard tables of New York.[63]

Dunlap, then, had no fewer than eight teachers, including his father, in his school career. Even for those who spent their whole

---

63. William Dunlap, *History of the Rise and Progress of the Arts of Design* (New York, 1832), I, 292, 294–295, 301.

childhood in the city, New York, unlike the isolated districts, offered a choice.

Both of these boys were in school in occupied New York. They add to the impression that schooling proceeded normally during the Revolution. The Revolution was more than a war, of course, but the creation of the Republic did not change schooling practices directly or quickly, as Chapter Two will show.

The legacy of the provincial period was not neglect of common schooling but a mode of schooling quite different in structure and operation from that to which we have been accustomed since the mid-nineteenth century. Schooling, in conjunction with apprenticeship, the family, and the church, was effective, but its effectiveness has eluded us because common schooling prompted little group support and no communitywide decisions.

Schooling in late colonial New York, appropriate to the city's economic and cultural requirements, provided training in rudiments for the many, and classical training for the few, plus some supplementary schooling in technical subjects. It allowed wide latitude for alternative patterns of education for different status groups, and it mirrored the city's religious and cultural diversity without enforcing any of these distinctions formally. While the conformism of the majority in the nineteenth century was born of social anxieties, the tolerance of the coexisting minorities in eighteenth-century New York was born of social necessity. There was an amalgamation in progress, however, and, as a survey of the 1790's will show, the same informal mode of schooling which allowed distinctive schools for cultural minorities also produced many schools in which children from a wide variety of backgrounds shared a common experience.

CHAPTER TWO

New York Schools in the 1790's

The schooling arrangements of the late colonial period persisted in the 1790's, and they served New York's children effectively. Access to common schooling was broad. Between the extremes of the church charity school and the expensive private tutors was a large group of independent schoolmasters and mistresses who presided over common pay schools that most parents could afford. The forces which prompt change in education were gathering, but neither the growth of the city nor the ideals of the Revolutionary generation had caused a social revolution in New York yet. Demographic, economic, political, and cultural changes had not yet been severe enough or rapid enough to make common schooling for social purposes a subject of serious debate. Anxieties about new social trends first generated educational discussion at the national, speculative level; at the local, functioning level there was a lag between social problems and educational solutions. Nevertheless, two efforts to bring some organization into schooling were made in New York City, a teachers' society and a plan for school support under a state law. The failure of these efforts illustrates that there was little pressure for the systematization of schools before the turn of the century.

NEW YORK CITY IN THE 1790's

In the 1790's, while Philadelphia took over as the nation's capital, New York was taking over as the nation's commercial center.[1]

1. See Robert G. Albion, "New York Port in the New Republic, 1783–1793," *New York History* (October 1940), pp. 388–403; Adna Weber, *The Growth of Industry in New York* (Albany, 1904), p. 6.

The city had an aura of cosmopolitan activity often noted by travellers. John Bernard said of New York in 1797: "The one great market to the enterprising foreigner, it was also a sort of Mecca to the hungry backwoodsman . . . It resembled a large fair or cluster of inns rather than an abiding city." In 1796 William Priest called New York "a London in miniature—populous streets, hum of business, busy faces, shops in style." Expecting a more provincial scene, William Strickland was amazed that in New York *"everything is perfectly English* . . . The town which has been almost entirely rebuilt since the peace perfectly resembles one of our large newbuilt commercial towns and strikingly so that of Liverpool."[2] Although New York was in large part "newbuilt," new buildings do not make a new city. There was continuity with its colonial past. The city was governed as before. About half of the white adult males were eligible to vote in city elections in 1790. The governor still appointed the mayor, and the ballot reform of the 1777 Constitution did not apply to city elections. Thus, viva voce voting remained a prop to merchant dominance. A majority of those eligible did not exercise their right to vote for alderman.[3] State elections were becoming important, however, and party rivalry in the expanding city made politicians aware of the growing importance of political persuasion among the general citizenry. Nevertheless, there was little political urgency to the notion, current among orators of the day, that the survival of the new republic depended on a well-educated democratic electorate.

Despite rising costs and enduring unemployment, the 1790's were years of improvement for many New Yorkers. The postwar depression had begun to lift in 1787, although a newspaper writer still complained in 1791 that "many of our industrious small tradesmen, cartmen, day labourers, and others dwell upon the border of poverty

2. John Bernard, *Retrospections of America* (New York, 1887), p. 50; James G. Wilson, ed., *The Memorial History of the City of New York* (New York, 1893), III, 150; William Strickland to the Rev. John Robinson, September 21, 1794, Strickland transcripts, NYHS.

3. Sidney I. Pomerantz, *New York, an American City, 1783–1803* (New York, Columbia University Press, 2nd ed., 1965), pp. 68–72; Wilson, *New York*, I, 12–14. There is disagreement about the interpretation of suffrage figures; see Staughton Lynd and Alfred Young, "After Carl Becker: The Mechanics and New York City Politics, 1774–1801," *Labor History* 5 (Fall 1964), 221–222.

and live from hand to mouth."[4] Wages for laborers did not rise
from 1785 to 1792, it seems, when they averaged about 50 cents
a day. By 1795 workmen's rates had increased to about $1.00 a
day, with wages for skilled workers as high as $2.00. A laundress,
said a French observer, earned 50 cents a day in 1794, and a sailor
$1.75.[5] These wages may be compared to the usual price for the
pay schools of the day, two dollars per quarter. It is difficult to
estimate how marginal two dollars was to a New York workingman,
especially without specific information about rents, but at two dollars, schooling was within the reach of many workingmen.[6] The
relation of schooling costs to average wages was roughly the same
as before the Revolution.

Other aspects of New York's economic and cultural life in the
1790's are relevant to education but are even more difficult to assess.
Apprenticeship may have begun to decline, but the evidence is not
clear.[7] The only indentures that have survived in quantity are for
the Almshouse children. Of 135 pauper children bound out from
1792 to 1794 all were placed with masters in the traditional skilled
trades except eleven of the youngest, who were sent out of the
county to learn farming.[8] Table 1 shows that craftsmen were a

4. *Advertiser*, January 13, 1791, cited in Pomerantz, *New York*, p. 216;
on the economics of the 1780's, see E. Wilder Spaulding, *New York in the
Critical Period, 1783–1789* (New York, Columbia University Press, 1932),
pp. 28–29.

5. Pomerantz, *New York*, p. 216; Kenneth Roberts and Anna M. Roberts,
eds., *Moreau de St. Méry's American Journey, 1793–1798* (New York, Doubleday, 1947), pp. 157–160. These sources imply that the wage increases represented increases in real income.

6. On commodity prices, see Roberts, *Moreau's Journey*, pp. 157–160; on
rents, see Wilson, *New York*, II, 21, and Pomerantz, *New York*, pp. 169,
227–228. The best proof that working men could afford school tuition is
that so many of them in fact appear in the pay school lists analyzed below.

7. See Paul H. Douglass, *American Apprenticeship and Industrial Education*
(New York, Columbia University, Studies in History, Economics and Public
Law, No. 216, 1921); Samuel McKee, Jr., *Labor in Colonial New York*
(New York, Columbia University Press, 1935); Richard B. Morris, *Government
and Labor in Early America* (New York, Columbia University Press, 1946).
Douglass wrote that apprenticeship was unchanged after the Revolution and
began to decline with industrialization after the War of 1812, while McKee
(p. 62) sees signs of decline before the Revolution, and Morris (p. 200)
says the system began to decline at the close of the Revolution. There are
no figures available to document any of these contentions, but impressionistic
evidence, such as is presented here, indicates that although apprenticeship
may have begun to "decline," it had not, by any means, "declined."

8. New York City, Apprentice Indentures, 1792–1794, MS, NYHS. By 1850,
in contrast, there was less demand for craft apprentices in the city and

TABLE 1. Occupational Categories in the 1796 Directory.

Category	Explanation	Number	Percent of sample
Laborer	Includes porter, stoker, and stevadore	56	5.5
Mariner	Includes boatman, excludes captain	38	3.7
Cartman	Includes coachman	93	9.5
Skilled craftsman	All crafts; includes rigger, printer	443	43.1
Clerical worker	Clerk, accountant; includes inspector, measurer	21	2.0
Proprietor	Grocer; tavern, boardinghouse and stable keeper; includes brewer, tobacconist	147	14.3
Professional	Doctor, lawyer, minister	41	4.0
Merchant	Includes broker, warehouse and shipyard owner	133	13.0
Others	No clear category; e.g., ship captain (17), teacher (4), gardener (4), cigar manufacturer (3), dairyman (3)	55	5.4
Total		1027	100.0

Source: Men whose last names begin with A and B in [Low's] *New York Directory for 1796* (New York, 1796), pp. 1–28.

prominent group in the occupational structure of New York in 1796.[9] The economic system of New York still offered much oppor-

a trend toward exporting the children. In 1850–51, 58 of 108 poor children were sent away to become farmers, and 21 more were bound to craftsmen outside New York City. New York City Apprentice Indentures, Boys, 1850–1853, MS, NYHS.

9. The assumption that city directories underrepresent common laborers and especially mariners is probably correct, though the directories of the late 1790's seem to be more inclusive than the first efforts of the 1780's or the later nineteenth-century directories. Low's *New York Directory for 1796* (New York, 1796) contains approximately 10,100 entries, of which approximately 1900 are female household heads or redundant firm names, leaving 8200 male adult entries. The estimated population for 1795 is 46,397 (see n. 30 below), of which about 25 percent, or 11,579, were white males over 16. This would yield an inclusion percentage of 70.8 percent. However, the male adult figure (based on the percentage in the 1800 Census, 25.3 percent) is for whites whereas the *Directory* included some black household heads. This would make the inclusion figure too high, perhaps by 5 percent. On the other hand, and more importantly, many men between 16 and 21, or even older, were apprentices or still lived with their families and thus would not appear in the *Directory* as heads of households. This would more

tunity for the skilled manual worker, and thus for meaningful apprenticeship. Housing and ship construction occupied many carpenters, and iron production employed many blacksmiths. In these businesses craftsmen worked in larger groups, for example, in the shipyards, sail lofts, or air furnaces. However, the small workshop and partnership were still more typical. Small work units meant that more men were likely to work where they lived. Both craft and literary education within the family were thus more possible than in later years.

The living patterns of the city were in transition between the mixed neighborhoods which had reinforced the personal deference traditions of the colonial town and the impersonal, economically segregated neighborhoods of the nineteenth-century city. Slum areas were already developing in New York by the 1790's. Poor people crowded into the low, marshy areas around the Collect and on the East River. With stagnant water in the cellars and uncollected garbage in the narrow streets, these areas were more prone to disease.[10] Noah Webster pointed out that while the wealthy could escape summer epidemics by leaving the city, "the poor, whose lot it is to labor daily for bread, must remain in their crouded hovels, where their infants pant for fresh air and die." New York was beginning to experience the problems of urban density that would plague the city as the nineteenth century progressed. Moreau noted that the crime rate was much higher than in the state as a whole and said that "in many parts of the city whole sections of streets are given over to street-walkers," especially in the area "called 'Holy Ground' by the irreligious." The city's wards were

than compensate for the omission of blacks in the population estimate. Thus (granting that the total population figure is hypothetical), Low's *Directory* seems to have included over 70 percent of the city's male adults. Furthermore, we must not assume that those omitted were all common laborers or mariners; indeed, in this case we can disprove it. Fortunately, a competing directory for the same year survives, Longworth's *New York Directory for 1796*, which includes well over 1000 names of male adults not found in Low's *Directory*. The occupations of the first ten nonduplicated names are as follows: tobacconist, cartman, mason, ropemaker, carpenter, laborer, gold-beater, mason, cartman, mariner. Therefore, although Table 1 may somewhat underrepresent laborers and mariners, it is not a great exaggeration.

10. See Alvin F. Harlow, *Old Bowery Days* (New York, D. Appleton and Company, 1931), p. 90; Elinor Barnes, "The First Federal City, New York in 1789," *New York History* 21 (April 1940), 163; and Alfred Young, "The Mechanics and the Jeffersonians, New York, 1787–1801," *Labor History* 5 (Fall 1964), 260–261.

becoming differentiated economically, and by the 1790's the general pattern of a merchants' downtown and a mechanics' uptown had emerged.[11]

Nevertheless, economic segregation was not thorough in the city. Residential patterns were in transition; although some historians have emphasized the contrast with the more integrated colonial period, the contrast with the increasingly fractionalized nineteenth century is equally important. Table 2 shows that the wards were quite similar in the percent of electors in 1790. The West Ward is low with 12.8 percent, and Harlem, then "a little Dutch village," was notably prosperous with 22.4 percent eligible to vote in state elections. With the exception of these wards, however, the variation in total eligible electors ranged only from 16.0 percent to 21.4 percent, and the differences among categories of voters are not striking.[12] The living standards of the rich and the poor varied greatly, of course, but the variety still existed within each ward. Alleys, rented rooms, and backyard cottages provided many of the poor with housing among the more substantial residents. Narrow, unpaved streets, unpotable water, and refuse were not unique to the poor areas but were problems throughout the city. Speaking of the slums, the historian of the Bowery notes that "other well-to-do and prominent persons lived just around the corner from this ugliness."[13] The persistence of integrated living patterns in the 1790's is further illustrated by the mixed enrollment of the common pay schools, which will be analyzed below. Compared to 1850, the city of the 1790's was still small and its residential patterns were still mixed. This integration, one suspects, helped maintain the city's precarious social stability.

11. Noah Webster to William Currie, December 20, 1797, in Harry R. Warfel, ed., *Letters of Noah Webster* (New York, Library Publishers, 1953), pp. 168–169; Roberts, *Moreau's Journey,* pp. 156, 166; Alfred Young, *The Democratic Republicans of New York* (Chapel Hill, University of North Carolina Press, 1967), pp. 471–474.

12. The higher concentration of renters in some wards and owners in others was increasing and is emphasized in Young, *Democratic Republicans,* e.g., p. 474. The remark of Young and Lynd, however, that "the suffrage bottle may be viewed as half full or half empty," in "After Carl Becker," p. 223, applies to residential segregation as well. It is a matter of emphasis. The description of Harlem is from Bernard, *Retrospections,* p. 50.

13. Harlow, *Bowery,* p. 91; see also Kenneth D. Miller, *The People Are the City: 150 years of Social and Religious Concern in New York City* (New York, Macmillan, 1962), p. 25.

TABLE 2. New York State Census of Electors and Inhabitants, City and County of New York, 1790.

Ward	Freeholders at £100		Freeholders at £20		Tenants at 40 s.		Freemen		Total electors		Population			
	No.	Per-cent	No.	Per-cent	No.	Per-cent	No.	Per-cent	No.	Per-cent	Male	Female	Slaves	Total
North	173	3.8	174	3.8	528	11.5	0	0	875	19.0	2,001	2,333	264	4,598
West	152	2.5	151	2.4	479	7.8	7	0.1	789	12.8	2,777	3,089	303	6,169
Dock	86	4.7	82	4.5	147	8.0	0	0	315	17.0	793	813	248	1,854
East	225	6.2	200	5.5	350	9.7	1	0	776	21.4	1,572	1,567	488	3,627
South	11	0.6	54	3.1	253	14.4	19	1.1	337	19.2	797	845	114	1,756
Montgomery	308	4.6	304	4.5	584	8.7	3	0	1,199	17.9	3,056	3,215	427	6,698
Out Ward	214	4.4	215	4.5	289	6.0	63	1.3	781	16.0	2,141	2,374	304	4,819
Harlem	40	8.0	41	8.2	31	6.2	0	0	112	22.4	193	193	115	501
Total	1,209	4.0	1,221	4.1	2,661	8.9	93	0.3	5,184	17.3	13,330	14,429	2,203	30,022

Sources: Advertiser, January 15, 1791; Heads of Families at the First Census of the United States (Washington, 1908).

This does not mean, necessarily, that the poor and the well-to-do liked each other better or helped each other more because they lived closer and sometimes went to neighborhood schools together. Stephen Allen's reaction to class mixing in schools of the late 1770's suggests quite the reverse: "In all schools of the day, there was an evident partiality shown by the Master in his treatment of the children of those persons in eligible circumstances. This was the fact here [at Mr. Wingfield's], for it was plain to me that the children of those who were considered rich, were not only treated with more consideration and lenity than others differently situated, but they were seated in more conspicuous places in the school."[14] The point is not that there was more equality because of the mixing but rather that social stratification was learned and enforced in personal relationships. As economic segregation by neighborhoods increased in the nineteenth century, people in different economic groups learned to live apart as "rich" or "poor." Institutional relationships were interposed in place of personal contact.

In the 1790's this process had barely begun, but the decade saw other ominous demographic developments. After the relatively placid coexistence of Dutch and English cultures in the colonial period, New York in the 1790's experienced a new ethnic conflict which took on political and class dimensions and foreshadowed the great problems of nineteenth-century immigration. Tensions became politicized in the mid-1790's as the Federalist-Republican rivalry grew fierce, and French and Irish immigration alarmed the natives. Although the number of non-English immigrants settling in New York City in the 1790's was small compared to the great nineteenth-century waves, the numbers were increasing, and, in addition to New Yorkers' traditional fear of Catholicism, two characteristics made immigration more threatening to conservatives than it had been in colonial times: they began to associate immigrants first, with radical politics and second, with poverty and crime.[15] The arrival of French West Indian refugees and United Irishmen made the Federalists worry about maintaining social order and political

14. Allen, *Letters*, p. 22.
15. See Richard J. Purcell, "Immigration to the Canal Era," in Alexander C. Flick, ed., *History of the State of New York*, 10 vols. (New York, Columbia University Press, 1934–1937), VII, 7–15; Young, "Mechanics and the Jeffersonians," p. 264, and *passim;* Maldwyn A. Jones *American Immigration* (Chicago, University of Chicago Press, 1960), pp. 64–65.

control; indeed, they thought the two were synonymous. New societies were begun to aid the destitute, and schemes were discussed
both for providing work for the idle and for limiting future immigration, but even these responses tended to be partisan, the Republicans promoting assistance, while the Federalists were concerned
about limitation. Tammany and the Mechanics' Society lost their
nonpartisan character and swung to the Jeffersonian party. In 1794
the Republicans formed a "Society for the Information and Assistance of Persons Emigrating from Foreign Countries" and announced they would help newcomers find "the most eligible mode
of establishing themselves in their several professions." By September 1795, they were receiving "*numerous* and *distressed* appli-
cations." Noah Webster, a Federalist, wrote in 1795, "I consider
as a matter of infinite consequence the cautious admission of
foreigners to the rights of citizenship . . . Many of them are warm
democrats; and the Emigration Society here is headed by Democrats of our own—in short, the opposers of our government are
literally wriggling themselves into all sorts of company to carry their
points." There was tension between political partisans over the re-
ception of Citizen Genêt as ambassador and over other demonstra-
tions of support for the French Revolution. In 1798 the quelling
of the Irish Rebellion sent a new group of impoverished radicals,
or so the Federalists thought, to the port of New York. The editor
Hugh Gaine recorded simply in that year, "Too many United Irishmen arrived here within a few Days."[16]

The fears aroused were due in part merely to the Federalists'
justified assumption that French and Irish immigrants would increase Republican strength. But there was also uneasiness with cultural values different from the mainstream of Protestant New York,
prompting, for example, a more stringent Sabbath law from the
Common Council. In 1794 the Presbyterian minister John Rodgers
became president of the new Society for Promoting Christian
Knowledge and Piety, which aimed to distribute Bibles and tracts
among the poor.[17] This kind of response was to become widespread
in the nineteenth century. The new urban missionaries began to

16. Pomerantz, *New York*, pp. 334, 337–338; Stokes, *Iconography*, May
22, 1794; *Argus*, September 3, 1795; Webster to Theodore Sedgwick, January
2, 1795, in Warfel, *Letters*, p. 124; Pomerantz, *New York*, p. 203.
17. Wilson, *New York*, III, 84; *Argus*, June 11, 1795.

connect foreign birth with poverty and crime. In 1795 the Commissioners of the Almshouse reported a disproportionate number of Irish among the city's paupers, and by 1802 the *American Review* reported that three-fourths of the criminals in New York City were foreign born.[18] Enumeration by foreign and native birth became a standard feature of prison and almshouse reports in the nineteenth century, always with the same worrisome implications about increasing immigration.

Still, these problems were new, and their scale was not yet oppressive. First approaches to postwar immigration and ethnic complexity did not affect schooling. It was the adults, not the children, who were the problem, and New Yorkers turned to tract societies, employment schemes, and proposals that would restrict poor immigrants from entering their city. Immigration, like the other social changes suggested above, did not prompt a fundamental change in New York's mode of education in the 1790's. One important but generally unrecognized reason for this lack of action was that the city already had extensive provision for common schooling under the same conditions that had prevailed during the late colonial period. When a state law for common education did provide the city officials with an opportunity to systematize schooling, tradition, confusion, and political animosity combined to prevent any substantial innovation. The remainder of this chapter is devoted to examining how the informal mode of schooling worked and why it did not change overnight.

THE TEACHERS

In 1788 Noah Webster assured the readers of his *American Magazine* that the schools of New York were much improved. Nevertheless, he thought, there were not enough first-rate teachers, especially in the lower schools. With his usual zeal, he said he would "almost adore the great man, who shall make it respectable for the first and best men to superintend the Education of youth."[19] If they were not the "first and best men," however, at least some of New York's teachers achieved respect and middle-class income. *The New York Directory for 1796*, the 1796 New York tax lists,

18. *M.C.C.*, II, 125; The *American Review* report of 1802 is cited in Roberts, *Journey*, p. 166.
19. *Amer. Mag.*, I (1788), 215.

and a survey of schools made by the Common Council in the same year provide information which, although not statistically sophisticated, is at least suggestive.

Table 3 gives the tax groups for ninety-one teachers engaged in teaching general subjects.[20] The "no listing" category tells us little, but the other listings provide some useful information.[21] Over one-half of the men teachers were assessed at £20 of personal property or more, and nine owned their houses. Actual income is revealed by the extant reports to the Common Council (Table 3, part B). The lowest teaching income reported was £46, the highest, £208. The average income of the eighteen teachers whose incomes are known was £122. This was not a great income at the time, but considering that many teachers supplemented their income, and some received fuel in addition to their fees, the occupation seems to have been a relatively attractive one, perhaps comparable in income potential to the skilled crafts, but with the additional advantage of easy entry into the occupation. It also required little or no capital, which may be why teaching attracted some talented men on their way to other careers. As with merchant or cordwainer, the occupational designation "teacher" covered a wide range of personal fortunes. Easy entry into the occupation provided an even greater attraction for women than for men because few jobs were open to women, and widowhood provided recruits for New York's

20. [Low's] *New York Directory . . . 1796*. The *Directory* lists ninety-seven teachers for 1796; four others have been added from other sources. When the Columbia professors and the dancing and music teachers are eliminated, the number is reduced to ninety-one teachers engaged in precollegiate academic schooling. The figure is probably low because some wives who were not listed separately probably taught, and some ministers, like the Rev. Christopher Peter of the United Brethren Church, were also schoolmasters. See Christopher Peter to the Common Council, May 18, 1796, NYMA. The Rev. Mr. Staughton advertised for grammar scholars in 1795, and his wife opened a full school for girls. *Argus*, August 14, 1795. Instructors such as these tend not to appear in directories as teachers.

21. The group for whom no tax listing was found is ambiguous. Some were rated at less than £20 and thus paid no taxes; for example, teacher Jeremiah Connor was listed, probably by error, then rated at £0. Others, however, had simply moved between the time the *Directory* was prepared and the property assessments were made; for example, teacher Samuel Rudd was not listed in the tax rolls at the address given for him in the *Directory*, but at a different address in the tax lists, rated at £25. It was not possible to check the entire tax list for all names. Sources: *1796 Directory;* New York City Tax Lists, MS, 1796, NYHS; Teachers' Reports to the Common Council, May-July, 1796, MS, NYMA, Box 6459, hereinafter Teachers' Reports. Twenty-three reports are extant.

TABLE 3.   Financial Status of New York
City Teachers, 1796.

A. *Tax assessments*[a]

	Men	*Women*
No listing	26	30
Renters, personal property valued at:		
£20–25	5	0
£26–50	16	0
£51–100	4	0
House owners	9	1
	60	31

House-owning teachers

Name	*Ward*	*Real and personal property*
John Collins	5	£ 250
Daniel Smith	5	300
John West	Bowery	300
Malcolm Campbell	4	400
Treat Crane	1	450
John Campbell	1	500
Samuel Van Steenburgh	2	600
Gerard Smith	1	700
Benjamin Romaine	4	1750
Mrs. Mary Henshaw	3	1800

B. *Annual incomes*[b]

Name	*Income reported, April 1, 1795–April 1, 1796*
Daniel Smith	£ 46
Samuel Dodge	50
Robert Piggot	60
James Gibbons	66
William Gum	73
John Roe	73
James Liddell	81
Thomas Richardson	100
Martin Evans	101
Nathaniel Mead	107
Richard Paterson	120
George Youngs	133
John Collins	172
George Bement	199
Benjamin Romaine	199
Samuel Rudd	200
Stanton Latham	200
Donald Fraser	208

Sources: Teachers' Reports to the Common Council, May–July, 1796, MS, NYMA, Box 6459; New York City Tax Lists, 1796, MS, NYHS.
[a] N = 91 teachers.
[b] N = 18 teachers.

dame schools.[22] As in the colonial period, the lack of regulation allowed diverse members of society to join in teaching on a short-term basis. This openness may have invited the incompetent to teach, but it also encouraged teaching by future lawyers or ministers. Success depended solely upon satisfied customers. The number, quality, and cost of schools in the city were determined by demand, not by social policies which decided who needed to be educated. The charity schools were exceptions to this generalization, but the pay schools were the characteristic mode of common schooling.

The men teachers had many backgrounds and skills. As in the colonial period, some pursued another occupation while teaching or changed occupations during their careers. John Collins was listed in the *Directory* as "schoolmaster and grocer," and Stanton Latham, master of the Dutch Charity School, not only doubled as chorister in the Dutch Church, but was reported to have run a grog shop as well. Washington Irving had three teachers in this period, not including the mistress of his dame school; of these, the first, Benjamin Romaine, went into commerce, the second, Josiah Henderson, into the ministry, and the third, Jonathan Fisk, into the law.[23] Some men stayed in teaching a long time. From the Bowery Robert Piggot reported to the Council that he was "the antientest Teacher in this City having spent upwards of thirty four years in the Occupation." The rate of turnover is suggested, however, by earlier and later directories. Of the ninety-one teachers of precollegiate academic subjects in 1796, thirteen had been listed at the beginning of the decade. Of the same ninety-one, thirty-five remained in 1800. Only eight masters were teaching on all three dates.[24]

22. Of the thirty-one women, none was assessed at even £20 except the wealthy widow Henshaw, who owned and operated a "young ladies academy." Thirteen were listed as widows, eight as "Mrs." (some of whom, like Mrs. Henshaw, were widows), one as "Miss," and nine whose marital status was not given.

23. On Latham, see Harmon C. Westervelt, "Schools, Schoolmasters, Colleges, and Universities . . . ," MS, NYHS, p. 3, and Henry W. Dunshee, *History of the School of the Reformed Protestant Dutch Church in New York, 1633–1883* (New York, 2nd ed., 1883), p. 68; on Irving's teachers, Pierre M. Irving, *Life and Letters of Washington Irving* (New York, 1862), p. 36.

24. Robert Piggot, Teacher's Report; *New York Directory . . . 1789;* Longworth's *American Almanac, New York Register and City Directory . . . 1800* (New York, 1800).

The schoolmasters of the 1790's resemble their unorganized predecessors of the provincial period. Teamwork in teaching was not characteristic. Combinations among New York teachers of the 1790's were generally confined to husband-and-wife teams or short-lived partnerships. As long as easy entry and short tenure characterized teaching, no differentiated ranks of teachers, or a training system for those at the bottom, could develop. Larger schools, with a division of labor, rationalized programs, and hierarchical staffs, developed only later, as the problems of urbanization caused the systematization of the schools.

THE COMMON PAY SCHOOLS

The services of these independent masters were not expensive. Among the extant school reports, sixteen gave the quarterly rates of tuition, and the average beginning rate is about sixteen shillings, or two dollars. Masters charged slightly more for advanced subjects, but the rates vary only slightly from one school to another. Table 4 indicates that masters teaching elementary subjects generally conformed to the sixteen- to twenty-four-shilling range. The Rev. Christopher Peter, whose school enrolled fifty-five children of the poorer members of his United Brethren Church, charged eight shillings for readers to sixteen shillings for writers and grammarians. He said these fees were possible because he paid no rent and he desired to educate the poor, and he described the rates as "rather lower than in other schools."

The impression that the city's pay schools were limited to the wealthy, then, is incorrect. The description of these schools as simply "private" is misleading, first, because it has a connotation of exclusiveness that developed at a later time, and, second, because "private" education in the 1790's, as in the colonial period, often meant home tutoring, in contrast to "public" classroom instruction. Thus, in a sense, the private pay schools, with the charity schools, *were* the public schools of New York City in the 1790's. Although nomenclature is not important per se, the term "common pay schools" better conveys the function of the schools described here. They were common in three ways: first, they were the most common, or prevalent, kind of schools; second, most of New York's schoolmasters were engaged in giving children what was called a

TABLE 4.   Tuition Charges for Common Pay
Schools, 1796.

Name	Quarterly tuition[a]
William Gum	16s
Daniel Smith	14s to 20s
Robert Piggot	14s to 20s
Christopher Peter	$1 to 2
George Bement	20s to 24s
O'Hagarty & Carroll	20s to 24s
John Collins	20s to 24s
Martin Evans	20s to 24s
Donald Fraser	22s to 24s
James Gibbons	16s to 20s
James Liddell	14s to 18s
Nathaniel Mead	16s to 20s
Richard Patterson	16s to 24s
John Roe	$2 to 3
George Youngs	16s to 40s
Benjamin Romaine	24s to 28s

Source: Teachers' reports to the Common
Council.
[a] £ = $2.50.

common education; and third, attendance at these schools was common to the children of families with a broad range of income and occupations. This third fact is the most important, for it is this sense of the word that was central to the ideology of the "common school" reformers of the nineteenth century. The data below suggest that their reform, whether they knew it or not, was an attempt to restore the social mixing that had existed, at least in New York, before the creation of the free schools. The difference, of course, is that as the century progressed, economic and ethnic differences greatly increased, and the independent pay schools were not adequate to meet new educational problems. Nevertheless, it is important to note that this arrangement was working rather well in the 1790's, a fact hitherto masked by the absence of data about schooling in the period and by the denigration of "private" schools by early writers anxious to promote the fledgling public system.[25]

25. See Albert Fishlow, "The American Common School Revival: Fact or Fancy," in Henry Rosovsky, ed., *Industrialization in Two Systems: Essays in Honor of Alexander Gerschenkron* (New York, Wiley, 1966), pp. 40–67, esp. pp. 41, 46.

TABLE 5. Profile of Dutch Charity School Students, 1796.[a]

Student's name	Father's occupation	Tax assessment (£) Real	Tax assessment (£) Personal	Ward	Whites 16+ Male	Whites 16– Male	Whites Female	Other Free	Other Slaves	Religion	Age April 1, 1796	Basis of parental identification	Admitted	Withdrew
Armstrong, Elizabeth	Laborer	0	0	6	0	1	—	—	—	(All assumed to be Dutch Reformed)	13	Baptism	'92	'96
Deacon, James	(Mother:nurse)	0	0	1	—	—	3	0	0		—	Dunshee	'92	'95
Covenhaven, Nicholas	Cartman	200	0	6	2	4	4	0	0		—	Dunshee	'92	'98
Romine, Ob	Taylor	0	0	7	—	—	2	0	0		—	Dunshee	'92	'96
Vonck, Catherine	Cartman	0	0	7	0	0	—	—	—		—	Dunshee	'92	'96
Van Benschoten, Cornelius	Cartman	0	0	7	1	0	2	0	0		—	Dunshee	'92	'96
Morris, Rachel	Cartman	0	0	6	—	—	7	0	0		—	Dunshee	'93	'95
Morris, Susan	Cartman	0	0	6	—	—	7	—	—		—	Dunshee	'95	'97
Lyon, Michael	(Mother:mantua maker)	250	30	4	2	3	4	0	0		12	Baptism	'93	'97
Stagg, John	Cartman	0	0	6	1	1	2	0	0		10	Dunshee	'94	'96
Ackerman, Lawrence	Grocer	0	0	7	—	—	—	—	—		—	Baptism	'94	'99
Decker, John	Potter	0	0	6	1	0	3	—	—		—	Dunshee	'94	'95
Colbert, John	(Mother:seamstress)	0	0	4	1	2	1	0	0		8	Dunshee	'94	'99
Rykeman, Mary	Cartman	0	0	6	1	1	3	0	0		—	Dunshee	'95	'98
Emmett, George	Measurer	0	50	3	3	3	5	0	0		—	Dunshee	'95	'02
Slidell, Nicholas	Shoemaker	0	20	3	3	1	5	0	0		—	Dunshee	'95	'98
Wandell, Catherine	Shoemaker	0	20	1	—	—	—	—	—		—	Dunshee	'95	'98
Wandell, Mary	Silversmith	0	0	3	—	—	—	0	0		—	Dunshee	'95	'98
Skarts, Harmon	(Guardian:Widow Kip)	0	0	7	1	1	3	0	0		—	Dunshee	'95	'97
Smith, Edward	Cartman (guardian:Andrew Fash)	100	0	7	1	1	3	0	0		—	Dunshee	'95	'96
Acker, Laney }		100	0	6	—	—	—	—	—		—	Dunshee	'95	'96
Acker, Rachel }												Dunshee		
Ayers, Tobias	Blacksmith	0	0	6	—	—	—	—	—		6	Dunshee	'95	'97
Ayres, Daniel	Blacksmith	0	0	3	—	—	—	—	—		—	Dunshee	'96	'02
Penny, John	Pilot	0	0	6	2	2	1	0	0		—	Dunshee	'95	'96
King, Jacob	Cartman	0	0	6	1	4	3	0	0		10	Dunshee	'95	'97
Kiersted, James	Brass founder	150	0	2	2	2	3	0	0		—	Dunshee	'96	'01
Mead, John	Tavernkeeper	0	50	2	2	2	3	0	0		—	Dunshee	'96	'99
Mead, Mary	Tavernkeeper	0	50	5	2	3	3	0	0		9	Baptism	'95	'99
Amerman, Isaac	Cartman	0	50	6	—	—	—	—	—		—	Dunshee	'95	'98
Nicholas, Henry	Blacksmith	0	0	4	1	—	2	0	0		—	Dunshee	'95	'99
Van Dyke, Charles	None:Almshouse	0	0	6	2	2	2	0	0		11	Dunshee	'95	'98
Deklyn, Peg	None given	200	50	6	—	—	—	—	—		9	Dunshee	'95	'96
Miner, James	Cartman	200	0	6	—	—	—	—	—		9	Dunshee	'96	'99
Ver Valen, Andrew	Shoemaker	0	50	6	—	—	—	—	—		9	Dunshee	'95	'95
Lang, Daniel	Shoemaker	200	0	6	—	—	—	—	—		9	Dunshee	'96	'99
Devoe, Laney	Wood inspector	200	50	1	—	—	—	—	—		9	Dunshee	'95	'97

Sources: Henry W. Dunshee, History of the School of the Reformed Protestant Dutch Church in New York, 1633–1883 (New York, 2nd ed., 1883); see also n. 26, this chapter.

[a] Total enrollment, 101; parents identified, 32; sibling pairs, 5; children of parents identified, 37.

43

TABLE 6. Profile of Benjamin

Student's name	Father's occupation	Tax assessment (£) Real	Personal	Ward	Whites 16+ Male	16− Male	Female	Other Free	Slaves
Quackenbush, David	Dry goods	300	0	4	2	4	3	0	0
Burger, Elizabeth	Block & pump maker	1000	900	5	3	2	3	0	1
Burger, Gerald	Block & pump maker	1000	900	5	3	2	3	0	1
Fish, John	Library supervisor	0	500	4	1	1	3	0	2
Carr, Mary	Grocer	400	100	5	1	2	4	0	0
Swartout, Anthony	Merchant	500	0	4	1	6	2	0	1
Swartout, James	Merchant	500	0	4	1	6	2	0	1
Crolius, Thomas	Stoneward mfg.	500	100	6	4	3	3	0	1
Kingsland, Catharine	Oyster picker	0	0	5	1	1	3	0	0
Stagg, Benjamin	Grocer	0	200	4	4	4	4	0	1
Ruckel, Philip	Baker	0	80	4	—	—	—	—	—
Schultz, Elizabeth	Brewer	700	400	7	—	—	—	—	—
Schultz, Michael	Brewer	700	400	7	—	—	—	—	—
Heerman, Frederick	Druggist	0	100	4	—	—	—	—	—
Utt, John	Cooper	850	0	4	2	3	6	0	0
Holdup, William	Tavernkeeper	0	100	3	—	—	—	—	—
Haight, Abigail	Sadler & cap maker	1200	200	4	2	1	5	0	1
Haight, John	Sadler & cap maker	1200	200	4	2	1	5	0	1
Post, Elizabeth	Master builder	1400	300	4	2	2	5	0	1
Post, Ann	Master builder	1400	300	4	2	2	5	0	1
Brower, Catherine	None given	0	0	6	1	0	2	0	0
Stanton, Agnes	Measurer of lime	500	100	4	1	0	6	0	0
Lebrun, Peter	Grocer	0	0	6	1	2	4	0	0
Link, George	Tobacconist	0	0	5	—	—	—	—	—
Shrady, John	Shoemaker	0	0	5	3	2	1	0	0
Steddiford, William	Auctioneer	0	250	4	1	3	6	0	0
Steddiford, Catharine	Auctioneer	0	250	4	1	3	6	0	0
Irving, Washington	Dry goods	1500	350	3	—	—	—	—	—
Hasen, Catherine	Mariner	0	0	4	2	1	4	0	0
Gunn, Mary	Silk & wool dyer	700	100	3	—	—	—	—	—
Cromwell, Sarah	Grocer	2800	200	3	1	2	2	0	0
Romaine, Samuel	Teacher	1650	100	—	1	1	2	0	0

Sources: Benjamin Romaine, Teacher's Report to the Common Council, June 1, 1796, NYMA, Box

a Total enrollment, 108; parents identified, 26; sibling pairs, 6; children of parents identified, 32.

b Probable identification. A general combination of probability factors—whether the name was less close to the school, and whether the family structure of that household head (as recorded in the federal itive identifications.

The common pay schools were not an educational utopia, of course. It is impossible to determine how many truly poor children attended school, but they were undoubtedly underrepresented; at the other end of the scale, although many quite substantial families sent their children to the common schools, others opted for tutors and more expensive boarding schools. Nevertheless, the mix was broad, and the contrast between charity and pay school families,

Romaine's Students, 1796.[a]

Religion	Age April 1, 1796	Basis of parental identification	Subjects studied					Days attended	Tuition due (rate 24–28 s/ quarter) (£-s-d)
			Read.	Writ.	Spell.	Arith.	Gramm.		
Dutch	12	Baptism	x	x	x	x	x	155	2-13-7
Dutch	15	Baptism	x	x	x	x	—	39	0-11-6
Dutch	12	Baptism	x	x	x	x	x	155	2-13-7
Episc.	16	Baptism	x	x	x	x	x	117	1-19-2
Episc.	11	Baptism	x	x	x	x	x	27	0-12-0
Episc.	7	Baptism	x	x	x	—	x	83	1-10-4
Episc.	—	Sibling	x	x	x	—	x	142	2-8-10
Dutch	10	Baptism	x	x	x	x	x	155	2-13-7
Episc.	8	Baptism	x	x	x	x	x	101	1-14-9
Dutch	9	Baptism	x	x	x	x	x	155	2-13-7
Episc.	11	Baptism	(Bookkeeping)					54	2-0-0
—	—	Probable[b]	x	x	x	x	x	101	1-14-9
—	—	Probable[b]	x	x	x	x	x	44	0-15-7
—	—	Probable[b]	x	x	x	—	x	155	2-13-7
Episc.	15	Baptism	(Bookkeeping)					54	2-0-0
Episc.	7	Baptism	x	x	x	—	—	27	0-9-4
Episc.	13	Baptism	x	x	x	x	x	116	1-19-11
Episc.	9	Baptism	x	x	x	—	x	155	2-13-7
Dutch	11	Baptism	x	x	x	x	—	121	2-1-9
Dutch	8	Baptism	x	x	x	x	x	81	1-8-0
Dutch	7	Baptism	x	x	x	x	—	155	2-13-7
Episc.	9	Baptism	x	x	x	x	—	108	1-17-0
Cath.	8	Baptism	x	x	x	—	x	81	1-8-0
—	—	Probable[b]	x	x	x	x	x	155	gratis
—	—	Probable[b]	x	x	x	x	x	155	2-13-7
Dutch	15	Baptism	x	x	x	x	x	147	2-9-5
Dutch	—	Baptism (n.d.)	x	x	x	x	x	131	2-5-3
Presb.	13	Baptism	x	x	x	x	x	85	1-9-3
—	—	Probable[b]	x	x	x	—	—	81	1-8-0
—	—	Probable[b]	x	x	x	—	—	75	1-5-11
Episc.	13	Baptism	x	x	x	—	—	62	1-1-8
Dutch	6	Baptism	x	x	x	—	x	155	gratis

6459; see also n. 26, this chapter.

than common, whether there was only one such adult listed in the *Directory*, whether that adult lived census of 1790) allowed the possibility of a child of the right age and sex—yielded probable but not pos-

though real, was less distinct than one might expect. An analysis of the children enrolled in the Dutch charity school and in Benjamin Romaine's pay school will illustrate these points. The results are not easily conveyed in statistical form, especially because the tax category, "not listed," is ambiguous, and because the same information was not available for every child. Tables 5 and 6, therefore, present all the relevant information available for

the two schools. Generalizations can then be drawn from
this data.

Of the 101 children who attended the Dutch charity school between April 1795 and April 1796, the parents of 37 have been
identified. There were five pairs of siblings; thus, thirty-two families
are involved.[26] Nineteen of the thirty-two families were not listed
in the tax lists at the address given in the *Directory* and thus either
had no property worth more than £20, which is quite likely for
widows and low-paid laborers, or they had moved. More interesting
among the charity scholars' parents are the thirteen who were successful enough to be taxable. Cartmen were the most numerous
among these parents, which is not surprising, for they belonged to
an economically diverse occupational group. There were 811 licensed
New York cartmen in 1796, and some of them did quite well.[27]
Of the 11 cartmen whose children attended the charity school, 5
were taxed; 4 of these owned their own homes. These men could

26. Student names were linked with parents in several ways. The Dutch
school parents were all listed on the register, but only thirty-seven of these
were found in the *Directory*. The register is reprinted in Dunshee, *Dutch
Church*. Second, for other schools, the most secure identifications were through
baptisms. Except with very common names, these identifications are fairly
certain. Third, children with the same family name, especially if listed next
to each other, were generally assumed to be siblings, so some baptismal
identifications led to further matching of brothers or sisters with parents.
These three means of identification provided the parents' names for about
half of the final sample. The others were identified from wills or, with less
certainty, by the general combination of probability factors, i.e., whether the
name was less than common, whether there was only one such adult listed
in the *Directory*, whether that adult lived close to the school, and whether
the family structure of that household head (as recorded in the federal Census
of 1790) allowed the possibility of a child of the right sex and age. These
factors were combined in judgments that yielded probable, but not positive
identifications. Many possible matches were discarded. The materials used,
in addition to the school reports (see n. 21, above, this chap.), Low's 1796
Directory, and the 1790 Census, *Heads of Families* . . . (Washington, United
States Bureau of the Census, 1908), included: First Presbyterian Church
(12 W. 12th Street), Baptisms, MS, vol. I (1728–1790), vol. II (1791–1802);
Trinity Church, Baptisms, transcript, New York Genealogical and Biographical
Society, vol. I (1749–1813); Methodist Episcopal Church Records, vol. 233,
Baptisms, NYPL; Tobias A. Wright, ed., *Records of the Reformed Dutch
Church in New Amsterdam and New York: Baptisms, 1731–1800* (New York,
New York Genealogical and Biographical Society, 1902; repr., Gregg Press,
Upper Saddle River, New Jersey, 1968); Rev. James H. McGean, "The
Earliest Baptismal Register of St. Peter's Church, New York City," *Historical
Records and Studies,* vol. I (part I, 1899, part II, 1900), 97–107, 387–399;
and New York City Wills, New York Surrogate's Court, Room 402.

27. See Pomerantz, *New York,* pp. 211–212; Moreau said that "a good
city cart horse" cost 72 to 75 dollars, Roberts, *Moreau's Journey,* p. 159.

have afforded to pay for education, and indeed many cartmen did, but, whether from frugality or an attachment to the Dutch church, these 5 men were getting free schooling for their children, thanks to the Dutch consistory, which apparently had a rather loose definition of eligibility. The other tax-paying parents included 2 city workers—a wood inspector and a measurer—2 shoemakers, a tavernkeeper, a blacksmith, and a brass founder. The Dutch charity school, then, was not simply a pauper's school. The point, however, should not be overemphasized. The school did serve primarily workingmen, many of whom probably would have found education difficult to finance.

Romaine's school contained only one free scholar, but, like the Dutch school, it brought together a collection of boys and girls whose parents represented diverse occupations and incomes. Twenty-six parents (of thirty-two students) were identified. At the lower end of the social scale they included a mariner, an oyster picker, and four others not listed on the tax list. The twenty who were taxed ranged from the substantial businessmen like Oliver Cromwell, William Irving, and Bernardus Swartout, to the baker John Ruckel, who rented quarters in Green Street but had £80 in personal property and sent his son first to Martin Evans's school and then to Romaine's. The most typical of Romaine's clients, however, were successful craftsmen, like master builder Anthony Post, sadler Benjamin Haight, silk dyer George Gunn, and stoneware maker John Crolius.

Fourteen of the twenty taxpayers owned their houses or shops. These were generally in the middle wards, three through six; the Bowery (Ward 7) was represented only by the children of Christian Schultz, a prosperous brewer. However, this was not strictly an economic bias; numerous pay schools were scattered throughout the city and charged similar prices. Therefore they tended to attract children from a smaller area than the six charity schools, whose religious affiliations influenced attendance. James Liddell's school, located in the Bowery on the line between the sixth and seventh wards, attracted more students from the eastern part of the city than Romaine's, which was on the west side, but it also had at least two pupils from quite far downtown. Table 7 gives information on the twelve parents of Liddell's students who have been identified. One might expect them to be less prosperous than

TABLE 7. Profile of James Liddell's Students, 1796.[a]

| Student's name | Father's occupation | Tax assessment (£) | | Family structure, 1790 | | | | | | | Age April 1, 1790 | Basis of parental identification | No. of quarters attended | Tuition paid | |
		Real	Personal	Ward	16+ Male	16– Male	Female	Free	Slaves	Religion				(£)	(s)
Marshell, Thomas	Storekeeper	0	0	7	—	—	—	—	—	Episc.	6	Baptism	2	1	16
Marshell, Rebecca	Storekeeper	0	0	7	—	—	—	—	—	—	—	Sibling	2	1	16
Marshell, Gilbert	Storekeeper	0	0	7	—	—	—	—	—	—	—	Sibling	2	1	16
Marshell, John	Storekeeper	0	0	7	—	—	—	—	—	—	—	Sibling	1	—	18
Gerald, Eliza	Merchant	0	100	1	—	—	—	—	—	—	—	Probable[b]	3	2	14
Gerald, Fanny	Merchant	0	100	1	—	—	—	—	—	—	—	Sibling	1	—	18
Andens, James	Cartman	0	0	6	—	—	—	—	—	Presb.	14	Baptism	3	2	14
Andens, William	Cartman	0	0	6	—	—	—	—	—	Presb.	10	Baptism	3	2	14
Andens, Samuel	Cartman	0	0	6	—	—	—	—	—	Presb.	8	Baptism	2	1	16
Andens, Mary	Cartman	0	0	6	—	—	—	—	—	—	—	Sibling	2	1	16
Stead, Fanny	Carpenter	0	0	5	—	—	—	—	—	—	—	Probable[b]	2	1	16
Shanon, Jean	Mason	0	0	6	—	—	—	—	—	—	—	Probable[b]	1	—	14
Tetes, Eliza	(Mother:market woman)	0	0	3	—	—	—	—	—	—	—	Probable[b]	1	—	14
Dickson, Ann	(Mother:none given)	0	0	7	—	—	—	—	—	—	—	—	1	—	18
Dickson, Thomas (eve.)	(Mother:none given)	150	0	7	—	—	—	—	—	—	—	Sibling (?)	1	—	16
Mitchell, Andrew	Merchant	2000	500	4	1	4	3	0	2	Presb.	10	Baptism	1	—	18
Mitchell, Fanny	Merchant	2000	500	4	1	4	3	0	2	Presb.	—	Sibling	1	—	18
Fundie, Isaac	Cartman	0	0	7	—	—	—	—	—	—	—	Probable[b]	1	—	15
Fundie, Mary	Cartman	0	0	7	—	—	—	—	—	—	—	—	1	—	14
Furman, Henry	Painter-glazier	300	100	5	—	—	—	—	—	Episc.	10	Baptism	1	—	16
Hibner, George (eve.)	Sawyer	0	0	7	—	—	—	—	—	—	—	Probable[b]	1	—	16
Casilear, John (eve.)	Mariner	300	25	7	1	3	5	0	0	—	—	Probable[b]	1	—	16

Sources: James Liddell, Teacher's Report to the Common Council, May 31, 1796, NYMA, Box 6459; see also n. 26, this chapter.

[a] Total enrollment, 70 (61 day, 7 evening); parents identified, 10; children of parents identified, 22.

[b] Probable identification. A general combination of probability factors—whether the name was less than common, whether there was only one such adult listed in the *Directory*, whether that adult lived close to the school, and whether the family structure of that household (as recorded in the federal census of 1790) allowed the possibility of a child of the right age and sex—yielded probable but not positive identifications.

Romaine's clients, since the eastern area included more laboring people. This impression is borne out, to the extent that fewer of the twelve were found on the tax lists, but the same broad range of occupations and wealth is also evident. At Liddell's school the children of wealthy merchant Andrew Mitchell, assessed at £2,500, mingled with the son of middling-class painter-glazier Henry Furman, assessed at £400, as well as many children from poorer homes.

The reports from Romaine, Liddell, and the Dutch school, with those from the eleven other masters who provided the Common Council with lists of students, show that these schools offered children a common experience in other ways. Table 8 describes these lists and indicates the size of the sample under discussion. Each school shows a mixture not only of family wealth, neighborhoods, and occupations but also of age, sex, and religion. The median age of the students was ten, with 75 percent between the ages of eight and thirteen, but the range was quite broad for each teacher.[28] Romaine, for example, had to cope with both a six-year-old and a sixteen-year-old in his classroom. All the common schools enrolled both boys and girls, in a ratio of about two to one, unlike the sexually segregated common schools of the nineteenth century. Nor was religion a segregating factor; baptisms are extant for eighty-eight children on the pay school lists. As Table 9 illustrates, religion was not a determining factor in school choice among the predominant Protestant denominations.[29]

Access to a common education seems to have been widespread. In addition to the charity schools' contribution, some pay school masters reduced or omitted fees for poor parents. Donald Fraser's statement to the Council includes the following entries: "T. Poor abated 28s being a poor widow's child; D. McColl abated 24s being an orphan; Wm. Block one quarter Gratis, his father pleads poverty; Wm. Faike abated 16s his mother being a widow; D. Miller

28. N = 108, those students whose age was known and whose parents were identified.

29. The extant Catholic baptisms begin with 1789–90, which means that they include only those children age six or less in 1796. This is unfortunate; considering the conflict which developed between Catholic and Protestant schools in the nineteenth century, it would be interesting to know whether there were very many Catholics in the pay schools of 1796. Only one, young Peter Lebrun, the son of a grocer, showed up in the limited sample described here.

TABLE 8. New York City Teachers' Reports, 1796, Listing Students by Name.

Reports	No. of children listed	No. of children whose parents were identified				No. of families	Tax assessments listed		
		Boys	Girls	Not clear	Total		None	£20–100	£100+
A. Charity schools									
African Free	51	4	0	0	4	4	3	1	0
Presbyterian	69	4	7	0	11	11	7	1	3
Dutch	101	24	10	3	32	19	19	7	6
Subtotal	221	32	17	3	52	34	29	9	9
B. Pay schools									
O'Hagarty-Carroll	40	5	4	2	11	8	5	1	2
Collins	83	9	3	2	14	12	3	3	6
Evans	48	15	3	2	20	15	5	3	7
Fraser	96	12	6	8	26	19	4	5	10
Gibbons	66	18	7	0	25	16	6	4	6
Liddell	69	12	10	0	22	12	7	1	4
Mead	79	10	4	1	15	12	3	3	6
Patterson	63	5	14	1	20	9	3	1	5
Roe	60	11	3	1	15	8	2	1	5
Romaine	107	19[a]	13	0	32	22	5	3	14
Youngs	56	8	1	0	9	8	4	3	1
Subtotal	767	124	58	17	209	141	47	28	66
TOTAL	988	156	75	20	261	175	76	37	75

Sources: Teachers' Reports to the Common Council, May–July, 1796, MS, NYMA, Box 6459; see also n. 21, this chapter.
[a] Omits two students from Romaine's list who also appear on other lists.

TABLE 9.   Religion of Common Pay School Students, 1796.

School	Episcopal	Dutch Reformed	Presbyterian
O'Hagarty & Carroll	0[a]	0	1
Collins	3	1	1
Evans	6	0	6
Fraser	3	3	4
Gibbons	4	2	3
Liddell	2	0	4
Mead	1	1	3
Patterson	3	4	2
Roe	2	1	3
Romaine	11	11	2
Youngs	1	0	0
Total	36	23	28

Sources: Teachers' Reports to the Common Council, May–June, 1796, NYMA; First Presbyterian Church (12 W. 12th Street), Baptisms, MS, vol. I (1782–1790), vol. II (1791–1802); Trinity Church, Baptisms, transcript, New York Genealogical and Biographical Society, vol. I (1749–1813); Tobias A. Wright, ed., *Records of the Reformed Dutch Church in New Amsterdam and New York: Baptisms, 1731–1800* (New York, New York Genealogical and Biographical Society, 1902; repr. Gregg Press, Upper Saddle River, New Jersey, 1968).

[a] Zero does not imply that no Episcopal children attended O'Hagarty & Carroll's School, but only that of their students whose religion could be determined none was Episcopal.

Alex Miller, Their father pleads poverty, abated 24s." Romaine has one similar entry, and William Payne informed the Council that "for this year, and for several before I have taught two poor Scholars gratis."[30]

Although it is impossible to know exactly how many children from different income groups were in school, a rough estimate can be made of the total school enrollment. Table 10 multiplies the total number of schools in each category by the average number of pupils per teacher at the schools where enrollment is known. This total enrollment, compared to the estimated number of children age five to fifteen in 1795, results in a remarkable enrollment rate: 52 percent.[31] Even if this estimate were high by 10 to 15

30. Teachers' Reports, May-July, 1796, MS, NYMA, Box 6459.
31. The estimated population in 1795, on the basis of a simple arithmetic increase between the 1790 and 1800 federal census returns (which tends to overestimate 1795 population) is 46,397. The percentage of children 0 to 15 (i.e., under 16) was estimated to be 41 percent on the basis of the

TABLE 10.   Total Estimated School Enrollment, 1795–96.[a]

Schools	Reported (partial)			Estimated (total)
Charity schools	African free	51		71.5 students per school
	Trinity charity	86		×6 charity schools
	Presb. charity	69		429.0 estimated charity school
	Dutch charity	80		enrollment
		286		
	Average: 71.5			
Pay schools, men	Carroll	40 day	0 eve.	69 students per school
	Collins	83	41	×60 men teachers
	Evans	48	24	4140 estimated pay school
	Fraser	96	0	enrollment, men teachers
	Gibbons	66	0	
	Liddell	61	8	
	Mead	49	30	
	Patterson	63	12	
	Roe	60	0	
	Romaine	107	0	
	Youngs	56	41	
	Bements	98	0	
	Gumm	31	0	
	Smith, D.	20	8	
	Piggot	50	0	
	Peter	55	0	
	Rudd	25	0	
		1008	164	
	Average: 69			
Pay schools, women	No reports extant			20 students, estimate
				×31 women teachers
				620 estimated pay school
				enrollment, women teachers
Almshouse school	Enrollment: 60			60 students
Total	Reported (partial): 1518			Estimated (total): 5249

Sources: Teachers' Reports to the Common Council, May–June, 1796, NYMA, Box 6459; [Low's] *New York Directory . . . 1796* (New York, 1796); see also n. 20, this chapter.
[a] Excludes college, dancing, and music students.

percent, the enrollment rate would still be impressive, especially because it compares attendance in a given year with all children age five to fifteen, while actually very few individuals would have gone to school every year during that whole twelve-year span. Modern enrollment rates reflect not only compulsory education laws

following known figures: the ratio of such children to total population was 40.1 percent for whites in 1786, 39.9 percent for whites in 1790, 42.2 percent for whites in 1800; 42.9 percent for blacks in 1747, 35.7 percent for blacks in 1771. Using this 41 percent figure, children 0–15 are estimated at 17,023 in 1795. The ratio of children 5 to 15 is estimated to be 59 percent of the 0–15 figure on the basis of the slightly strained analogy that 61 percent of children 0–14 were 5–14 in 1850 and 57 percent in 1855, the closest relevant figures available. The estimated school age population for 1795, then, is 59 percent × 17,023, or 10,043. The estimated enrollment, 5,249 children, is 52.2 percent of the estimated school age population.

but an assumption that children need continuous education throughout their school age years. In the 1790's, however, a man decided what was appropriate for his children: nothing, or a few semesters for reading, or three or five years for a good common education, or a few more for accounting or navigation, or a full grammar education. Therefore, many children not yet sixteen would already have been bound to a trade (although some of these might be among the evening school students counted); others, especially those five to seven years old, might not have gone to school yet but would in the future. Nevertheless, in the twelve months from April 1795 to April 1796, it seems, about half of all of these children attended some kind of school for some time. The estimate of 52 percent, then, if accurate, does not mean that 48 percent of New York's children never went to school. Schooling was such a discontinuous and informal procedure that a 52-percent enrollment rate might occur in a given year even if 80 or 90 percent of the population received some schooling during their childhood.

Materials are not available to correlate common schooling with occupational success. Schooling had a closer relationship to success in some occupations than in others, of course. Above the level of common laborer, cartman, and other unskilled jobs, and below the level of the professions, there were many jobs where a good common education could contribute. For the skilled craftsman a knowledge of arithmetic and some accounting might mean the chance to become a manufacturer employing others and branching out; for the mariner training in reading and some navigation might mean the chance to rise to able seaman or mate at double and triple the wages.[32] Clerks and civil servants were a small proportion of the labor force in the 1790's (see Table 1), but innkeepers, grocers, brewers, and other proprietors comprised nearly 15 percent, and schooling could help them too. Table 11 was computed to see if parents in these categories patronized the common schools in disproportionate numbers. The results hint that this was true, but the differences are too small to be statistically significant with such small samples. More important than the slightly different percentages is the general use of the common schools by all occupational groups.

---

32. See Pomerantz, *New York*, p. 430; for seamen's wages, see Stanley Lebergott, *Manpower in Economic Growth; the American Record Since 1800* (New York, McGraw-Hill, 1964), p. 531.

TABLE 11. Occupations of School Children's Parents, 1796.[a]

Category	Number of parents	Percent of school parents	Percent of directory sample (Table 1)
Laborer	4	2.4	5.5
Mariner	8	4.8	3.7
Cartman	21	12.6	9.5
Skilled craftsman	66	39.5	43.1
Clerical worker	10	6.0	2.0
Proprietor	31	18.6	14.3
Professional	0	0	4.0
Merchant	13	7.8	13.0
Other	14	8.4	5.4
Total	167	100	100

Sources: Teachers' Reports to the Common Council, May–June, 1796, NYMA, Box 6459; [Low's] *New York Directory* . . . *1796* (New York, 1796); see also n. 26, this chapter.

[a] Includes both charity and pay school parents. See Table 1 for explanation of categories.

Causal statements about the effects of education are very hazardous. Whatever the effects of this mixing of classes and religions, however, the mix was later assumed to be a desirable goal in the educational development of the city and the nation; but because of the profound changes in economic and ethnic composition of the city brought on by industrialization, immigration, and urbanization, it took the whole of the nineteenth century and beyond to recapture this situation in the schools of American cities. Indeed, New York City's common schools may have been more comprehensive in socioeconomic terms in the 1790's than today, if individual schools are considered. More important, the process of shaping an educational system to meet the problems of the city changed the nature of schooling and people's notions about schools, as the succeeding chapters will show. No ideologues promoted the schooling arrangements of New York in the 1790's; they just grew that way. Yet the 1796 school returns make it clear that education in the city was inexpensive, with independent masters serving a broad cross-section of the population.

EDUCATION BEYOND THE COMMON SCHOOLS

John Collins said that his students had studied reading, writing, spelling, arithmetic, English grammar, and morality; that is a good summary of a common education. The relation of such schooling to further literary education and to occupational training is difficult to define because there was no system. One did not "graduate" from common school, and no particular patterns prevailed except that many boys were apprenticed at age fourteen. Except for the fact that they both kept boys busy, schooling and craft apprenticeship were not closely related in purpose. Schooling did not cease, however, when apprenticeship began. All full-term indentures contained schooling clauses, usually for one quarter's schooling per year. These were perhaps as often breached as honored, but the commissioners attempted to enforce them in the case of Almshouse children. The board broke one indenture in 1794 for such an infraction, with the further notation that the master was "sharply reprimanded from the Chair, and on Motion a resolution passed unanimously that no poor Child of this house shall be bound to the said Thomas in the future."[33] The fact that seven of seventeen schoolmasters reporting to the Council kept evening as well as day schools indicates that many young men who worked in the daytime were in school at night.

Evening schools as well as specialized day schools offered young men a variety of subjects beyong the common curriculum; navigation, surveying, and modern languages were the most frequently advertised. But there is no positive information about the youths who attended these schools or how much good it did them. From newspaper advertisements it appears that both the ability to write and the backing of good recommendations were required to open the door to many desirable apprenticeships. In the *Diary* a man advertised: "Wants employment, Either in whole sale or dry good store or shipping house—a young man of unexceptionable charac-

33. New York City, Almshouse and Bridewell, Commissioners Minutes, 1791–1797, NYPL, September 15, 1794.

ter, who wishes to serve as an apprentice, writes a good hand, and well acquainted with common accompts, can produce the best recommendation." Another young man who knew accounting and French advertised for a place in a store or as a ship's clerk and said he could give security. The combination of acquaintances and abilities is again apparent in the advertisement of "a young man of genteel connections, writes a good hand, understands accounts, was regularly bred to the Dry Good bussiness."[34] A variety of jobs were open to men who had a little more than a common education.

A thorough liberal education was quite another matter. Especially if achieved at boarding school and college, it was anything but cheap, and, as in the colonial period, young men who were thus privileged did so for cultural and social reasons more than for occupational training. As Henry Seamans said in 1799, "at the time my sons take their degree at College they will be of an age to judge what occupation they are best fitted for." Also, as before the war, the different levels of educational institutions were disjointed. There was no concept in New York of an educational pyramid such as Jefferson envisaged for Virginia, whereby the best students from the common schools were to attend grammar schools, and the best of these were to attend college. There were a variety of ways to prepare for Columbia College, and all of them cost money. One could attend the common pay schools and then go on to one of the city's grammar schools, for example, William Best's, or Samuel Lilly's, where one could be "instructed in the Greek and Latin languages with elegance and grammatical purity." One could read grammar privately with a minister, or go to the Columbia Grammar School, or board at an academy out of town. The extreme flexibility of the sequence is well illustrated by Gulian Verplanck, who learned his Latin at home on Wall Street, entered Columbia at age eleven, and graduated at fourteen.[35] Because there were no set, expected patterns, the educational experience of a child was shaped to his personal abilities or desires, or those of his parents. For elites as well as commoners, the initiative in eighteenth-century

34. *Diary,* September 29, 1795; *ibid.,* November 28, 1795.
35. *Wills,* XV, 149; *Advertiser,* January 2, 1795; Robert W. July, *The Essential New Yorker, Gulian Crommelin Verplanck* (Durham, N.C., Duke University Press, 1951), p. 11.

New York was on the part of the consumers, not the dispensers, of education.

For New York's elites the city itself, or at least their part of it, was a great school. A young man's education went on in class, in the fashionable societies of the day, at tea, in public lectures, and in his rooms under his own direction. The diary of John Anderson, Jr., portrays the daily round of a young gentleman being educated in New York. On January 22, 1794, he delivered an essay on "the Utility of Afflictions" before the Athenian, a literary society. Two days later he spent the afternoon listening to the Supreme Court in session and then stayed at home in the evening, reading Pufendorf, practicing the violin, and doing some exercises on irregular French verbs. As he was then attending a series of lectures on electricity by Dr. Kemp of the college, he also read on that subject in the Encyclopedia. The next day Washington Irving came to tea and listened to Anderson play his violin. That evening Anderson had French class. Other days found him at college lectures, at the Law Society, the Society Library, the theater, and evening sermons. He spent one afternoon at the Tontine Coffee House discussing literature and another making an illustration for the Swords' *New York Magazine*.[36]

Thus were the confines of a classical education broadened in the 1790's. Music, art, drama, debating—it was all very alluring. As one Columbia student said, "in a town like this there will ever be company to attract our attentions." He assured his father, who had inquired from Poughkeepsie about his late hours, that "few of my company and none of my intimates are in the least exceptionable," and that he had to see them at night because he studied all day. The next year he wrote that he could get by on the little money his father allowed him only if he could be more liberal in the spring, a plea common to all ages. The son was probably right, however. The activities and associations of the gentleman student were indeed expensive. Evening French lessons cost Alexander Anderson, then a Columbia medical student, six dollars a season in 1793. The entrance fee to the Law Society was eight shillings, and a share in the Society Library cost $15, plus annual fees of about

36. John Anderson, Jr., Diary, 1794–1798, NYHS, pp. 1–30.

$1.25. Only those with considerable resources could enjoy the full benefits of a gentleman's education in New York.[37]

The education of young ladies was similarly varied, often emphasizing the social more than the intellectual. In 1801 Governor Trumbull of Connecticut sent his daughters to the metropolis, where they boarded with Catherine Duer, the famous widow. Their endless round of teas and promenades are recorded in letters home. "Lady Kitty Duer has a great many Books," wrote Maria Trumbull to her mother, "though we don't find much time to read as we go four times to dancing-school—three to drawing and Hariet takes a music lesson three times a week."[38]

In contrast, Theodosia Burr's education in New York was remarkably academic, and because her father had an intense interest in her preparation, their correspondence records her progress in detail. Aaron Burr took pleasure in showing his daughter's best letters to Benjamin Rush and other friends in Philadelphia. His letters in return are loving, but bantering and demanding. At age eleven Theodosia began Greek, and he assured her that she would find it the most charming language. He made her keep a journal of her lessons and activities and send it to him so he could chide her when she was slack. In September 1795, he calculated, "You ought to be out of the Odyssey before this will reach you, counting only two hundred lines a day since we parted. You may begin the Iliad, if you please." Even her mother's illness became the subject of a vocabulary lesson: "Be able, upon my arrival, to tell me the difference between an *infusion* and *decoction;* and the history, virtues, and the *botanical* or medical name of the bark," he wrote. She had several tutors at once, including the fashionable Mr. Leslie, who missed too many lessons to suit Burr. Even Theodosia's education could not be entirely intellectual, however, and Burr occasionally gave her advice on social life and exercise. He was determined that she would become a learned and important woman. When she was fifteen, he wrote, "if you should abandon the attempt, or

37. Samuel Jones, Jr., to Samuel Jones, Sr., February 25, 1787, and January 26, 1788, NYHS; Alexander Anderson, Diary, typescript, Columbiana Collection, CU, I, October 25, 1793; John Anderson, Diary, p. 10; Austin B. Keep, *History of the New York Society Library* (New York, DeVinne Press, 1908), pp. 247, 250.

38. Maria Trumbull to her mother, March 5, 1801, in Helen M. Morgan, ed., *A Season in New York, 1801* (Pittsburgh, University of Pittsburgh Press, 1969), p. 133.

despair of success, or relax your endeavours, it would indicate a feebleness of character which would dishearten me exceedingly."[39]

Much more congenial, but just as thoroughly involved in his children's education, New York's theater producer, William Dunlap, tutored his children personally. Entries in his diary in the summer of 1797 show how their lessons mingled with his activities and his own reading. On June 15: "Walk out to Williamson's with my boy. Read with both the Children aided by maps." The next day: "Read with John—Go with Samuel Bowne to collect subscriptions for the use of the African free school . . . Hear Margaret read. Read Mandeville." The next day he paid salaries, read geography to the girl and arithmetic to the boy. At the end of the week he recorded that his son's "mind is attracted to a great variety of objects during these lessons & by answering his questions my mind is exercised & my knowledge increased."[40]

From parents as well as schoolmasters, from public lectures, courts, sermons, and clubs as well as from tutors, children learned about the world of ideas and the world of affairs. The education of children was part of the life of adults. Just as apprentices learned from their masters things they could not learn in school, wealthy children learned their adult roles from adults in general, not just from teachers. In this regard, elite education was just a more full-blown example of the general state of schooling and education in New York at the time: education was informal, discontinuous, and varied. Schooling was plentiful; it played an important but not a predominant role in education, and it did not serve to isolate children from the rest of the world.

The more resources a family or a whole community has, both financial and intellectual, the more successful such informal modes of education can be. New York society emerged from the colonial period with a tradition of spontaneous, unregulated education supplemented by a modicum of charity schooling. A largely literate society with a common language, New Yorkers did not rely solely on schools to teach basic skills. A society without disruptive racial or ethnic tensions, it did not rely solely on schools to transmit a code

39. Mark Van Doren, ed., *The Correspondence of Aaron Burr and His Daughter Theodosia* (New York, Covici-Friede, 1929), pp. 12–13, 24–25, 29, 42, 47.

40. *The Diary of William Dunlap,* vol. I, 1786, 1788, 1797–98 (New York, NYHS *Collections,* 1929), pp. 69–71.

of morality. A society integrated enough socioeconomically not to
rely solely on schools to teach deference, New York nevertheless had
schools within the reach of most families' means, schools in which
the children of mechanics and merchants mingled.

POTENTIAL SYSTEMATIZATION:
THE SOCIETY OF ASSOCIATED TEACHERS

No urgent social needs prompted schoolmasters or philanthropists
to organize schools in this period, but other influences led to organization and, potentially, to a systematization of the schooling
of New York's children. During New York's postwar period of population growth there was a great proliferation of associations, some
on an ethnic basis, like the Friendly Sons of St. Patrick (1784),
and some on occupational lines, like the cartmen (1792), the
printers (1794), or the more broadly based Society of Tradesmen
and Mechanics (1785). There were political groups, like the Democratic Club (1794), and literary societies, like the Calliopean
(1788) and the Drone (1792). Many of these associations, to the
Federalists' alarm, had a decidedly Republican cast. It was thus
typical of the period that in 1794, fifteen schoolmasters met to form
a society, and several of their number were active Republicans.[41]

Among the teachers who attended the organizational meetings
of this Society of Associated Teachers of New York City in May
and June were Donald Fraser, author of a famous textbook, *The
Young Gentleman and Lady's Assistant,* John Campbell, whose
schoolroom they often used for meetings, John Collins, the successful grocer-teacher, Irving's mentor, Benjamin Romaine, Bowery
schoolmaster James Liddell, and Cornelius Davis, teacher of the
African Free School. By September twenty-nine teachers were on
the rolls. Each member was asked at first simply to communicate
"anything which he conceives may have a tendency to promote
useful knowledge."[42] In addition to a weekly evening of conviviality

41. Society of Associated Teachers of New York City, Minutes, MS, NYSL,
published in full in the *37th Annual Report of the State Superintendent
for the School Year . . . 1889–90* (Albany, Department of Public Instruction,
1891), to which page references cited here and below refer. For May and
June meetings, see pp. 245–251. On the Republican complexion of the Associated Teachers, see Young, *Democratic Republicans,* p. 406.

42. Associated Teachers, Minutes, p. 250.

and the discussion of shared problems, the Society provided teachers for the first time with a potential mechanism for developing group standards. A committee was established to "make enquiry into the merits and abilities of any person who shall apply to this Society for a Testimonial." The Society also acted as an accrediting group concerning textbooks. Fraser's *Young Gentleman and Lady's Assistant* carried their approval, as did a geography by Charles Smith, a speller by John Barry of Philadelphia, and a revision of *Dilworth's Assistant* by one of their members, James Gibbons.[43] The Society established a small professional library, including Smith's *History of New York*, a life of Franklin, and a volume on education by Joseph Priestley, a Republican hero of the day.[44] The activities of the Society illustrate its political as well as its fraternal purpose. For example, they met at Gad Ely's schoolroom in 1794 to march out as a group along with other associations to help build the fortifications on Governor's Island, an anti-British gesture. Like the Cartmen's and Mechanics' Societies, the Associated Teachers extended aid to indigent members.[45]

The Society attempted to coordinate some practices among the city's schools. A committee appointed to propose changes in school holidays suggested that a regular summer holiday of fourteen to twenty days in August be substituted for the customary scattered holidays. Members were asked to discover in the ensuing week "the sentiments of teachers, not belonging to the Society, respecting the proposed alteration of holidays." At another meeting it was resolved that "when any Scholar shall behave so disorderly as to oblige the Master to expel him, it shall be the duty of the teacher to report the same to the Society, together with his reasons for so doing."[46] The Society, it appears, was trying to prevent unmanageable children from making the rounds of the city's classrooms.

The Associated Teachers' most important activity was debating. Each week a question of educational theory or practice was argued and voted upon, and the minutes tell us what interested the teachers of the day and how they felt. The conclusion as to "whether a Republican or Monarchical form of government is most advan-

43. *Ibid.*, pp. 253, 255, 266, 267, 309.
44. *Ibid.*, p. 287.
45. Stokes, *Iconography*, May 10, 1794; Associated Teachers, Minutes, p. 290.
46. Associated Teachers, Minutes, pp. 280, 263.

tageous in a school," was not recorded, unfortunately, nor was the vote on "whether Silence or studying aloud be the most conducive to the improvement of scholars in a public school." Some strictly methodological questions were argued; it was decided in 1796 that a more "systematical" method of teaching penmanship was desirable. The question, "might not schools be well governed without corporal punishment?" the pedagogues decided in the negative. Not surprisingly these schoolmasters also decided, after "copious discussion," that "a private education in a family" was not as advantageous as that acquired in a school.[47] A debate in the fall of 1796 resulted in a reaffirmation that the Bible was a proper school book, and, on the related question, "ought any religion further than morality to be inculcated in schools?" President Benjamin Romaine requested that another man take the chair so that he could argue. Religion prevailed again.[48]

In December 1797, Benjamin Romaine posed the nature-nurture question for debate: "Does the difference of ability, so apparent among mankind arise from a superior intellect or from external causes?" The tie vote was considered important enough to record the aye's and nay's in the minutes, along with a decision to reconsider. Fraser, for example, voted for "original" differences, while Romaine argued the environmentalist position. Another prominent member, Jonathan Fisk, declared himself "doubtful." The votes of Romaine and Fisk against inherited differences is indicative of the optimism that informed their oratory as educational leaders. In his inaugural address as President of the Society in March 1797, Romaine declared, "The unmeaning names of Titular Distinctions and hereditary privileges are discarded, substituting in their stead the standard of merit, to the most exalted stations in Government . . . when America (to whom seems reserved the perfecting of human establishments) shall arrive at meridian Glory, the virtuous and indefatigable school man shall stand as a bright shining light."[49]

Fisk, invited to give the anniversary oration in 1798, carried the doctrines of Lockean psychology and republican philosophy even further. Children are "docile, tractable, ambitious," he said, and

47. Associated Teachers, Minutes, pp. 265, 267, 281, 282, 288.
48. *Ibid.*, pp. 289, 284.
49. Associated Teachers, Minutes, pp. 300, 274.

education can "stamp the character of parents and make the fortunes of their child." The teacher shares the duties of the parent for moral education, Fisk argued, and whatever their differences in politics and religion, "all will cordially unite in applauding the virtuous." Since few have the opportunity to go beyond a common education, "it is on the success of our common schools, that the well-fare, and hopes of the community must rest."[50] The importance of education in protecting liberty has been proved by the American Revolution, he declared, for in that crisis, "few were the soldiers called to bear their muskets, who were unable to read the complaints, and decide on the merits of their injured countrymen." Fisk carried the two themes of environmentalism and republicanism to their logical conclusion in a peroration that presaged his later success as a lawyer:

> Tho *Genius* may be the gift of heaven; it is not the precious possession of a chosen few: But like the animating beams of light and heat, is diffused among all classes, and colours, who have the form and feelings of men. If the means of cultivation were equal to all, we should not be able to find that vast disparity in their improvements which many have been ready to imagine . . . The doctrine of native superiority is nearly exploded, and we are at this day taught the humane, and benevolent creed, that all men are naturally equal, the children of one great family. If all have by nature equal rights, all ought to be informed of those rights, that they may estimate them suitably, enjoy them freely, and preserve them inviolate.[51]

Such views, needless to say, were not self-evident to all New Yorkers; indeed, they were considered dangerously partisan by the reigning Federalists. Thus it is not surprising to find, in the *New York Argus* for May 21, 1796, a news item, claiming to describe a meeting of the Associated Teachers, which exposed the group's political sentiments: "several moral and patriotic songs were sung, and many toasts were drank." Among the toasts, the writer said, was one to the United Republics of France and Holland—"May the valors of their arms crush to insignificance the hirelings of despotism, and may the British ravagers be the first to fall"—and

---

50. Jonathan Fisk, "On Education," Anniversary oration to the Society of Associated Teachers of the City of New York, May 19, 1798, MS, NYHS, pp. 5, 12, 21.
51. *Ibid.*, pp. 21, 30–31.

another, "Bread to the hungry, peace to the belligerent powers upon terms honorable to the French, and prosperity to faithful schoolmasters." John Campbell immediately wrote a rebuttal, in which he labelled the story a malicious fabrication but only half denied that the toasts were accurately reported: "That some toasts were drank that evening will not be denied . . . as they were not committed to writing by the secretary, it would be difficult—nay, I might say impossible, for any member thereof to give an exact statement of them. Suffice it to say, that party spirit on that occasion did not dare to raise its dangerous head." Campbell's refutation is not convincing. His own political affiliation is suggested by his membership in the Republican-dominated Emigrants Society. Also, in 1795, the Teachers' Society had regularly adopted the title "Citizen" in their minutes. Furthermore, in the aftermath of the newspaper attack the Associated Teachers passed a resolution that "no member of this society shall publish or cause to be published in any Newspaper, any of their proceedings, without their leave."[52] The educational rhetoric of the Society's leaders and their public activities as a group demonstrate the Society's Republican orientation.

This association with Republican politics was surely one reason why the Common Council rebuffed the Society's effort to obtain public funds for the city's schoolmasters, but there were other reasons more important for the future of public education in the city. The Council's decision—to allocate government funds only to denominational charity schools—was a blend, like many public policy decisions, of tradition, confusion, and political animosity. The elements of tradition and confusion will emerge from an analysis of the Council's interpretation of the New York State law of 1795 for the encouragement of common schooling.

POTENTIAL SYSTEMATIZATION: THE 1795 LAW

In 1795 the New York State legislature, spurred on by the example of the New England states, the appeals of Governor George Clinton, and the availability of funds from state land sales, passed a bill for aid to common schools. Clinton argued that the colleges

52. On Campbell, see *Argus,* June 2, 1795; *Argus,* May 21, 1796; *Argus,* May 24, 1796; Associated Teachers, Minutes, p. 279.

and academies assisted by the state Regents served only the "children of the opulent" and that "a great proportion of the community is excluded from their immediate advantages." He urged the establishment of common schools.[53] Led by upstate common school advocates, the legislature passed in April 1795 an "act for the encouragement of schools," which appropriated £20,000 a year for five years, to be apportioned to the counties on the basis of population.[54] Counties were required to match one-half the amount of their share with school taxes in order to receive the state aid. New York County's share from the state was £1,888; they therefore had to raise £944 for schools as part of the city's property tax.

The law stated that the money should be used to maintain schools where children learned English, arithmetic, mathematics, "and other branches of knowledge as are most useful and necessary to complete a good English education." In a rural district where there had been a single schoolmaster or none at all the local school commissioners would have no problem parcelling out the money. But in New York City, where there were nearly a hundred teachers offering a common education, the distribution posed a problem for the Common Council. Recognizing that the city was a special case, the law had stipulated that there the Common Council could act in lieu of school commissioners and that the money could be used to support the charity schools as well as "all other schools" where the common subjects were taught.

This did not solve the problem of who should receive the money, however. A committee on schools appointed by the Council in June 1795 did nothing until the following spring, when the Society of Associated Teachers began lobbying for a decision favorable to their interests. In March 1796, the Society appointed a committee "to solicit a conference with the Commissioners who may be appointed to put the Law of this State in force," but this committee was unsuccessful because no such commissioners were appointed. In May the teachers assigned a new group "to wait upon the Recorder to obtain information respecting the public law for the support

---

53. George Clinton, opening speech to the legislature, July, 1782, in Charles Z. Lincoln, ed., *State of New York Messages from the Governors* . . . (Albany, J. B. Lyon Company, 1909), II, 350.

54. Samuel S. Randall, *History of the Common School System of the State of New York* . . . (New York, 1871), pp. 7–10; *New York Laws*, 1795, chap. 75.

of *schools*." In that month the Council committee recommended that a survey be taken of existing schooling arrangements. Accordingly they directed the clerk to publish in the newspapers a request that all schoolmasters "employed in teaching the English language" submit a report on the number of students taught, the subjects studied, the length of attendance, and tuition charged. The results of this survey have been summarized above.[55]

The Teachers' Society, encouraged by the fact that they were asked to submit reports on their schools, awaited the Council's decision with great interest. By September, however, the law was seventeen months old, and the Council had not acted. Since the state aid was not only optional, but conditional upon local taxation, the teachers feared that New York City would forego the opportunity. In a petition on September 12, 1796, they urged the Council to take action before the upcoming session of the legislature. They told the Council that they understood the reports requested of them had been "a part of the duty which a late Act of the State enjoins." The act had required county commissioners to collect individual school reports similar to those the Council had requested the previous spring, as the basis for distribution within the counties, and the New York City teachers, not unreasonably, had assumed that the Council had already determined to apportion the money to them. "Under this view, we did not hesitate to comply with a demand which being unprecedented was not otherwise to be accounted for," they argued. "We consider ourselves as a Party contemplated in the Act," they wrote, ". . . an Act which could not have been intended for an unequal Distribution of its Benefits."[56]

Here, then, was a critical point in the development and systematization of New York's common schools. The state legislature had left decisions on the distribution of aid in the hands of the Council. The teachers, recently organized and capable for the first time of collective action, argued that the money designated for common school education should be theirs. That they were already providing common education for large numbers of the city's children was indisputable; that they charged tuition was no automatic

55. *M.C.C.,* II, 154; Associated Teachers, Minutes, 273–279; *M.C.C.,* II, 237.

56. Petition of the Teachers of the City of New York to the Commissioners of Schools in and for the City and County of New York, September 12, 1796, NYMA, Box 6415; *M.C.C.,* II, 154.

barrier, for upstate common schools did so as well and continued to until 1867. The schools of men like Romaine, Fraser, and Campbell were public, common, and eligible under the New York City clause of the 1795 law to share in the school money. The charity schools, on the other hand, though free, enrolled only a small portion of the city's schoolchildren (about 8 percent, see Table 10), and were restricted to children of their respective denominations. They represented the received English tradition of church charity education.

THE FAILURE OF SYSTEMATIZATION

The Common Council, however, did not analyze the situation the way the teachers did. The Councillors' definition of a public school was not clear, but they decided that the common pay schools did not qualify. On September 23, 1796, "the Committee on Schools made a verbal report; question was raised if it would be proper to distribute any part of the Monies granted by the Legislature and raised by Tax in this City among the Schoolmasters or Teachers in the City. Unanimous negative."[57] Because the report was verbal, nothing more of the debate survives. Although their reasons are obscure, their vote was unequivocal. They obviously could not conceive of the Council distributing £2,832 to a constantly shifting multitude of common school teachers over whom they had no control. It would have been legal, but also, quite apart from the question of the teachers' politics, it would have been too intricate for a governing body that had never had anything to do with education. Upstate communities typically hired schoolmasters on salary; they could thus subtract from the necessary tuition bills any state aid received. But in New York City a teacher's income varied according to enrollment. If aid had been distributed according to the number of students taught, masters like Romaine and Fraser, who earned substantial teaching income, would get more aid than teachers like Liddell and Gum in the Bowery, who earned much less.

The Council apparently made a distinction between a single teacher hired on salary by the inhabitants of a defined area and

57. *M.C.C.,* II, 281.

a group of nonsalaried teachers competing in a free market. The former they looked upon as engaged in public education and eligible for assistance in the same manner as in upstate counties, but they had few such schools. The inhabitants of Bloomingdale village, in the outer reaches of the Bowery ward, provide the contrast which illustrates the point. They had engaged a teacher in 1797 on the promise of £120 a year, but they found they could only raise £80 by subscription. In November they petitioned the Common Council for assistance, explaining that "the Situation of this place being Such, that the Greatest part of those who support the School in Summer, Remove to town in Winter, a Number of Children Remaining, several of whose parents are not able to pay for Tuition." They prayed some aid from the money provided by the legislature. The Council awarded the trustees of this school £20, half of the deficit.[58]

The petition of the Teachers' Society, however, was another matter entirely. Never having collected or distributed any money for common education, the Council was suddenly forced by the state's action into developing a definition and a plan for governmentally sponsored common schooling. Since the need for such schooling had not been widely felt in the city, and the pressure for a program came only after the state had provided the money, the Council was able to procrastinate. They had not yet received the state's share for 1796, and they voted, eight to three, to distribute the amount collected from city taxes, £944, to the city's six charity schools.[59]

The Council had resolved at the time of their September decision to apply to the legislature "for legal provision to establish public schools in the city." Accordingly, in October, after receiving the state share, they drafted a memorial in which they informed the legislature that they complied with the provisions of the law and received their money, but "from the manner in which the private Schools in the said City are conducted it is impracticable to distribute the said monies according to the Direction of the Act." Having made its decision, the Council began using the terms "pri-

58. Petition, Trustees of the Bloomingdale School to the Common Council, November 30, 1797, NYMA, Box 6415; *M.C.C.*, II, 410.

59. *M.C.C.*, II, 281; Report of the Committee on the Distribution of Monies to the Charity Schools, October, 24, 1796, NYMA, Box, 6459, Folder 1320.

vate" and "public" in a manner roughly equivalent to our modern usage. The Council asked the legislature to determine what portion they should distribute to charity schools in the future and to authorize them "to apply the Residue to the erecting and supporting of one or more public Schools in the said city." The Council by this time seems to have been thinking of public schools in terms of buildings, and the funds from the Act of 1795 had been limited to salaries.[60] The distinction between salary and construction was not simply a budgeting decision. It sealed the Council's rejection of the independent masters' claim to public funds and committed the Council to a concept of "public school" which involved first erecting a public building similar to other official edifices like City Hall and the Almshouse. Until now, "public school" had generally meant places open to the public where children learned together; henceforth it was to mean places of education erected and maintained with governmental assistance and administered either by governmental representatives or a surrogate board acceptable to them.

The legislature complied with the Council's request and passed a supplemental law in 1797 which allowed the city to use funds for school construction and to allocate one-sixth of the annual school moneys to charity schools, leaving five-sixths for the promised public schools, which were by this time significantly restyled "free schools."[61] Considering the absence of real functional demands, it is not surprising that they continued to postpone their commitment. The city's urban problems—disorder, ethnic diversity, and poverty—were ominous but not urgent enough to precipitate a new relationship between government and education. Each year the Council apportioned one-sixth of the funds to the charity schools (£472) and set aside five-sixths.

In 1800 the school law expired, and the efforts of Governor John Jay and other school supporters were not sufficient to get its renewal through a budget-conscious Senate. The funds available from state land sales and the interest on surplus capital had not proved sufficient for the statewide school program, and in 1799 the state had

60. *M.C.C.*, II, 281; Memorial of the Mayor, Aldermen, and Commonalty of the City of New York to the Legislature of the State of New York, October 24, 1796, draft, NYMA, Box 6459, Folder 1319.

61. Elsie G. Hobson, *Educational Legislation and Administration in the State of New York, 1777–1850* (Chicago, University of Chicago Press, 1918), p. 83.

to institute a direct property tax, for the first time in its brief history, to meet its commitment. This the Federalist Senate was not willing to continue.[62] School taxes in the city had been slight—in 1797, for example, the required £944 was 2 percent of the city's tax budget—but the city's program, having been initiated by the state law, ended with the failure of repassage. The termination, moreover, allowed the city an excuse to divert the funds earmarked for public schools to the charity school subsidies. The school committee had declared in the spring of 1800, despite the accumulation of nearly $30,000, that establishing free schools "upon as liberal and extensive a Plan as the Funds will admit" was not advisable. The Council decided to invest the money in United States or other bonds for later use. After the rejection of the 1795 law, however, the Council requested, and the legislature passed, another new bill allowing them to divide the capital itself among the eleven charity schools then operating in the city.[63]

These charity schools were now styled "free schools," and the city's earlier plans for erecting "free schools" was dropped. The accumulated funds were paid over to the trustees of the various schools, who were required to invest them and use the interest to operate their schools.[64] Clinton, back in the governorship in 1802, said of the discontinued common school law that "the failure of one experiment for the attainment of an important object, ought not to discourage other attempts."[65] As applied to New York City, however, the law was neither experimental nor was its aid discontinued. It was used to sustain existing charity schools rather than create new common schools, and the Council continued the aid after 1800 by using the unexpended five-sixths of the capital. The money had been provided by a law to encourage common schools on the New England model, but New York City already had an adequate, though different, arrangement for common schooling. In the end the Council was completely traditional. They refused to allocate the money to the independent masters, which would

62. *Ibid.*, p. 29; Randall, *Common School System*, pp. 9–11; see also Robert F. Seybolt, *The Act of 1795 for the Encouragement of Schools and the Practice in Westchester County* (Albany, New York State Local History Service Leaflets, 1919), copy in NYPL.

63. *M.C.C.*, II, 309; II, 628; III, 12.

64. The extant required reports on these grants are found in NYMA, Box 2990.

65. Lincoln, *Messages*, II, 512.

have required new standards for judging schools and disbursing funds; but they also delayed and finally abandoned their commitment to build new public schools directed and supported entirely by the city. The old arrangements worked; there was no crisis. They allocated the money where tradition suggested, to church charity schools.

The ambiguous use of terms by both the Council and the Associated Teachers during these five years illustrates the prevailing confusion about the role of the government in education. The schoolmasters had reality on their side, but not precedent. They were in fact in charge of the common education of most children in the city, but the allocation of tax funds to them would have required a complicated involvement of the government in schooling which the Council was not prepared to undertake. By delay and by amendment of the law the Council chose a course which affected fewer children but for which there was long-standing precedent: aid to charity schools. Through occasional grants and privileges, government had customarily extended this kind of aid as far back as pre-Reformation England. Far from seeing a conflict between church and state, the Council reinforced this tradition of aiding churches to educate the poor. There was no establishment and no favoritism; all denominations shared alike. However, the decision also reinforced an association of state intervention in education with charity to the poor. While the Regents assisted colleges and academies which were too expensive for all but the wealthy (at least as far as New York City was concerned), the city aided common education only for those too poor to pay. Both policies tended to increase segregation of education on class lines in the city as the nineteenth century progressed and made it difficult for the free schools aided by the city to become a truly common school system. What was settled in the years 1795 to 1800 was that a common school system in New York City would evolve from the free charity schools and not from the common pay schools.

THE DECLINE OF THE SOCIETY OF
ASSOCIATED TEACHERS

When they first organized in the summer of 1794, the Associated Teachers had established a fine of 12½ cents for absence except for illness or travel. This they soon repealed. Although the organization had a small group of active members, many others were elected who only attended a few times. The severe yellow fever epidemic of 1798 caused meetings to cease from July to November, and by 1799 the Society was moribund. In 1800 they decided to eliminate all delinquent members from the rolls, and the treasurer duly reported in May that there were only ten members left, and "all others who have signed the Constitution have withdrawn or are deceased."[66]

Why the Society failed initially to attract a majority of the city's teachers is not clear, nor do the minutes reveal clearly the reasons for its decline at the turn of the century. The Society's failure to bargain successfully for state aid money must have been disappointing, but the rate of turnover in the occupation was probably a more important factor. Most teachers were not committed to staying in the classroom all their lives. By 1800, when the treasurer trimmed the rolls, Jonathan Fisk had been lost to the law; Benjamin Romaine was still active in the Society but had already gone into commerce. Although the Constitution was signed by seventy-six men in the whole span of the Society's existence (1794–1807), by 1800 they often could not raise a quorum of seven. Gathering to elect officers in February 1801, the only members present were the officers. Their response to this dilemma showed persistence and a nice sense of the absurd: the vice-president was elected president, and the president became secretary. The secretary took up the duties of steward, while the steward became treasurer. The treasurer, of course, was elected vice-president. The Society's new officers held no further meetings until July and after that met only sporadically. During their remaining six years of existence the pattern was similar, and there were no meetings from March 1805, to February 1807, a month before the Society disbanded.[67] An ignominious postscript to this first teachers' association, which had begun with such grand optimism, was provided in 1861. George Batchelor, addressing the New York Teachers' Association in that year, read a paper pretentiously entitled "A History of all the Teachers' Associations ever established in the City of New York." Although he claimed to have combed the records, Batchelor was unaware of

66. Associated Teachers, Minutes, pp. 253, 255, 316.
67. *Ibid.*, pp. 317, 333.

the Society of Associated Teachers and confidently reported that the first such society began in 1819.[68]

Batchelor's ignorance of the educational developments of the 1790's indicates the discontinuity between these premature efforts to organize schooling and later developments in the City. The coincidence of the Teachers' Society and the Law of 1795 had provided the possibility of a very different organization of common education, but the need was not pressing, and most men had not yet related new urban conditions to education.

In fact, active reform in education seemed to be fading on all fronts in the city by 1800. The hopes that had been generated at Columbia with the arrival of President William Samuel Johnson in 1787—hopes that had been partly fulfilled by increased enrollment and Johnson's creation of new professorships—were dissipated after 1796 in what Croce calls a period of "decline and disappointment." Enrollment in the medical program decreased from fifty-nine in 1791 to twenty-nine in 1797. James Kent's law lectures, the first in an American college, attracted forty to fifty students in the 1794–95 academic year, but the next year only two showed up, so he read his lectures to them in his office and decided to discontinue the course. Legislative assistance to the college was dropped in 1799, which forced Johnson to resume teaching rhetoric, logic, and moral philosophy himself. Ill and discouraged, he resigned in 1800.[69]

The 1790's, then, did not see substantial change in education in New York. The colonial legacy persisted: financial support for charity schools and no interschool regulation. New York's problems, however, did not go away. They got worse, and in the very next decade increasing poverty and ethnic diversity prompted new reform efforts in education. These efforts culminated by 1850 in a standardized hierarchical system of schooling, with opportunity beyond the common school level and clear procedures for advancement, a system that took the initiative for schooling rather than

68. George Batchelor, *History of all the Teachers' Associations ever established in the City of New York: a study read before the New York Teachers' Association* (New York, 1861).

69. George C. Croce, *William Samuel Johnson, A Maker of the Constitution* (New York, Columbia University Press, 1937), p. 187; William Kent, ed., *Memoirs and Letters of James Kent, L.L.D. . . . .* (Boston, 1898), chap. III.

responding to parental initiative, a system that aimed to include all the children of the city. The chapters that follow examine the major forces that shaped these developments. As they will show, the most significant changes that occurred in these fifty years involved differences in the organization rather than in the relative amount of schooling provided in the city, in the mode of schooling rather than in the percentage of children schooled. As the ethnic and economic structure of the population changed after 1800, the old colonial mode of elementary schooling became less effective, and, because all problems were multiplied by the tremendous expansion of the city, basic changes in the provision of education became imperative.

CHAPTER THREE

Socioeconomic
Influences on
Schooling,
1800 to 1850

In the period 1800 to 1850 the number of poor people in New York City was increasing. This was the most important economic trend that affected schooling by mid-century. It has not been demonstrated in quantitative detail; statistical determination of the number of poor people in early nineteenth-century New York would require better income and price information than is presently available. But contemporaries did not doubt that it was occurring, and the increase of poverty was real, relatively as well as absolutely. Indigence was increasing disproportionately to population.

The trend toward greater disparity of income was apparent by the turn of the century, and, as the new century progressed, an increasing number of charitable organizations attempted to ameliorate the lot of orphans, widows, debtors, the sick poor, black people, and other specially distressed groups. In response to increasing crime and poverty New York philanthropists urged prison reform, including separate facilities for juvenile offenders, temperance, work for all who were able, education through charity schools, and the dissemination of Bibles and tracts.[1] These reforms, however, had no effect on the living and working conditions of New York's lower class, and the city became less and less habitable, especially for

1. Sidney I. Pomerantz, *New York, an American City, 1783–1803; A Study of Urban Life* (New York, Columbia University, Studies in History, Economics, and Public Law, No. 442, 1938), chap. VI; Kenneth D. Miller, *The People are the City: 150 Years of Social and Religious Concern in New York* (New York, Macmillan, 1962), pp. 1–17. See also Raymond A. Mohl, *Poverty in New York, 1783–1825* (New York, Oxford University Press, 1971).

children. Although New Yorkers could hardly imagine how serious a social problem immigration would become, the new Society for the Prevention of Pauperism set the dominant theme for philanthropy in the decades to come by labelling immigration as a principal cause of increasing poverty in 1819.[2]

In the second quarter of the century the trend continued. Poverty increased, and class lines tightened. By 1830, perhaps half of New York's workingmen were unskilled. Immigration turned a labor shortage into a labor surplus, and in the 1830's and 40's workers' wages did not generally keep pace with prices.[3] With real wages declining and employment insecure, more and more of the city's workers had to live near the subsistence level. Periodic depressions, notably the one following the Panic of 1837 and another in the mid-1850's, swelled the numbers of the indigent. In 1847 nearly one-fourth of the population received some form of charity, and in the terrible winter of 1854–55 a workingmen's group estimated that 195,000 people, about 31 percent of the city's population, were destitute.[4]

By 1843 between thirty and forty organizations dispensed alms, which inevitably led to duplication and inequities of charity. The New York Association for Improving the Condition of the Poor, organized in 1844, attempted to regularize alms-giving through a "comprehensive, uniform, and systematic plan" of referrals and visitors. Its secretary, Robert Hartley, wrote in the Association's Report for 1845 that "when the population was small and the solicitations for aid infrequent, the character and the condition of applicants were so generally known," standardized procedures were not necessary. But, he reported, with the rapid growth of population and the influx of poor immigrants, "the number of dependent poor

2. Robert H. Bremner, *From the Depths: The Discovery of Poverty in the United States* (New York, New York University Press, 1956) p. 8.

3. Robert Ernst, *Immigrant Life in New York City, 1825–1863* (New York, King's Crown Press, 1949), pp. 15–17, 101–102; Douglas T. Miller, *Jacksonian Aristocracy: Class and Democracy in New York, 1830–1860* (New York, Oxford University Press, 1967), pp. 47, 50 and chap. II, *passim*. Stanley Lebergott, *Manpower in Economic Growth: The American Record since 1800* (New York, McGraw-Hill, 1964), p. 162, supports what native workers claimed at the time, concluding that "heavy increases in the flow of immigrants tended to depress wage increases despite rising real factor productivity."

4. Miller, *Jacksonian Aristocracy*, p. 96; Associated Workingmen's Committee of New York, cited in David M. Schneider, *The History of Public Welfare in New York State, 1609–1866* (Chicago, University of Chicago Press, 1938), p. 269.

permanently augmented, in a ratio far exceeding that of the population."[5]

Charles Loring Brace, Hartley's counterpart in the Children's Aid Society, saw the special dangers of the "great multitude of unhappy, deserted and degraded boys and girls." They "will soon form the great lower class of our city," he warned, and they will "poison society all around them." By the late 1850's Samuel Halliday estimated that half a million New Yorkers lived in tenement houses, about two-thirds of the population. He concluded that New York "may be said (comparatively), to have no longer a middling class . . . There are many rich, but more than ten times as many that are abjectly poor."[6] Halliday overstated the case with regard to a middle class, but his descriptions of the poor tenement dwellers were widely corroborated. These, then, were the brute economic trends facing New York philanthropists and educators in the first half of the nineteenth century: a poor class expanding even faster than the rapidly expanding population, periodic epidemics, periodic economic depressions, rampant health and crime problems, and, in the judgment of many observers, increasing distance between the classes.

RESIDENTIAL SEGREGATION

The economic distance between classes was mirrored by increasing geographic separation, which intensified social problems. New York had always had particularly fashionable streets, especially those around southern Broadway and Greenwich Street, where wealthy merchants built their homes, and by the turn of the eighteenth century, slum areas had developed in the marshy eastern sections of the city. But the city was small, and in most parts of it income levels were mixed. As commerce and manufacturing increased, however, property in the downtown wards became more valuable, while the noise and dirt levels rose. Prosperous residents began to sell their homes for commercial use or apartment dwell-

---

5. A.I.C.P., *Annual Report* (New York, 1845), pp. 18, 44; see Roy Lubove, "The New York Association for Improving the Condition of the Poor: The Formative Years," NYHS *Quarterly* 43 (1959), 307–327.

6. Charles L. Brace, *The Children's Aid Society: Its History, Plan and Results* (New York, 1893), p. 4; Samuel Halliday, *The Lost and Found, or Life Among the Poor* (New York, 1859), pp. 190, 201.

ings. They moved uptown to the Greenwich Village area on the west side, or, leapfrogging over the old upper eastern wards that had become predominantly working class, to new wards above the Bowery. Thus the earlier pattern of a merchants' downtown and a mechanics' uptown was reversed, and from the 1820's on, the long narrow island acted like a centrifuge, forcing society's dregs into the dense tenements while those who could afford to move gradually rose into the more spacious upper wards. The old "Knick-erbocker" mansions, reported an Assembly investigation committee in 1857, had been divided into smaller and smaller apartments and allowed to degenerate into "squalid deformity." They had be-come filled, "from cellar to garret, with a class of tenantry living from hand to mouth, loose in morals, improvident in habits, de-graded or squalid as beggary itself. This, in its primary aspects, was the tenant-house system, which has repeated itself, in every phase, as it followed the track of population from ward to ward."[7]

Institutions that promoted social stability, especially the church and the family, were weakened in poor areas. In 1817 an early urban missionary named Ward Stafford, "exploring the destitute sections of the city," found a shortage of churches and a surplus of taverns. About 89,000 New Yorkers did not attend church, he calculated, compared to 31,000 who did, and in the poorer wards over half the families had no Bible. These conditions—physical separation, mutual alienation, and the breakdown of institutions which wealthier New Yorkers considered crucial—spurred the urban missionary movement in the 1820's and 30's. The alienation was already serious. Stafford reported that "a respectable man, not long since, who was distributing Bibles, was attacked, knocked down, and had his clothes literally torn off, and was so beaten as to lose considerable blood."[8]

Missionary efforts and Christian charity notwithstanding, the situation grew worse. Population density increased in the seven low-

7. *Report of the Select Committee Appointed to Examine into the Condition of the Tenement Houses of New York and Brooklyn,* March 9, 1857, New York State Assembly, Doc. 205, 1857, pp. 10, 12; see also Ernst, *Immigrant Life,* pp. 19–20, 39–40.

8. Ward Stafford, *New Missionary Field, a Report to the Female Missionary Society for the Poor of the City of New York and its Vicinity* (New York, 1817), pp. 5–6, 15; see also Charles I. Foster, "The Urban Missionary Move-ment, 1814–1837," *Pennsylvania Magazine of History and Biography* 75 (1951), 47–65.

est wards from 94.5 per acre in 1820 to 163.5 per acre in 1850. The subtenantage system exploited the poor by inflating slum rents.[9] In 1850 police reported that 18,456 people lived in cellars; by that time, virtually all of the fourth ward was a slum. Immigrants in the lower wards, said the Association for Improving the Condition of the Poor in 1853, lived "like cattle in pens." Meanwhile, fashionable New Yorkers developed such neighborhoods as East 14th Street, "the glory of snobdom," north of the old city.[10] The children of cellar dwellers were "always sick in a never-ending rotation." Increasing infant mortality figures indicated that the toll of the tenement system was more than just exorbitant rent. The principal causes of disease, a doctor wrote, were crowding and lack of ventilation. "Many persons are ignorant of the large number of people that are in one house among the poor. The average number in an ordinary sized house is about 50."[11]

Ignorance of the true condition of the poor was widespread; most wealthy natives did not follow Charles Dickens' example and visit the inside of a slum tenement in the notorious Five Points neighborhood. Periodic beatings of missionary "visitors" in the slums showed that alienation worked both ways. Mike Walsh, a flamboyant political editor of the 1840's, expressed the workers' resentment at a meeting of Democratic candidates: "There are many men in the party who fawn upon us and call us the bone and sinew of the country, upon the platform, and who would use us until there was nothing but bone and sinews left of us. And then go to their palaces in the Fifteenth Ward, where they'd order their servants to throw a pail of water on one of the bone and sinew if he came to sit down and rest himself upon their stoop."[12]

9. Ernst, *Immigrant Life,* p. 149; L. Maria Child, *Letters from New York* (New York, 2nd series, 1845), p. 20; A.I.C.P., *Report of the Committee on the Sanitary Conditions of the Laboring Classes* (New York, 1853), pp. 8, 23.

10. "Philopedos," *A Few Remarks about Sick Children in New York, and the Necessity of a Hospital for them. By Philopedos, an ex-dispensary doctor* (New York, 1852), p. 8n; Herbert Asbury, *The Gangs of New York* (New York, Alfred Knopf, 1928), pp. 48, 52; A.I.C.P., *Sanitary Conditions,* p. 7; [William Bobo], *Glimpses of New York* (Charleston, 1852), p. 76.

11. "Philopedos," *Remarks,* pp. 3, 4, 8; on infant mortality, see Halliday, *Lost and Found,* pp. 230–231.

12. Charles Dickens, *American Notes for General Circulation* (New York, 1868), pp. 39–41; Asbury, *Gangs,* p. 16; Mike Walsh, *Sketches of the Speeches and Writings of Mike Walsh* (New York, 1843), p. 10.

The indifference of the well-to-do to the poor was made easier by residential segregation; conversely, there was a decline in traditional deference on the part of the urban poor.

The city's leaders increasingly saw informal socialization in poor families as untrustworthy or, more often, as a negative influence. Immigrants brought strange customs, and they swelled the ranks of a religion which Protestants viewed as alien or, worse yet, they often attended no church at all. Crowded living quarters in the tenements strained the integrity of the family by forcing several families to live together in the same room and by creating intolerable crowding, from which children could only escape to the streets. Respectable New Yorkers could no longer rely upon informal means of socialization among the poor, partly because poverty eroded the family environment and partly because there simply was no longer a consensus of values among the city's inhabitants.

Daily schooling is the most comprehensive means, short of complete institutionalization, by which one group can attempt to influence the socialization of another group's children. When the poor class continued to grow, and church affiliation in the slums declined, public-spirited citizens saw that some new extension of schooling arrangements was necessary. Because schooling as a public effort had traditionally been linked to charity, they naturally attempted to solve the problem by expanding charity school facilities, and they sought government assistance in their effort. The New York Common Council, it was noted in Chapter Two, had rejected the more radical innovation of operating public schools in 1800, and had continued to assist charity schooling by appropriating state funds to the city's church schools. This was the legacy of the Revolutionary period and the starting point for new efforts to meet the new problems of the nineteenth century.

THE EXTENSION OF CHARITY SCHOOLING: THE FREE SCHOOL SOCIETY

Thomas Eddy, prominent in the effort to provide more schooling, epitomizes the movement's leaders: he was active in several other reforms in New York, he was aware of English models, and he was a Quaker. As Sydney James has shown, the Friends were anxious to broaden their philanthropic efforts beyond the bounds of their denomination in the post-Revolutionary period.[13] This impulse in Quakerism to serve the whole community placed the Friends at the forefront of several New York reforms in the early nineteenth century, but their nondenominational emphasis had particular significance in the development of schooling.

It was only after nondenominational charity schooling gained large-scale governmental support that men began to interpret the appropriation of public funds to the city's denominational charity schools as illegal. In New York City, for the first fifty years of the nation's history, practice contravened any such theoretical barrier; state funds were appropriated to sectarian schools until 1825. The seeds of a challenge to this practice were sown in 1805 with the founding of the Free School Society by Eddy and his associates, but their initial intention was only to supplement the efforts of the churches. The Quakers' extradenominational philanthropic impulse had simply coincided fortuitously with the increase of religiously unaffiliated poor people, prompting the establishment of a nondenominational charity school.

Eddy kept abreast of English charitable enterprises. He was influenced by the writings of Bentham on the poor and on penal reform, and particularly by Patrick Colquhoun, a police magistrate of London and a leader in various societies for poor relief and education.[14]

---

13. Sydney V. James, *A People Among Peoples: Quaker Benevolence in Eighteenth Century America* (Cambridge, Harvard University Press, 1963), pp. 281–288; The Female Association, which opened a nondenominational charity school for girls in 1802, was founded by Quaker ladies. John Murray, Jr., a Quaker, worked as governor of the New York Hospital for 37 years, supported the Manumission Society, penal reform, savings banks, and societies for widows and orphans. Six of the eleven initial trustees of the Manumission Society School (1786f) were Friends, as were most of the women on the board of the Mission School for Colored Adult Women (1815). Quaker ladies founded the Association for the Relief of the Sick Poor (1798) and the Orphan Asylum Society (1806). John Griscom, a noted chemist, lecturer, and a Quaker, founded the Society for the Prevention of Pauperism (1818), which included Eddy, Matthew Clarkson, and other Friends. A. Emerson Palmer, *The New York Public School* (New York, The Macmillan Company, 1905), pp. 17–18; Thomas Eddy, *Memoir of the late John Murray jun read before the governors of the New York Hospital* (New York, 1819), pp. 4–5; John Cox, *Quakerism in the City of New York, 1657–1930* (New York, 1930), p. 62, and *passim;* K. Miller, *The People are the City,* p. 38; Pomerantz, *New York,* p. 382–383.

14. William W. Cutler, Philosophy, Philanthropy, and Public Education: A Social History of the New York Public School Society, 1805–1853, unpub. diss., Cornell University, 1960, pp. 37–41, with whose kind permission I draw upon and cite his unpublished material; Samuel L. Knapp, ed., *Life of Thomas*

Although remembered primarily for his efforts toward penal reform, Eddy was early convinced of the crucial importance of educating the poor. Colquhoun warned him in 1803 that if America's school facilities did not keep pace with its rapidly expanding population, the deficiency would be "manifested by extreme ignorance and immoral conduct, as it respects a considerable proportion of the lower classes of society."[15] Colquhoun forwarded reports on education by the Society for Bettering the Condition of the Poor and other reform groups. Eddy was especially impressed with a pamphlet by Joseph Lancaster, reporting his success in training great numbers of poor children in monitorial schools, where the older children taught the younger by a strict regimen of drill and repetition. Eddy wrote his friend, "I have been so much pleased with the outlines of it, that I have had one thousand copies printed in this city and Philadelphia. I flatter myself his plan will be adopted in our schools, when it becomes more generally known."[16] Eddy was therefore quite prepared for a visit in 1805 by his friends, John Murray, Jr., and Matthew Franklin, who proposed that the Quakers open a charity school for poor children not affiliated with any church. Eddy urged them to invite some non-Quakers to join the initial trustees, which they did, and Eddy was soon avidly corresponding with Colquhoun about further developments in monitorial education and the possibility of adopting them at the new Free School in New York.[17]

Eddy (London, 1836); for Colquhoun's career, see Sir Leslie Stephen and Sir Sidney Lee, eds., *The Dictionary of National Biography* (London, Smith, Elder & Co., 1885–1901).

15. Colquhoun to Eddy, February 16, 1803, in Knapp, *Eddy*, p. 149.

16. Eddy to Colquhoun, June 20, 1804, in *ibid.*, pp. 164–165.

17. *Ibid.*, pp. 127, 170–182. The history of the New York Free School Society, which became the Public School Society in 1825, has been written several times. William O. Bourne, *History of the Public School Society of the City of New York* (New York, 1870), cited hereafter as *PSS*, displays the partiality of a commissioned history but has the virtue of including numerous lengthy reports and debates verbatim. Two other early histories, both by Board of Education personnel, are Thomas Boese, *Public Education in the City of New York, Its History, Condition, and Statistics* (New York, 1869), and Palmer, *New York Public School*, cited above. The Society has been subjected to more critical thought in two recent dissertations, that of William Cutler, cited above, and Julia A. Duffy, The Proper Objects of a Gratuitous Education: The Free-School Society of The City of New York, 1805 to 1826, unpub. diss., Teachers College, Columbia University, 1968, with whose kind permission I draw upon and cite her unpublished material.

In 1806 the Society opened its first school in rented quarters in the fourth ward. In the next three years the trustees gained state and municipal assistance, built a large school designed especially for monitorial instruction, and announced their intention to establish not just a single school but several, not just for the churchless poor, but for "all children who are the proper objects of a gratuitous education."[18] For the first time in the city's history, an organization decided to establish a set of schools, something that could become a system.

Any organization that aspired to educate all of New York's poor children would need to be either very rich or very efficient. The resources of New York's Free School Society were limited; thus it is not surprising that they accepted with enthusiasm the new plan from England developed by Joseph Lancaster. Eventually the system became widely criticized for its rigidity and superficiality; but the population was increasing rapidly and the poor were increasing faster than the population. Thus, per capita resources for schooling were reduced while the social need for education became more intense. Lancaster offered a panacea for this dilemma.

Lancaster, a young schoolmaster and converted Quaker, opened his first school in Southwark in 1798. By experimenting with student monitors and homogeneous grouping, he was able to increase the enrollment from about 60 to 1000 by 1805.[19] His success came to the attention of some English noblemen, and in 1805 he even gained the patronage of George III. Thomas Eddy was not alone in supporting the new discovery in America. Benjamin Perkins, the Secretary of the Society, had visited Lancaster's school in England. In 1807 Perkins published in New York an edition of Lancaster's *Improvements in Education* . . . , in which the system was first fully elaborated. DeWitt Clinton, Matthew Franklin's son-in-law and the nominal head of the new Free School Society, became an ardent proponent of the monitorial system in America.[20]

18. Duffy, Proper Objects, pp. 122–126; early state and municipal aid is summarized in *An Account of the Free-School Society of New-York* (New York, 1814), p. 60.

19. Joseph Lancaster, *Improvements in Education, as it Respects the Industrious Classes of the Community* (New York, from the 3rd London ed., 1807), pp. 1, 18; see Carl F. Kaestle, ed., *Joseph Lancaster and the Monitorial School Movement: A Documentary History* (New York, Teachers College Press, forthcoming).

20. *Account of the Free-School Society*, pp. 7–8; Bourne, *PSS*, p. 9; John

He declared that Lancaster was "creating a new era in education" and that his system was "a blessing sent down from heaven to redeem the poor and the distressed." In 1814 the Society expressed the hope that the system would "yet include, within the sphere of its operation, the whole indigent population of our country."[21]

Quaker activism, Anglo-American cooperation, and the ingenuity of a young English schoolmaster had combined to present an apparent solution to the problem of educating the poor of New York, who, "brought up in ignorance, and amidst the contagion of bad example, are in imminent danger of ruin." At the dedication ceremonies of the first building in 1809, Clinton noted that Colonel Henry Rutgers had donated two additional lots in Henry Street, which was in the populous Bowery, and argued that if some generous citizen would do the same on the opposite side of town, all the poor would be supplied for years. Trinity Church answered this call by giving a site on the west side of the city, where School No. 2 opened in 1811.[22] Eddy wrote Colquhoun in 1816 that the Society had 1000 scholars in two schools and intended to add two new schools the following year. "It is owing to thy very valuable correspondence with me, that our New York Free School is in so flourishing a situation as it is at present, and that the condition of the poor, in many respects, have been considerably improved." The building program continued as petitions came to the Society from different sections, and the trustees selected sites "where the blessings of elementary instruction among the lower orders were not enjoyed." In 1825 John Griscom, at the opening of his monitorial New York High School, proudly claimed that a total of 20,000 children, "taken from the most indigent classes," had attended the Society's free schools, which by then numbered eleven.[23]

F. Reigart, *The Lancasterian System of Instruction in the School of New York City* (New York, Teachers College, Columbia University, Contributions to Education, No. 81, 1916), pp. 17–18; the DeWitt Clinton Papers, on microfilm at Columbia University, contain numerous letters concerning the Lancasterian system.

21. Bourne, *PSS*, p. 19; *Account of the Free-School Society*, p. 8.

22. Bourne, *PSS*, pp. 7, 22, 25.

23. Eddy to Colquhoun, May 4, 1816, in Knapp, *Eddy*, pp. 189–190; Bourne, *PSS*, p. 35; John Griscom, *Monitorial Instruction: An Address Pronounced at the Opening of the New York High School* (New York, 1825), pp. 19–20.

EXTENSION OF FREE SCHOOLING:
THE PUBLIC SCHOOL SOCIETY

In the same year, 1825, the Free School Society expanded its horizons again. They called for public schools for all the children of the city, rich and poor, and they called for an end of public assistance to denominational schools. Their *Annual Report* of 1825 argued:

> Our free schools have conferred the blessings of education upon a large number of the children of the poor, but still it is to be lamented that a description of public school is wanting amongst us, where the rich and the poor may meet together; where the wall of partition, which now seems to be raised between them, may be removed; where kindlier feelings between the children of these respective classes may be begotten; where the indigent may be excited to emulate the cleanliness, decorum and mental improvement of those in better circumstances; and where the children of our wealthiest citizens will have an opportunity of witnessing and sympathizing, more than they now do, with the wants and privations of their fellows of the same age.[24]

This rhetorical shift was rather abrupt, especially since fertile fields still remained for charity schools. A committee of the Free School Society reported in 1822 that thousands of children were vagrants because of poverty and because free schools were either full or too far from their neighborhoods.[25] Yet in 1825 the Society announced the ambitious goal of providing schools for those who could afford tuition as well as those who could not.

A number of factors caused this shift. The trustees were reflecting, to some extent, the egalitarian philosophy that was growing in the 1820's. They said that constructive contact between all classes in school was "no mere fanciful theory," but had been demonstrated at the high school in Edinburgh. They admitted that full equal opportunity might be "impracticable," especially considering "the peculiar local circumstances of this city," but hoped that inequalities might be "principally confined to the lower schools."[26] They were also by this time more conscious of the example of New England, where, they thought, "the child of the poorest citizen feels on a

24. FSS, *Annual Report* (New York, 1825), p. 7.
25. Bourne, *PSS*, p. 45.
26. *Ibid.*, pp. 114–115.

perfect equality with his richer classmate . . . and where all feel
the dignity of receiving their instruction as a right."[27]

However, the provision of democratic opportunity was not the
Society's main motive for trying to expand. Their dispute with the
Bethel Baptist Church also influenced their new ambitions. That
church had established its first school in 1820, and had gained
legislative permission to use surplus money from the school fund
to erect new buildings, rather than just to pay salaries, a privilege
the Free School Society had hoped to enjoy alone. By 1824 the
Bethel Baptist Church had three schools, admitting children of all
persuasions, and one of their schools was directly competing for
students with a Free School Society school.

In 1823 Clinton wrote, "The obtrusion of Charity Schools on
our System has done much evil. I was opposed to it from the
start—but how to get rid of it, is difficult."[28] The Society objected
to scattered denominational schools not as much because they were
sectarian as because they made the Society's enrollment, and therefore their space requirements and financial aid, uncertain. They
competed with the Society's schools, and the Society had decided
that competition was not the best way to provide schooling. The
trustees campaigned vigorously in Albany to eliminate subsidies to
denominational schools. In 1824 the legislature, in order to avoid
alienating either side, decided to let the Common Council distribute
the school fund in the city. As usual, the state authorities decided
that New York City was a special case in educational matters. The
Free School Society persuaded the Council that they could do the
job of schooling best, and in 1825 the state funds were limited
to them and specialized agencies like orphanages.

The shift to a common school concept, coupled with a campaign
against aid to sectarian education, was, in part at least, a rationale
for engrossing all the state money for education in the city. The
Society's efforts to increase its services over the years had produced
a momentum of its own. Men had given time and money to help

27. FSS, *Annual Report,* 1825, p. 7.
28. DeWitt Clinton to Isaac Collins, December 27, 1823, DeWitt Clinton
Papers, Columbia University, vol. 20, p. 525. The Bethel Baptist Church
controversy is discussed in Duffy, Proper Objects, pp. 159–168, Charles J.
Mahoney, *The Relation of the State to Religious Education in Early New
York, 1633–1825* (Washington, Catholic University of America Press, 1941),
pp. 134–201, and in Bourne, *PSS,* chap. III.

the Society grow; they believed it to be the most efficient and morally useful educational organization in the city, and they wanted it to continue to grow. Seen in this context, the shift to a common school ideal was not so discontinuous.[29]

A committee of the Free School Society, reporting in 1825 on the distribution of the state's common school fund in the city, related the Society's efficiency principle to both the charity schools and the city's independent pay schools. It concluded not only that it was improper that "a fund designed for the civil education of the youth of this State is in part placed at the disposal of religious Societies" but that it was much less efficient to have several groups divide the money than if a single agency directed general education in the city. The report stated that many of the city's 400 private schools were conducted in cramped and stuffy quarters by unqualified teachers, some of "doubtful morals."[30] An outside observer had commented in 1824 that "folks in the middle stages of society, who may be pushed and pinched from day to day" received no benefit from the free schools. "Knowledge is indeed positively imparted to the rich and the poor; while those who are of neither order, get it also, if they can."[31]

The Society proposed to the legislature in 1825 that they be allowed to change their name to the Public School Society, charge nominal tuition fees to those who could afford them, and open their facilities to all children. A report to the public in that year cited instances in Ireland and England where the requirement of nominal tuition had increased the number of scholars and improved the attitude of poor parents.[32] The legislature approved this plan in 1826, and the new Public School Society set out to attract to their schools children from a broad mixture of backgrounds.

The Society's strategy worked in one sense: expanding their clients sustained their growth. But their immediate tactic, that of charging tuition, did not. Their optimism that tuition payment would increase people's respect for the public schools and thus boost

29. The momentum of the organization to expand is discussed further in Chap. Six below.

30. Bourne, *PSS*, pp. 86–87.

31. Samuel H. Jenks, quoted in Bayrd Still, "New York in 1824: A Newly Discovered Description," NYHS *Quarterly* 46 (April 1962), 164.

32. PSS, *On the Establishment of Public Schools in the City of New York* (New York, 1825), pp. 6–7.

enrollment was wishful thinking. The first effect was that the attendance dropped from 4059 in 1825 to 3739 in 1826. In 1827 the enrollment climbed back to 4565, of whom 2874 paid, but still the Annual Report for that year regretted that "the advantages of this alteration to the poor themselves, have not been so fully appreciated as was anticipated." By 1832 tuition revenues had dwindled and the psychological uplift of paying for one's education had proved mythical. The Society therefore discontinued tuition charges. They did not, however, reinstate the poverty requirement for admission.[33] The tuition experiment thus played an important, if short-lived, role in the expansion of the Society. The trustees had seen "those in the middle walks of life" as a potential source of income and a potentially good influence on poor children in the schools.[34] Now they forgot the tuition and argued simply that the alienation between classes, which had grown much worse in the past quarter century, could be reduced by putting children together in schools. It had taken more than the example of New England public schools to convince them of this. It took the social realities of an increasingly stratified city, plus the momentum their organization had gained in providing schools for the poor, to convince the trustees that a single comprehensive school system was possible and desirable.

SOCIOECONOMIC STATUS AND PUBLIC SCHOOL ATTENDANCE

The doors of the public schools were open to all classes, but whether all would come in was another question. In their effort to attract a broad range of classes to the public schools the Society faced difficulties with groups in both directions, those who could afford private schooling, and those who were very poor. Statistical analysis of class backgrounds is impossible because no nineteenth-century enrollment lists are extant, but from the public and private school enrollment totals, and from the appeals and reports of schoolmen, it can be inferred that the public schools attracted children predominantly from working-class families. The increasing at-

33. Bourne, *PSS*, p. 150; Palmer, *New York Public School*, p. 70.
34. The phrase is from PSS, *Annual Report, 1827.*

tendance probably reflected some success in attracting "those in the middle walks of life," as officials claimed, but the comprehensive common school ideal was impaired by the schools' persistent difficulty in attracting both the wealthy, who went to increasingly expensive private schools, and the very poor, whose chaotic tenements produced the vagrancy and juvenile delinquency problems the schools were largely designed to solve.

The percentage of children going to school remained roughly the same in the second quarter of the nineteenth century, between 50 and 60 percent, but the percentage of those school children attending public rather than private schools rose dramatically, from about 38 to 82 percent (see Table 12). Much of this shift was due to the successful competition of the public schools with the

TABLE 12.   Children in School, 1829 and 1850.

A. Available data

	All attending	*Just age 5–15*
1829		
Public, corporate, & church charity schools	9,632	9,312
Private schools	15,320	13,631
Total	24,952	22,943

No. of children 5–15 not in school: 20,000 est.
Percent of children aged 5–15 in school: 53.4

	All attending	*Just age 5–15*
1850		
Public	45,509	
Private	10,175	not given
Total	55,684	

No. of children 5–15: 101,106 est.

B. Computations
1. Ratio of children attending (including those age 4 or 16+) to the number of children aged 5–15 in the population. (This slightly overstates the real percentage attending but makes the figures from the two years comparable.)
   1829: 58.2%   1850: 55.1%
2. Ratio of children in public schools (i.e., free schools, including corporate and charity schools) to the number of children attending school.
   1829: 37.8%   1850: 81.7%

Sources: PSS, *Annual Report,* 1829, p. 20; *7th Census of the United States: 1850* (Washington, 1853), Table 7.

TABLE 13.　Public School Attendance in Lower, Middle, and Upper
Wards, New York City, 1851.

Wards	White popula- tion	Age 5–15 (est.)	Whole number taught	Average atten- dance	Percent of children 5–15 attending, average attendance
Lower (1–7)	135,433	27,545	26,957	8,874	32.2
Middle (8–11, 13–15, 17)	254,888	49,944	61,033	22,052	45.9
Upper (16, 18–20, 12)	111,411	21,837	20,709	7,541	33.0

Sources: New York City Board of Education, *Annual Report for 1851*, in New
York State Superintendent of Common Schools, *Annual Report for 1852* (Albany,
1852); map locating all schools in New York City Board of Education, *Manual*,
1850.

Note: Attendance figures for all three areas omit corporate schools like
orphanages because their students were drawn from the whole city, and the
purpose here was only to differentiate between residential areas. Figures for
average attendance are used because the figures for "whole number taught" in
Board of Education reports are obviously inflated and do not represent the
number of different children who attended school. This was partly the result
of frequent moves from school to school during the year.

lesser pay schools. By 1850 public schools were operating in all
parts of the city, in contrast to the period 1805 to 1825, when
schools had been deliberately placed in the poorest sections. The
Board of Education surveyed popular education in 1851 and reported that many parents had switched from private to public
schools.[35] As Table 13 shows, attendance was roughly equal in the
lower and upper wards. This does not mean necessarily that the
wealthy used the public schools equally as much as the poor, for
although the city tended to have a north-south income gradient,
and the tenement districts isolated the poor, there was still some
spread of income in all wards. The middle wards, where public
school attendance was higher, included both fashionable districts

35. New York City Board of Education, *Annual Report,* year ending April,
1851, in *Annual Report of the Superintendent of Common Schools of the
State of New York . . . January, 1852* (Albany, 1852), p. 90.

and tenement neighborhoods. For example, Grammar School No. 3 was in the old Greenwich Village area of Ward 9, which, with the early exodus of wealth uptown, had become a predominantly well-to-do area. Among the graduates of this school were a number of bankers, civil servants, and lawyers, including Schuyler Colfax, later Grant's Vice-President. In 1918 the alumni of this school prided themselves on the fact that throughout the nineteenth century, old No. 3 had been "a distinctively American school" in its enrollment.[36] Some of those in better circumstances, then, had been drawn to the public schools. Although the amount of social class mixing in individual schools, which is the crux of the public school ideal, cannot be determined, the similar attendance rates in the upper and lower sections of the city show that the public school system had been successfully diffused throughout the city for those who wanted to use it. In some areas, where neighborhoods were more mixed, the common school ideal seems to have succeeded. One graduate recalled that at the old Fifth Street School, near the shipyards in the eleventh ward, children of different classes mingled.[37]

SCHOOLING AND THE WEALTHY

Nevertheless, several factors militated against the realization of the common school ideal in socioeconomic terms. Besides the economic segregation of neighborhoods, which especially affected the numerous primary schools begun in the 1830's, there were constraints on the rich and the poor which tended to keep them out of the public schools wherever they lived and thereby to narrow further the socioeconomic enrollment base.[38] The private pay schools, which in the 1790's had been largely responsible for common elementary education, came more and more to represent

36. Charles A. Hale, *Historical Sketch of Grammar School No. 3* (New York, 1918), pp. 6, 19.
37. A. W. Moynihan, *The Old Fifth Street School and the Association which Bears Its Name* (New York, 1887), pp. 10–13.
38. The creation of separate primary schools, as opposed to primary departments in the upper schools, had class overtones. The shift to separate primaries not only relieved upper schools of the numerous primary children, but also increased the class homogeneity by establishing smaller, neighborhood schools. See the report on primary schools, PSS, Minutes, 1832–1843, PSS Records, vol. 34, NYPL, December, 1832.

schooling with different concepts and methods. The Lancasterian system of the Free School Society, whose mass pedagogy had been justified as a means of educating the expanding poor population, remained in force when the public schools attempted to broaden their enrollment. Thus, the fact that the public schools developed from the charity schools rather than the pay schools left them not only associated with the stigma of poverty but also committed to an organization and pedagogy designed explicitly for the poor. Although New York enthusiasts had at first looked on monitorial instruction not only as an economic but pedagogical improvement, fewer and fewer people accepted that argument, outside of the Public School Society, as time went on. In 1825 John Griscom said that the public schools, although "rising in public estimation, were deemed to belong to the working classes, and accordingly were regarded as charity schools."[39]

Private schooling became different not only because of the pedagogical luxuries that smaller groups afforded, but because of its content and purpose. *The Academician,* published by the private schoolmasters Albert and John Pickett, defended the classical curriculum in 1818 and pointed out that "the sordid and ignorant cannot, by the most direct reasoning, be made to comprehend the value of these studies, the most important object of which is to purify the taste, harmonize the affections, improve the understanding and heart, and enhance the dignity of human nature."[40] These goals contrasted with the emphasis in the monitorial schools on inculcating "habits of cleanliness, subordination, and order."[41]

The Public School Society schools gradually displaced the lesser pay schools; private school enrollment actually declined from 1829 to 1850 (see Table 12). In 1829, there were 430 private schools in the city, of which 157 were for higher branches, the rest being minor pay schools, dame schools, and "2nd class" female schools (arithmetic, geography, and needlework). By 1850 only 138 private schools remained, and the greatest decrease was undoubtedly among the lower schools, which were in competition with the public schools.[42] Increasingly, private schools became places to refine a

39. Griscom, *Memoir of John Griscom* (New York, 1859), p. 203.
40. *The Academician,* September 19, 1818.
41. FSS, *Annual Report* (New York, 1824), p. 6.
42. PSS, *Annual Report* (New York, 1829), pp. 21–22; *Seventh Census of the United States: 1850* (Washington, 1853), Table VII, pp. 114–116.

child's sensibilities through personal attention, not to teach him temperance, frugality, and cleanliness by mass drill.[43]

The private day schools of New York in 1850 included some expensive, and some within the range of middle-income families, but the trend was toward higher costs. Pay schools run by special groups exemplify this trend. The General Society of Mechanics and Tradesmen opened a school in 1820 which admitted free scholars, the children of their poorer members or members' widows, as well as the children of substantial artisans who could pay. However, the increasing proportion of paying customers is indicated by comparing the enrollment figures of 1824, when there were 53 free scholars in a body of 117, to the enrollment in 1851, when there were only 64 free scholars among 580 students.[44] Trinity School's history illustrates the same pressures that were affecting independent pay schools. After the Public School Society succeeded in persuading the Common Council to withdraw School Fund money from denominational schools in 1825, Trinity charity school became the Protestant Episcopal Public School, which mixed pay scholars with scholarship students. In 1832 most of the students' fathers were craftsmen, but after a reorganization in 1838 the enrollment was reduced, and the school gradually took on a more decidedly middle-class character.[45]

While the rich continued to provide private education for their children, those with more limited resources gradually lost their alternatives to the public schools when the middle-priced private schools, both independent and corporate, became more exclusive or closed. Although there are no statistics to prove the case, it seems that the rich remained largely out of the system, while the children of those with middle- and working-class incomes moved into the expanding public schools.

43. For a detailed account of school life at the fashionable Abbott's Institute in 1848, see Sarah Jane Bradley, Diary, typescript, NYHS. For schools that boasted individual attention, see New York Merchants School for the Education of Young Gentlemen, *Annual Circular* (New York, 1852), Joseph M. Ely's Private School for Boys, *Prospectus* (New York, 1848), and Hopper S. Mott, *New York of Yesterday: A Descriptive Narrative of Old Bloomingdale* (New York, G. P. Putnam's Sons, 1908), p. 94.

44. Thomas Earle and Charles Congdon, eds., *Annals of the General Society of Mechanics and Tradesmen of the City of New York from 1785 to 1880* (New York, 1882), pp. 57, 70, 84.

45. Edward S. Moffat, Trinity School, New York City, 1709–1959, unpub. diss., Columbia, 1963, pp. 92, 112–114, 124–126, 131, with whose kind permission I draw upon and cite his unpublished material.

SCHOOLING AND THE POOR

If there were constraints against the use of public schools by the wealthy, who disdained the former charity schools in favor of a more personal, genteel experience for their children, there were even stronger reasons why the children of the poor would not be found in the proposed comprehensive schools. There were limits on the occupational relevance of elementary school training, and child labor provided a conflicting attraction for those who could barely pay rent and eat.

If a child proceeded successfully through all nine classes offered in the monitorial public schools, he would, presumably, read and write fairly well and know something of history, geography, mathematics, and English grammar. And, if these abilities greatly increased his chances of getting a white-collar job, the common schools would have contributed significantly to economic opportunity; but it seems improbable that the schools were having much effect in this direction during the period considered here, first, because for various reasons, most children did not go through the whole curriculum and second, because the main trend in the occupational structure was from skilled to unskilled labor, not from manual to nonmanual.

The rate of drop-outs from the public schools was very high. Part of the rationale for the establishment of primary schools was the early leaving age of most pupils. The Society's *Annual Report* for 1832 stated: "Experience proves that the labouring classes of society will, to a great extent, withhold their children from school, the moment they arrive at an age that renders their services in the least available in contributing to the support of the family." In October 1835, Primary School No. 2 reported that "of 14 promoted to the higher schools but 2 entered in them." In one of the upper schools, over one-third of the enrolled children were discharged in a single quarter in 1836.[46] The annual reports of the Primary School Committee from 1837 to 1842 (Table 14) convey the high rate of leaving at the lower school level. In three of the five years reported, the numbers admitted and discharged were

46. PSS, *Annual Report* (New York, 1832), pp. 5–6; PSS, Primary School Committee, Minutes, October 5, 1835; PSS, Minutes of Public School No. 14, November, 1836.

TABLE 14. Primary School Attendance, 1837–1842.

Year ending May 1	No. of primary schools	Number admitted	Number discharged						Year-end no. on register	Aver. attendance
			To priv. sch.	To pub. sch.	To work	Irregular—expelled	Unknown	Total		
1837	26	4568	459	643	404	846	1087	3954	3321	2320
1838	28	5267	380	768	590	1062	1543	4802	3731	2898
1839	36	6479	531	1110	910	1046	1794	5396	4765	3489
1840	46	7667	551	1361	1123	1174	1347	6484	9889	4463
1841	47	5104	420	806	1060	914	—	4333	6320	4915
1842	48	8422	572	1536	1782	2017	1189	7879	6003	4738

Source: Primary School Committee, Minutes, vol. I, 1832–1845, PSS Records, vol. 60, *passim.*

greater than the year-end enrollment, that is, the turnover rate was over 100 percent. Of those discharged, some may have gone to other primaries, or were in and out of the public schools several times, which helps account for the inflated figures for "whole numbers taught" in some reports of the Society. Of those accounted for more specifically, the number leaving to attend private schools was about 10 percent and was decreasing in the five-year period, while those leaving for work rose from about 12 percent to nearly 25 percent of the year-end number registered. Nearly all those who had not left school by the age of fourteen left then, the traditional age for beginning an apprenticeship. The trustees reported in 1850 that "the children of our common schools, are, necessarily, taken from them at an early age. The boys must be placed somewhere, to learn an art or trade, to support themselves or assist their parents."[47]

Most poor children who began school, therefore, did not finish the curriculum and gained only a smattering of the rudiments. They were, at any rate, destined to manual labor when they entered the labor market. It was in this area of the labor force that the greatest changes were occurring. Traditional craft apprenticeship declined as New York manufacturers began to mechanize and mass produce. It is difficult to trace this process, however, for evidence in industrial histories is sparse. Although there were some large manufacturing enterprises, New York did not follow the same pattern of industrialization as New England mill towns did.[48] In 1820 the major manufacturing establishments were the iron foundries, sugar refineries, breweries, and distilleries; by 1832 the city had nine iron furnaces, employing 465 men, and the development of smelting with coal boosted the industry after 1833. By 1850 New York was producing 150,000 stoves a year, as well as steam engines and other heavy iron products.[49] By mid-century it was also the country's clothing center, an industry which began to mechanize in 1846 with the invention of the sewing machine.[50]

47. PSS, *Annual Report*, 1850, in *Annual Report of Superintendent of Common Schools . . . 1852*, p. 109.
48. V. S. Clark, *History of Manufactures in the United States, 1607–1860* (Washington, McGraw Hill Book Company, 1929), p. 549.
49. Clark, *Manufactures*, pp. 412, 465n., 491, 503, 507–508; Thomas F. Gordon, *Gazeteer of the State of New York* (Philadelphia, 1836), p. 337.
50. Clark, *Manufactures*, pp. 430, 521; Ernst, *Immigrant Life*, p. 17.

Although the typical manufacturer at mid-century did not employ hundreds of workers, the number of larger establishments was increasing, and this development suggests two probable effects on education: first, more and more fathers worked away from home, eliminating the opportunity for informal training in the family-work unit, especially as the possibility of father-son apprenticeship declined. Second, the more manufacturing became concentrated, the less possibility there was of the journeyman artisan becoming master and then small entrepreneur, which might have given him a chance to use his school learning in taking orders, trading, or keeping accounts. The common expectation of the colonial craftsman, to rise within his trade, was reduced as the hierarchical apprentice system was undermined. Apprentices became laborers who were functionally immobile.

It did not take extensive mechanization and mass production to undermine apprenticeship. Surplus labor and the resulting depressed wages had more to do with vitiating the traditional training process. Even before 1820 journeymen complained that there were too many apprentices, and in 1828 the *Mechanics Free Press* charged that some masters were using only apprentices, as many as fifteen to twenty, with no journeymen. This practice was just as bad for apprentices as for journeymen, the paper argued, because there was no point in learning a trade only to be thrown out of work when you finished. "It is no wonder that so many young men, under such unfavourable circumstances, are ruined in their morals and reputations," they concluded.[51] In some trades, employers began to use apprenticeship as a substitute for adult labor. It became terminal rather than preparatory. By mid-century apprentice training was virtually gone in shoemaking and tailoring. A visitor to the city in 1852 described an establishment which had 500 girls sewing pantaloons at home, and he charged that milliners took apprentices at little or no wages and then let them go after six months. Native workers blamed cheap immigrant labor for the breakdown and called for restrictive legislation. Some observers, like Horace Greeley, regretted that apprenticeship was "out of fashion,"

51. Paul H. Douglass, *American Apprenticeship and Industrial Education* (New York, Columbia University Press, 1921), pp. 60–61; John R. Commons et al., *Documentary History of American Industrial Society* (Cleveland, A. H. Clark and Company, 1910–1911), I, 67.

and labor organizations called for its regulation, but nothing was done to prevent its distortion and decline.[52] In 1832 a New York State Assembly committee on apprenticeship and child labor had cited severe problems in Europe and recommended mild regulation for the state, but they also asserted the individual rights of manufacturers and cautioned against "severe penal codes." This caution was heeded, and no meaningful legislation on child labor or apprenticeship was passed until late in the century.[53]

It is difficult, for several reasons, to determine how much child labor was used in New York and whether it increased as apprenticeship training decreased. First, the word "apprentice" was used loosely to describe child laborers, for example, in the absurd case of chimneysweeps, who, when they reached journeyman's age, would either be dead or too big to get into chimneys. Second, written indentures gradually fell into disuse; whatever bona fide craft apprenticeship remained was arranged through verbal agreements.[54] Third, one cannot tell from census reports whether children who are listed as employed were doing menial labor for labor's sake or were receiving occupational training. Finally, employers lied about the number of children they employed.[55] It is therefore very difficult to assess the relationship between declining craft apprenticeship, increasing child labor, and school attendance. The trends are clear, but their magnitude is not. It does not seem, however, that decreasing apprenticeship caused a transfer of the occupational training function to the schools, because the age groups were different. The schools concentrated on the pre-14-year-old group, and apprenticeship was typically a post-14-year-old status.

To the extent that mass production techniques were converting skilled into unskilled trades, the decline of apprenticeship caused

52. Ernst, *Immigrant Life,* pp. 103, 109; [Bobo], *Glimpses,* pp. 107–108; Ernst, *Immigrant Life,* p. 103; Horace Greeley, *Recollections of a Busy Life,* (New York, 1868), p. 64; Douglass, *Apprenticeship,* pp. 60–64. Homer Folks, *The Care of Destitute, Neglected and Delinquent Children* (New York, J. B. Lyon Company, 1900), p. 41, says that apprentice indentures were in disuse by 1875.

53. New York State *Assembly Documents,* 1832, vol. IV, No. 308, April 24, 1832; Adna F. Weber, *Labor Legislation in New York* (Albany, 1904), pp. 3–7; Jeremy P. Felt, *Hostages of Fortune: Child Labor Reform in New York State* (Syracuse, Syracuse University Press, 1965), pp. 1–8.

54. License of Henry King, Chimney Sweeper, March 25, 1814, NYMA, Box 2990; Douglass, *Apprenticeship,* p. 68.

55. See Douglass, *Apprenticeship,* p. 57, on reports of the 1830's, and Felt, *Hostages,* p. 3, on the 1870's.

no training problem: some men just worked all their lives at jobs that required less initial training. The boy who had previously worked beginning at age fourteen for his training, his tools, and his keep, came increasingly to start working at the same age or earlier, for low wages, no keep, and no tools. Once children began work, the schools had little concern with them. The decline of apprenticeship did not cause a custodial problem for society either, for it primarily affected those fourteen and older, and most of the youths thus displaced were taken up by wage labor.

In the younger age group, as the Primary School Reports show (Table 14 above), there was also some opportunity for wage earning, which kept children away from school. The Public School Society kept other poor children out by requiring minimum standards of appearance and attendance. The Workingmen's Committee of Philadelphia in 1830 said that in New York, as in Philadelphia, there were thousands of vagrant or laboring children because "very many of the poorest parents are totally unable to clothe and maintain their children while at school." In 1853 the common schools were still excluding many of the children of the poorest inhabitants; *Putnam's Monthly* noted that about 100 students, "of a lower grade than usually attend the public schools," attended a "ragged school" operated by St. George's church.[56] After 1850 this failure of the public schools to attract or admit the poorest students prompted renewed efforts by charitable societies to establish vocational and mission schools in the slums. In 1869 Matthew Smith wrote that there were 40,000 vagrant poor children, mostly of immigrant families, who "are too dirty, too ragged, and carry too much vermin about them, to be admitted to the public schools." Charles Loring Brace said in 1857 that estimates of vagrant children ranged from 20,000 to 50,000. "Whatever be the cause, here is the fact. It is idle to say 'let them go to the Public Schools.' They do not go, and they will not."[57]

One reason, then, that the public schools were unable to effect significant economic democracy through schooling was the pressure

56. Commons, *Documentary History,* V, 102; *Putnam's Monthly,* vol. II, No. 7 (July 1853), p. 11.
57. Matthew H. Smith, *Sunshine and Shadow in New York* (Hartford, 1869), p. 206; Charles L. Brace, *Address upon the Industrial School Movement . . .* (New York, 1857), p. 12; see also Charles Brace, *The Dangerous Classes of New York and Twenty Years' Work Among Them* (New York, 1872), p. 133.

on the poor to quit school and work. To this was added the public schools' exclusion of unkempt or irregular children. Another reason, however, which was beyond the schools' control, was that the economy did not call for substantially increased numbers of nonmanual laborers. Most of the poor were destined to manual labor whether they could read and write or not, and the schools could offer only a limited, sponsored mobility to those who stayed in the system.

SCHOOLING AND OCCUPATIONAL MOBILITY

Despite the economic changes that took place in New York City in the first half of the nineteenth century, the basic occupational structure in 1855 remained surprisingly similar to that of 1796. The data upon which Table 15 is based are not strictly comparable, for the 1796 *Directory* probably omitted more working-class people than the New York State Census of 1855, and category names sometimes mask changes in the nature of an occupation; but even allowing a margin for distortion, the comparison suggests no broad expansion of the professional, merchant, or proprietary groups relative to the whole work force, and the increase in clerical workers did not bring them to sufficient numbers to affect the job market very much.

More impressionistic evidence also suggests limited prospects for those starting without family background or financial resources. Visitors' accounts and immigrant guides, which often painted a rosy picture of economic mobility in the first quarter of the century, became more conservative as the city's labor market became tighter. Robert Hartley's memoirs describe the difficulty of finding a clerk's job; most of the "multitudes" who applied were disappointed. Merchant apprenticeships generally went to "gentlemen's sons," who received no pay for the first year. In 1832 one author warned poor immigrants not to stay in New York: "They can rarely rise in such places, and are likely to be doomed to the lowest, most groveling and vicious pursuits." Robert Ernst has shown that some immigrants were able to rise, mostly becoming proprietors or contractors, but "hard work and extremely frugal living" were more important to this success than schooling.[58]

58. Isaac S. Hartley, ed., *Memorial of Robert Milham Hartley* (Utica, 1882), pp. 75–76; Calvin Colton, *Manual for Emigrants to America* (London, 1832), p. 62; Ernst, *Immigrant Life,* p. 83.

The avenues to advancement were not entirely barred by considerations of family and wealth, of course. Searching the literature on life in the city in the first half of the century, one finds individual cases of persistent poor men getting ahead as a result of schooling. For a poor child entering the New York public schools, however, occupational mobility was not a likely prospect, nor was there a heavy emphasis on it in the promotional rhetoric of the Public School Society. When the Society addressed itself to the general public, whose support they needed, the usefulness of the schools was generally stated in terms of moral improvement and the reduction of crime. In the second quarter of the century, however, faced with the fact that many poor people as well as rich people did not appreciate the common school program, the trustees made some attempts to promote school attendance as a means of economic advancement for the individual. In 1838 the Society sent a letter to all the charitable organizations in the city, asking them to "urge upon the numerous families with whom they have intercourse, the great advantages of sending their children to the Public Schools," and in the same year they published and distributed free a pamphlet detailing those advantages. Although parents might be reluctant to give up the present earning power of their children, they urged, "give them a *good schooling,* and in a few years, they will be earning *ten, twenty, fifty or a hundred* times as much as they do now."[59]

The Society's pamphlet claimed that there was a great demand for good clerks, but most of their examples of success stories, significantly, were about public school students who became teachers. The Lancasterian system had given the teaching occupation in New York a structure it lacked in the colonial period; the use of monitors, assistant teachers, and principal teachers created a hierarchy and a form of apprenticeship. Promising students were trained in special monitors' schools begun in the 1830's, and in their pamphlet the trustees said they employed "more than 100 of their former scholars, at salaries of from 25 to 1,000 dollars a year." One of them, "who was so poor that his clothes were found for him, rose to be the Principal of one of the Public Schools. He afterwards had a large and profitable private school of his own, and purchased a very

59. PSS, Executive Committee Minutes, June 4, 1838; PSS, *Public Schools, Public Blessings* (New York, 1838), p. 22.

TABLE 15. The Occupational Structure of New York City in 1855, Compared to That of 1796.

| | 1796 | | | 1855 | Number of workers | |
Category	Percent of work force	Subcategory		Percent of work force	Sub-category	Category[a]
1. Laborers	5.5	1a.	Laborers, porters	27.4	23,161	58,884
		1b.	Domestic workers; nurses		35,723	
2. Mariners	3.7	2	Sailors, mariners, boatmen	2.7	5,837	5,837
3. Cartmen	9.5	3	Workers in ground transportation	3.8	8,325	8,325
4. Skilled trades	43.1	4a.	Artisans & factory workers	41.2	32,330	88,610
		4b.	Building trades workers		22,187	
		4c.	Clothing workers		23,828	
		4d.	Machinists		1,714	
		4e.	Maritime workers		2,733	
		4f.	Metal workers		5,813	
5. Clerical	2.0	5a.	Clerks, accountants	7.7	13,907	16,448
		5b.	Government employees		635	
		5c.	Agents, auctioneers, wardens		1,906	
6. Proprietor	14.3	6a.	Proprietors: hotels, inns, stables	6.4	4,028	13,839
		6b.	Shopkeepers: grocer, bookseller		6,544	
		6c.	Dealers: fish, coal, ice, fruit		2,907	
		6d.	Brewers, distillers		360	

	%		%	Number	Total
7. Professions (law, med., clergy)	4.0	7a. Medicine, law, clergy	3.7	2,776	
		b. Teacher, artist, engineer, other		5,092	7,868
8. Merchants	13.0	8a. Merchants	3.5	6,001	
		b. Financiers, bankers, brokers		1,003	
		c. Speculators, investors		219	
		d. Importers		235	7,458
9. Other	5.4	9a. Policemen and firemen	3.7	1,434	
		b. Service workers		494	
		c. Pedlars		1,889	
		d. Other		3,870	7,687

Sources: Census of the State of New York for 1855 (Albany, 1857), pp. 178–195, and Table 1, Chapter Two, above. The categories are adapted from Robert Ernst, *Immigrant Life in New York City, 1825–1863* (New York, King's Crown Press, 1949), Appendix VII, pp. 206–212; the individual occupations included in the subgroups are listed there.

[a] Totals for 1855: 214,956 workers, 359 occupations.

valuable farm, on which to retire."[60] The school system, then, had a built-in means of limited, sponsored mobility. Beyond their schools the Society could offer only unexciting or uncertain prospects: for girls, the earning power of the needlework they would learn in school, or the ability to catch a smarter husband, and for boys, a chance to compete in the tight market for white collar jobs. But within their system, the ladder of advancement was clear, and many of the public school teachers rose from the ranks of the students.[61]

The ideal of at least a nominal equality of educational opportunity went a step farther at the end of this period. In the 1830's the trustees had arranged, first with Columbia, then with the new University of the City of New York (later New York University), for small numbers of students from the public schools to attend college on scholarship. Because the nine classes of public school included no preparation in Latin and Greek, the Society obtained additional scholarships to the Columbia Grammar School. Few students made it through the program, however, and in 1842, when it was discontinued, the trustees could boast only one graduate.[62]

Although this early experiment in sponsoring the higher academic advancement of the talented poor failed, a project on a much grander scale began in 1847 when the legislature authorized the new public Board of Education to establish a Free Academy in the city, subject to a referendum of the city's voters, who overwhelmingly approved the measure in June of that year. The city academy would eliminate the preparation gap students had faced between the public schools and the colleges. It would accept students who had attended the public schools for at least one year, on the basis of entrance examinations in the three R's, English grammar, and U.S. history. However, it was clearly designed to

60. PSS, *Public Blessings,* pp. 18–20; Reigart, *Lancasterian System,* p. 92.

61. PSS, *Public Blessings,* pp. 10, 17–18. In 1846 the Executive Committee noted that of 320 teachers in the white schools, 271 had been trained in the public schools. PSS, Executive Committee, Minutes, July 2, 1846. In the technical sense, the Public School Society schools were a "contest" mobility situation at the lower levels, but they could offer so little beyond their own bounds that the competition had little relation to job status. On the other hand, the monitor who became teacher, or the recipient of the school-sponsored scholarship to grammar school, are typical cases of "sponsored" mobility, as defined in Ralph H. Turner, "Sponsored and Contest Mobility and the School System," *American Sociological Review* 25 (1960), 855–867.

62. PSS, Executive Committee, Minutes, March 1, May 3, 1838; May 23, June 27, 1839; September 3, 1840; May 5, 1842.

function both as an academy and a college. The word "academy" had been used to ensure funding from the state's literature fund, which was limited to incorporated academies, but the trustees soon set up two five-year programs, one in classics, the other in modern languages, and promised bachelors degrees to their first graduating class in 1853 as soon as they were granted the power to confer them.[63]

The Whig papers had generally opposed the Free Academy, arguing against public funding of higher education and cautioning against the instability that might be caused by rising expectations. A "Mechanic" wrote in the *Journal of Commerce* that "to send the children of persons possessing small means to college, is doing them an injury rather than a favor. It is of this description of college educated individuals that the ranks of pettifoggers and quacks are filled. They are too proud of their superior education to work either as clerks or mechanics, or to follow any active business except what is termed 'professional.' " To critics who feared that higher education would only dissatisfy common men with manual pursuits, the Board of Education had replied that, on the contrary, an academy education including practical knowledge in chemistry, mechanics, and other sciences "would remove the foolish prejudice which now induces thousands to abandon the honest and healthy pursuits of their fathers, in order to establish themselves in professions, and mercantile pursuits which are already crowded to excess." This theme was prominent again at the opening ceremonies in 1849, where Robert Kelly, the new president of the Board of Education, stressed that the purpose of the Academy was to dignify all forms of work. There is a tacit assumption of occupational stability; Kelly spoke as if the students' occupations were already settled, stating that the Academy would be "elevating and equalizing the rank and respectability of their widely different occupations, making industry honorable."[64]

63. S. Willis Rudy, *The College of the City of New York: A History, 1847–1947* (New York, City College Press, 1949), pp. 31, 34–39.
64. *Journal of Commerce*, May 22, 1847, in Mario E. Cosenza, *The Establishment of the College of the City of New York as the Free Academy in 1847* . . . (New York, The Associate Alumini of the College of the City of New York, 1955), pp. 146–147; Townsend Harris et al., *Memorial . . . to Establish a Free Academy* . . . (New York, 1847), p. 7; *Addresses Delivered upon the Occasion of the Opening of the Free Academy, January 27, 1849* (New York, 1849), pp. 10–11.

The Democratic *Daily Globe,* in contrast, was openly in favor of occupational mobility and saw it as a key purpose of the Academy A *Globe* editorial said the new institution would "improve and illustrate one of the peculiar characteristics of our people," which was, "irrespective of their circumstances and business in life, to be looking up. Every man expects to be wiser and wealthier, and to rise in the estimation of his countrymen."[65] Whether the New York work force at mid-century really fulfilled this Tocquevillean image or not is doubtful, but the Democrats hoped the Academy would foster such aspirations. On the more radical Democratic side, however, the erratic Mike Walsh had reversed field and opposed the Academy, charging that poor men's sons would be eliminated by prejudiced examiners, despite assurances from the promoters that entrance examinations would be scrupulously impartial.[66]

The available evidence tends to vindicate the faith of the electorate and the intentions of the Democrat-dominated Board of Education, at least in terms of the range of backgrounds of those admitted to the Academy. In 1854 the Board published a list of the occupations of the fathers of all boys admitted since 1849. Table 16 summarizes that list in terms of the categories used in Table 15 to describe the 1855 Census of occupations. Compared to their proportion in the whole population, laborers' and servants' children were far underrepresented, but artisans and factory workers sent academy students almost in proportion to their numbers, clerical workers slightly over their numbers, proprietors in a ratio of nearly twice their numbers, and the professional and merchant groups in numbers over three times their proportion in the population. Considering that the matriculates had to be well versed in the subjects taught in the nine classes of the public schools, this enumeration indicates that the public schools—those of the Public School Society now bolstered by the new ward schools—had succeeded in producing a cream of the crop which included large numbers of working-class children, and that at least some children of higher-status men were also attending public schools. Black students were excluded from the Academy as from so much else, and the bottom

65. *Daily Globe,* May 25, 1847, in Cosenza, *Free Academy,* pp. 149–150.
66. *The Subterranean* (ed. Mike Walsh), vol. V, no. 3 (June 12, 1847); *Addresses upon Opening of the Free Academy,* p. 11.

TABLE 16. Occupations of Parents Whose Children Were Admitted to the New York Free Academy, 1849–1853.

Occupation category	No. of parents	Percent of Academy parents	Size of category in work force (percent)
Laborers & servants	19	2.3	27.4
Mariners	9	1.1	2.7
Ground transportation	59	7.2	3.8
Artisans & factory workers	290	35.4	41.2
Clerical	88	10.8	7.7
Proprietors	94	11.5	6.4
Professionals	105	12.9	3.7
Merchant	103	12.6	3.5
Other	49	6.0	3.7
Total	816		
Parent's occupation not given	174		
Total admitted	990		

Source: 12th Annual Report of the Board of Education of the City and County of New York (New York, 1854), pp. 13–14.

quarter of the work force was almost entirely absent; otherwise, the enrollment was quite mixed, and the term, "People's College," was not inappropriate.

Entering the Free Academy and graduating from it were, on the other hand, two very different things. The drop-out rate was high. In 1855, for example, there were 174 in the introductory class and 24 in the senior class.[67] Of the 160 students admitted in July 1853, 25 eventually graduated from the full five-year course. It is impossible to discover what benefit the Academy was to those who dropped out, whether it made them more dignified, intelligent mechanics, or gave them expectations which were frustrated, or whether a partial academy course could help them get a more desirable job. The occupations of the fathers of those who did graduate, however, were still quite varied. Attrition operated somewhat disproportionately against workers' sons, but the list of graduates' fathers from this one entering group still contained a tailor, a wheel-

67. Report on the Free Academy, in New York City Board of Education, *Annual Report*, 1855, p. 23.

TABLE 17.   Occupations of Graduates and Graduates' Fathers, New York
Free Academy, Entering Class of July 1853.[a]

Name	Graduating class	Father's occupation	Graduate's occupation
	1858		
Banks, William		Upholsterer	Merchant-Banker
Beneville, Emil		Brass turner	Lawyer
Childs, Augustus		Dry goods mer.	Bookkeeper
Clark, John		Cartman	None given
Crowther, Thomas		None (widow)	Clergyman
James, Charles		Lawyer	None given
Ketchum, Alex		Inspector	Lawyer
Kursheedt, Manuel		Merchant	Lawyer
McKee, Thomas		Machinist	Lawyer
Moriarty, Edward		Clerk	Theology student (died)
Pettigrew, John		Wheelwright	Bookkeeper
Plyer, Charles		Paper stainer	Insurance
Sands, Walter		Chemist	Lawyer
Sturges, Peter		Merchant	Merchant
Tompkins, Elliot		Bookkeeper	Clergyman
Vehslage, Henry		City missionary	Clergyman
	1859		
Howland, Elijah		None given	P.S. principal
Mackie, Simon		Clerk	Merchant
Man, William		Lawyer	Lawyer
Martin, Benjamin		Banker	Doctor
Merritt, Mortimer		Cartman	Architect
Quinn, William		Tailor	Lawyer
Sullivan, Dennis		Coal dealer	Bookkeeper
Tisdall, Fitzgerald		Agent	Greek prof.
	1860		
Gray, William		Dry goods mer.	Student of ministry (died)

*Sources: Twelfth Annual Report of the Board of Education of the City and County of
New York* (New York, 1854), Free Academy Report, pp. 70–73; *Register of the
Associate Alumni* of the College of the City of New York (New York, 1924).

[a] 160 admitted; 25 graduated.

wright, a machinist, and two cartmen. Table 17 also suggests that
most graduates who were not already from professional or merchant
families were upwardly mobile, and that, true to the conservatives'
gloomy predictions, those who made it all the way through to grad-
uation went predominantly into the professions, especially law.

Information on the family backgrounds of students at the city's pay colleges is not so readily available; but a sample of those parents of N.Y.U. graduates in the classes of 1850 to 1855 who could be identified in the *New York Directory* will give some perspective on the socioeconomic composition of the Academy's students. Of the twenty-five native New Yorkers who graduated from N.Y.U. in those years, the occupations of thirteen fathers could be determined. They included: three physicians, three ministers, a merchant, a broker, an architect, a building materials dealer, a clerk, a grocer, and the secretary of a charitable organization.[68] The sample is tiny, but it suggests the more exclusive character of the tuition colleges.

As an institutional precedent, the Free Academy was important in the development of the city's schooling system, providing for the first time tax-supported, tuition-free schooling beyond the common school level. It had a limited impact on the school population as a whole, but it did significantly alter the socioeconomic composition of college students in New York. It also provided the public school system with a further avenue of limited, sponsored mobility for its most promising students, in addition to the teaching positions the common school system could offer.

Thomas Jefferson had approved of a natural aristocracy as opposed to an aristocracy of wealth, but the system he proposed in Virginia to implement this goal was far from a meritocracy. Twenty boys a year were to be sent free to grammar school each year, and of these, half would be sent on to college. By this means, as he said, the geniuses would be raked from the rubbish.[69] Similarly, in the New York schooling system as it operated in 1850, the raking process left most in the dirt. This was perceived on both sides. Workingmen's groups regularly supported improved common schooling, but given the limited occupational relevance of the schools in a predominantly manual job market, their complaints about the pauper aura of the public school seem to have been mainly a means of expressing their displeasure about the social gap

68. *Biographical Catalogue of the Chancellors, Professors and Graduates . . . of the University of the City of New York* (New York, 1894); *Doggett's New York City Directory, 1850–1851.*
69. Thomas Jefferson, *Notes on the State of Virginia* (Chapel Hill, University of North Carolina Press, 1955), p. 146.

between the rich and the poor. In 1830 a group of "Mechanics and other Workingmen" in New York asked "if many of the monopolists and aristocrats in our city would not consider it disgraceful to their noble children to have them placed in our public schools by the side of poor yet industrious mechanics?"[70]

The men who fostered and directed the public schools had not designed them for economic democracy. They had built the system in response to the social problems of a city that was expanding rapidly, both demographically and economically, whose changing residential and production patterns had left great numbers of children resourceless, untended, and unschooled. They built it in response to a widening gulf of misunderstanding and animosity between the classes of its citizens, in response to rising crime rates and residential squalor. Most important, and underlying these other motives, they built the public school system in response to what they perceived as the moral failings and moral dangers of an uneducated poor class, many of whom were churchless or guided by a church alien to the city's Protestant leaders. Many of the city's problems were economic and would be solved only gradually and partially by economic developments; but the schoolmen saw the same problems as moral, and they sought moral solutions. The next chapter turns to those solutions and their consequences.

The relationship between economic systems and educational systems, in the long run, is reciprocal. Changes in economic growth, means of production, and income distribution prompt changes in the quantity, the mode, and the purposes of education. Conversely, changing the level and types of skills in the population affects the productive capacities and earning power of individuals and of collective groups like cities or nations. In the long run the American schooling system, despite its conspicuous failures, has advanced both the technological capabilities of the economic system and the material prosperity of most of the society's individuals.

In the period 1800 to 1850 one direction of the reciprocal relation between the economic and schooling system predominated. Economic conditions—poverty and class tensions—were more visibly effective in changing schooling than schooling was in altering the economic position of individuals or of the society as a whole. The moral training of the schools may have helped produce co-

70. Commons, *Documentary History*, V, 113.

operative workers, but this effect cannot be measured, and the transmission of more technical information was not a function of mass schooling. The clearest causal relationship between economics and education in this period involves immigration and urbanization. A great influx of surplus unskilled labor was exploited in ways that led to the degeneration of living conditions, institutional stability, and public order. The result was the creation of a schooling system, where none had existed before, intended to harmonize and reintegrate the members of the society. The system provided a modicum of occupational advancement through free schooling, but it was primarily an instrument of a moral crusade, bent on reestablishing consensus and cooperation in a community which in 1850 was vastly different in size and cultural complexity than the New York of 1750, or of 1800.

The effort to draw all classes into the public schools was hampered by socioeconomic factors which militated against attendance by the rich and the poor. It is not safe to assume, however, that the public schools became simply a middle-class institution. The schoolmen's efforts were persistent; thousands of poor children were marched (almost literally) through the schools, even if many only escaped out the back door. Some stayed and rose in the system; others stayed and did not. Most important, all were now confronted with a school *system*, a network of buildings and men, which took the initiative for schooling in the city.

CHAPTER FOUR

*The Moral
Mission of the
Schools*

Free schools in New York City were designed to give elementary education, moral training, and nondenominational, Protestant religious instruction to the poor. The tone and purpose of the public school enterprise in New York City were determined by these charity school origins. The purpose was moral, not economic or political. Although the training a child received in school might have some effect on his occupational and economic status, the relationship between school and job training, as explained in Chapter Three, was weak. Schoolmen professed to believe that an educated citizenry was crucial to the survival of republican government, but this theme too was minor. Training for a job or for intelligent voting were subordinate to the goal of character building. The schoolmen aimed to promote citizenship in a broad sense, encompassing daily attitudes and behavior. One need not be cynical or read between the lines to recognize that the public schools' dominant purpose in the city was to produce industrious, sober, punctual, God-fearing citizens. School trustees, like orphanage directors and tract missionaries, were motivated primarily by the leading urban problems of the day as they saw them: theft, vagrancy, idleness, intemperance, Sabbath breaking, and prostitution. To combat these, the Free School Society announced in 1821, the schools "are rapidly extending the benign influence of moral principles, inspiring self-regard, creating respect for the laws, diminishing the sources of pauperism and crime, and preparing for usefulness a large portion of what must soon compose our future active population, who might otherwise grow up in idleness, remain a burden on the community, and become victims to every species of vice and profligacy incident to extensive and populous cities."[1] Reformers recognized that there were virtuous and industrious poor, whose poverty came from unavoidable circumstances. They were the proper objects of outright alms. But reformers also believed, as the Reverend Ward Stafford said in 1817, that "almost all the sufferings of the poor in this, and other cities, are the immediate effect of ignorance and vice." The Association for Improving the Condition of the Poor reiterated this belief in 1847: "in most cases, their destitution and misery are owing to moral causes, and will admit only of moral remedies. Condition must consequently be improved, by improving character."[2]

Moral education was broadly conceived, then. On one side it was a kind of occupational training because it sought to inculcate habits of industry and promptness that would make good workers. On the other side it included religious training. God was always present in the schools, and although He was said to be nondenominational, He acted distinctly like a Puritan. Religion was the foundation of moral education in the public schools as it was for tract societies and Sunday schools. Religiously sanctioned moral education was the central function of the schools because everyone thought of urban problems in moral terms, and almost no one could think of morals as separate from God and the Bible. Moral education is discussed below in this broad sense.

MORAL EDUCATION AND VAGRANCY

Statistics on vagrancy in New York are quite unreliable. Vagrants were sometimes defined loosely as all those between the age of five and fifteen who were not in school, including even those who worked, despite the fact that school was not compulsory. Actual vagrant children who roamed the streets causing trouble, of course, were a smaller group. The problem was, nevertheless, sizeable enough and ominous enough to play a prominent part in school and police reports from the 1820's to mid-century and beyond. Police Chief Matsell's detailed enumeration of vagrants in 1849

1. FSS, *18th Annual Report* (New York, 1821).
2. Ward Stafford, *New Missionary Field . . .* (New York, 1817), p. 41; A.I.C.P., *Fourth Annual Report* (New York, 1847), p. 13.

gives an impression of the relative size of the different problem groups. In eleven patrol districts in the lower wards there were 2955 vagrant children, whom he classed in five groups: (1) boys who loitered around the piers, stealing from cargo and selling their loot to unlicensed junk shops (about 770 children); (2) beggars in rags, mostly girls (about 100); (3) prostitutes, more neatly dressed, masquerading as sellers of nuts or fruits but making $2 to $3 a day selling their bodies in alleys or shops (about 380); (4) homeless boys who carried luggage but often stole (about 120); and (5) boys who had homes but gathered on street corners in the evenings and on Sundays and caused trouble (about 1600). Thomas Harris, a minister who published Matsell's report with a sermon on the subject, estimated that one child of every ten in the lower wards was sent out daily to pilfer or beg.[3]

In a city with such abominable housing conditions, it is not surprising that children walked the streets; in a city where employment was uncertain and hard times frequent, it is not surprising that children begged; and in a city where gangs, brawling, and riots characterized slum life, where in the 1850's the mayor was arrested, and rival police forces fought it out in the streets, it is not surprising that many children grew up scrapping for survival, disregarding authority except when it was backed by force.[4] The children of the streets were presented with models of success antithetical to the version promoted by the schools and churches. They were thus the most resistant to moral education and the most difficult to bring into the schools. John Stanford, minister of the Almshouse, said that young children of the streets were instructed by older delinquents, who "form their criminal practices into a system." The higher learning takes place in jails, "so that, on the expiration of their sentence, it may be said of some of them, they are competent to take their first degree of *Bachelor* in the *Art* of crime." The same metaphor occurs again and again. A school report of 1856

3. Thomas L. Harris, *Juvenile Depravity & Crime in our City* . . . (New York, 1850), pp. 10, 13–14. Matsell's fifth category, boys who may or may not have attended school, illustrates the problem of definition. Not all vagrants were nonschoolers, just as not all nonschoolers were vagrants.

4. On gangs, riots, and the police during this period, see George W. Walling, *Recollections of a New York Chief of Police* (New York, 1887), pp. 43–46, 56–57; Herbert Asbury, *The Gangs of New York* (New York, Alfred Knopf, 1928), pp. 21, 28, 37–39, 65–66; James G. Wilson, ed., *The Memorial History of the City of New York* (New York, 1893), III, 339–345; and James F. Richardson, *The New York City Police: Colonial Times to 1901* (New York, Oxford University Press, 1970), chaps. 1–5.

complained that there were "between 20,000 and 60,000 children now being educated in our streets in habits of idleness, and a knowledge of vice, whence they will graduate, enemies to themselves and curses to the community, and enter upon careers of debauchery and crime."[5]

MORAL EDUCATION AND CRIME

Schoolmen often worried about the influence of this competing "system." Many children would not even be exposed to the moral influence of the school. They were confident of one thing, however: if they could get children into the public schools or some place where they received a good moral education, crime would be reduced. Not all vagrant children were criminals, but schoolmen were sure that school attendance and crime were inversely related. Thomas Eddy, active in both school and prison work, argued that schooling of the poor obviously reduces crime because only one boy who had attended the Free School Society's schools had been convicted of a crime, "although several hundreds who had not been at the Free Schools had been tried at the Quarter Sessions, and been committed to the City Penitentiary, for vagrancy and various other offences."[6] Prison wardens often reported the educational background of their inmates. In 1835, for example, New York's Auburn prison contained 747 persons: 4 with a college education, 8 with an academy education, 221 with a common education, 311 with a very poor education, and 203 with no education.[7] School supporters justified the cost of schools by the expected reduction in expenses for jails and welfare.[8]

The reformers' correlation of crime and ignorance was simplistic,

5. John Stanford, Discourse on Opening the New Building in the House of Refuge . . . , December 25, 1826, Stanford MSS, Box 2, NYHS, pp. 8–9; Samuel Halliday, *The Lost and Found, or Life Among the Poor* (New York, 1859), p. 346.

6. Samuel L. Knapp, *Life of Thomas Eddy* (London, 1836), p. 62. The Society made similar claims periodically; see, for example, FSS, *17th Annual Report* (New York, 1822), and DeWitt Clinton to the legislature, 1825, in Edward A. Fitzpatrick, *The Educational Views and Influence of DeWitt Clinton* (New York, Teachers College, Columbia University, Contributions to Education, No. 44, 1911), p. 54.

7. Thomas F. Gordon, *Gazeteer of the State of New York* (Philadelphia, 1836), p. 317.

8. New York City Board of Education, Report for 1851, in *Annual Report of the Superintendent of Common Schools of the State of New York . . . January, 1852* (Albany, 1852), p. 98.

but the frequent use of such statistics demonstrates the faith people had in the efficacy of moral instruction, and the importance of crime reduction among the functions of the school. New Yorkers considered moral education very important in attacking youthful vagrancy and crime, and, in the first half of the nineteenth century, they developed several types of schools to extend moral instruction where the church and the family were failing: public schools, Sunday schools, special supplementary institutions like mission schools and industrial schools, and finally, schools in residential institutions like the Almshouse, the orphanages, and the House of Refuge for juvenile delinquents.

AGENCIES OF MORAL EDUCATION:
PUBLIC SCHOOLS

One means of moral training in the public schools was straightforward catechism, as in this "persuasive charge" recited by teacher and students:

T: You must obey your parents.
S: I must obey my parents.
      (The pupils, at each repetition, place the right hand, opened, upon the breast, which gesture seems to make the sentiment more impressive)
T: You must obey your teachers.
S: I must obey my teachers.

The litany continues, with injunctions against lying, stealing, and swearing. Then, "slowly, and in a soft tone,"

T: God always sees you.
S: God always sees me.
T: God hears all you say.
S: God hears all I say.
T: God knows all you do.
S: God knows all I do.[9]

More effective in inculcating proper moral habits than the "persuasive charge," probably, were the routine and regulations of the schools. The schools required children to be silent, courteous, obedi-

9. PSS, *A Manual of the System of Discipline & Instruction* . . . (New York, 1850), pp. 19–20.

ent, prompt, clean, and faithful in attendance. Attendance was very important, for, as John Griscom noted in 1825, the few public school students who had been arrested "were children noted for great irregularity of attendance, and for the formidable habits of vice and insubordination which they were suffered to contract at home."[10] In an effort to stem such truancy, the Free School Society had established a policy of selecting the "most notorious delinquents" and then having the head monitor "proclaim round the school that those scholars were expelled on account of their neglect and bad conduct."[11] The self-defeating nature of this policy seems to have escaped the trustees; while they expelled the most irregular students from their schools, they continued their efforts to attract new ones from the homes of the irregular and undisciplined members of the lower class. Often the new students were just the old ones coming through again; the Society thus contributed to the transience of the student body despite the value they placed on faithful attendance.

Their visitation program illustrates this process. In 1827 the Society employed one of their trustees, Samuel Seton, as visitor and agent, to attempt to "persuade the indifferent and careless to send their children to school." In his first report Seton said that he had visited 1700 families.[12] Despite his efforts, however, the Society reported as usual in 1832 that "a very large number of children are found roaming the streets of our city." The Society determined to start primary schools to get children into the system earlier, and they persuaded the Common Council to pass a resolution declaring that people who refused to send their children to school would be considered "without the pale of Public Charities, and not entitled, in case of misfortune, to receive public favor."[13] The regulation proved as ineffective as the visitor, and in 1839 the Society's Committee on Coercive School Laws again urged the

10. John Griscom, *Monitorial Instruction . . . Address . . . Opening of the New York High-School* (New York, 1825), pp. 19–20.
11. Public School Society, Minutes, August 1, 1817.
12. A. Emerson Palmer, *The New York Public School: Being a History of Free Education in the City of New York* (New York, The Macmillan Company, 1905), p. 79; Thomas Boese, *Public Education in the City of New York: Its History, Condition, and Statistics* (New York, 1869), p. 121.
13. PSS, *Address to the Public* (New York, 1832); New York Common Council, Resolution, May 10, 1832, in PSS Records, vol. 41, NYHS.

Common Council to enforce more strictly the laws for the incarceration of vagrants and regulations against begging.[14] The schools obviously needed help in reducing the vagrancy problem.

Meanwhile, in the late 1830's, the Society hired some assistants for Seton. In August 1839, the Committee of Five on Vagrant Children reported that the visitors had induced 358 children to enroll during the preceding term, of whom 83 had never been to school before; 223 of these new pupils remained at the end of the term. Reports in following years show that the visitors had difficulty rounding up students who had never been to school before, and the number who remained in school declined. In March 1840, they reported an annual total of 706, of whom 602 remained in the schools, but only 105 were entirely new to the schools. In June they reported an additional 517 children brought in, but only 175 had remained; and in 1841 they reported a total of 1177, of whom 356 remained.[15] Those who stayed in school, of course, were receiving the desired moral training. Some, presumably, had been rescued from the influences of the streets; the missionary effort of the public school visitors must have helped some poor children into approved channels of work and conduct. How many children were influenced and in what ways is impossible to determine. Character building is an elusive claim for schools, especially in a voluntary system, because parents who already shared the values of the schools were more likely to send their children to school. Reinforcing this tendency, the schools expelled those who would not abide by their values. The public schools' probes into the slums demonstrate, however, that despite difficulties the schoolmen had not abandoned their commitment to the poor in general and the children of neglectful parents in particular.

Schoolmen sensed that the schools were excluding those whom they most wanted to reform. The Public School Society lamented in 1838 that the schools attracted "so small a number of those for whom they were originally intended." William Bourne, the Society's first historian, said that the shift to a common school ideal and the improvement of the Society's schools resulted in a "process of substitution." "In proportion as the comfortably-clad and cleanly and polished pupil makes his appearance, the opposite class shrink

---

14. PSS, Executive Committee Minutes, May 2, 1839.

15. PSS, Executive Committee Minutes, August 1, 1839, May 5, June 4, 1840, August 5, 1841.

from contact."[16] Unfortunately, analysis of actual income groups in the schools is impossible for the nineteenth century in New York City, and thus the "displacement" interpretation cannot be tested. It is true that the public schools were displacing the minor pay schools (see Table 12), but because their capacity was constantly increasing relative to the population, the poor could have continued to attend in as great numbers, relatively, as before. The cultural alienation implied in Bourne's displacement theory certainly existed, but we cannot determine quantitatively to what extent the alienation of the poor or the immigrant actually kept them out of the schools. The question remains open, and terms like "middle class" and the "poor" remain imprecise constructs in this context.

The visitors sometimes found the confrontation of values stark. The emphasis on moral training was but another expression of the distance between the city's establishment and its poor, a separation which was economic, residential, and cultural, but which was seen primarily as moral. One visitor described his difficulty in trying to bridge this gap:

> In searching for children for *Public School* we witness scenes enough to shock human nature. In one family I obtained the promise of two children. They were to be in readiness the next morning at 9 o'clock. I called at that time. Her Mother had represented herself as a Widow but to my astonishment I met with the Father who had been let out from state Prison the day before—rather sooner than had been expected by the Wife—On his arrival he found her intoxicated, quite unable to attend to her Children and she was in the same condition when I called for the children. On my appearance a Sceane commenced which cannot be discribed. Each tried to make the best story which was followed by blows and tumultous noise.—After waiting about 30 minutes I was compelled to leave with my mind made up that there are multitudes of children in this City who never will be benifitted by Education unless they can be rescued from such an influence.[17]

There in a single anecdote are many of the vices the visitors had to contend with: lying, crime, drunkenness, brawling, and

16. Boese, *Public Education*, p. 124; William O. Bourne, *History of the Public School Society of New York* (New York, 1870), p. 602. Julia Duffy accepts this interpretation in her study, stating that the middle class children "displaced" the children of the poor. Duffy, The Proper Objects of a Gratuitous Education . . . , unpub. diss., Teachers College, Columbia University, 1968, pp. 199 and 135–139.

17. Visitor's report, ca. December 3, 1840, addressed to the Rev. G. Orchard, President, loose MS in PSS Executive Committee Minutes, vol. 56.

neglect. It was difficult to recruit men who would go out into the slums to try to rescue the children. In May 1842, the Public School Society's Committee on Neglected and Vagrant Children reported that they could find no replacements for the visitors, and the program was discontinued.[18] Other programs, such as evening schools, attempted to reach a broad spectrum of working people, but many could not or would not come. Among them were many who were in greatest need, from the reformers' viewpoint, of moral education. As the Public School Society said, "We must have safe and consistent members of society."[19] Other organizations joined the crusade.

AGENCIES OF MORAL EDUCATION: SUNDAY SCHOOLS

In 1780 an English publisher named Robert Raikes, distressed by the "ragged, wretched, vicious state" of pinmakers' children in Gloucester, had started a Sunday school in "Sooty Alley." Without help from the clergy, and without doctrinal catechism, Raikes developed a system for popular religious instruction based on reading the Bible, using voluntary teachers and a version of monitorial instruction that preceded Lancaster. John Wesley and other prominent workers with the poor approved of Raikes' work, and in 1785 an interdenominational Sunday School Society was founded in London. Shortly thereafter the idea found its way across the Atlantic. In 1790 Benjamin Rush was instrumental in establishing a First Day Society in Philadelphia, and Matthew Carey, a Catholic, was among its directors.[20]

In 1801 and 1802 Mr. and Mrs. Divie Bethune, who were active in various charitable enterprises in New York, visited England and learned of the Sunday school movement firsthand. When they returned they opened such a school in Mott Street.[21] Their first efforts were sporadic, but they continued to correspond with English

18. PSS, Executive Committee Minutes, May 5, 1842.
19. Boese, *Public Education*, p. 122.
20. Edwin W. Rice, *The Sunday School Movement, 1780–1917, and the American Sunday School Union, 1817–1917* (Philadelphia, The American Sunday School Union, 1917), pp. 15–22, 45–46.
21. *Ibid.*, pp. 56–57; Theodore F. Savage, *The Presbyterian Church in New York City* (New York, Presbytery of New York, 1949), pp. 58–59; Kenneth D. Miller, *The People are the City; 150 Years of Social and Religious Concern in New York City* (New York, Macmillan, 1962), pp. 14–17.

acquaintances about the value of Sunday schools while they worked on other causes like orphanages and workhouses. Finally, at the urging of Eleazar Lord, who had observed the more organized efforts of Philadelphians in 1815, the Bethunes founded the Female Union Society for the Promotion of Sabbath Schools, for women, and the New York Sunday School Union Society, for men. John Griscom and Samuel Seton were active in the movement, and former mayor Richard Varick was the first president.

By the end of 1816 the two societies, who worked closely together and eventually merged, had begun about fifty Sunday schools with over 6000 pupils.[22] With this sudden expansion of activity, the Sunday schools became a matter of public discussion. Because they proposed to give secular and religious training to the poor on a nondenominational basis, the Sunday school enthusiasts had to define their relationship not only to the churches, but to the developing free school system. In the process, which took from 1815 to about 1840, the purpose and the clients of Sunday schools were substantially changed.

Sunday schools began, not as an effort of the organized churches to convert, but as an effort by reformers to solve social problems through moral education sanctioned by the Bible. They were intended for the children of nonmembers rather than churchgoers; they were rarely held on church premises, and when they were, it was essentially as a tenant, like the Free School Society, which also used church basement sites. Most ministers opposed the movement; detractors argued that the volunteer teachers were not competent, that the schools infringed on parental and pastoral prerogatives, and that Sunday schools, being nondenominational and partly secular in character, profaned the Sabbath.[23]

Although their initial relationship with the organized churches was somewhat hostile, the Sunday schools' relationship to the new free schools was congenial and mutually reinforcing. They were both engaged in the same enterprise, and many people were active in both. The Free School Society encouraged their students to attend Sunday school, and with the formation of the Sunday School Union

22. Rice, *Sunday School Movement*, pp. 57–58, 445–446.

23. Savage, *Presbyterian Church*, pp. 61–62; Shepherd Knapp, *A History of the Brick Presbyterian Church in the City of New York* (New York, 1909), p. 212; Rice, *Sunday School Movement*, p. 49.

in 1816 they discontinued their own program of Tuesday afternoon catechism by denominational representatives and their practice of requiring the free school children to report to schools on Sunday to be marched off to the church of their parents' choice. The Society often loaned its buildings for Sunday school use, and the Sunday School Union assured the public that Sunday school attendance would increase, not decrease, free school attendance.[24] Whatever the overlap between these two agencies of moral instruction, clearly they were both working with the same general population in mind: the poor, and especially, the churchless poor. William Dodge, a merchant-philanthropist, recalled that early Sabbath schools in the city "were designed only for the poor and neglected children. The children of churchgoers were instructed at home in the catechism, and in many churches were expected to recite every Wednesday afternoon in the session-room to the pastor and elder."[25] For the children of their own members, then, the churches had programs to relate family and church instruction, but the Sunday schools were trying to reach those who did not belong or did not attend church.

With little support from the churches, the Sunday schools had to rely on voluntary lay teachers. In the early years the main activity in many schools was the memorization of scripture, which led the American Sunday School Union to note in the 1820's that "it requires very little knowledge and experience to conduct them with ability."[26] The memorization fad may have helped the children learn to read, and memorizing whole books of the Bible seems to have satisfied the teachers of the children's religiosity, but the moral effect was dubious. In 1816 the Methodist teachers admitted that while the literary training was succeeding—some children could read who only knew the alphabet upon entrance—they were not sure the moral training was doing any good.[27] Of course, as in the weekday free schools, children were exposed in Sunday schools to the "precept and example" of the teachers. Periodic speeches

24. Boese, *Public Education*, p. 97; Rice, *Sunday School Movement*, p. 58.
25. William E. Dodge, *Old New York: A Lecture* (New York, 1880), p. 21.
26. Savage, *Presbyterian Church*, p. 63.
27. Methodist Branch of the New York Sunday School Union Society, Minutes, 1816–1819, Methodist Church Records, vol. 89, NYPL, April 30, 1816.

exhorted them to diligence and virtue. The Almshouse minister, John Stanford, told an assembly of Sunday school pupils that because they were not too young to die, they should give up swearing, nasty associations, and idleness; the more worldly William Dodge held up to his Sunday classes the example of a poor boy who, despite his drunken father, studied the Bible, learned to read, and became a rich businessman.[28]

The general enthusiasm for missionary work in the 1820's and 1830's benefitted this nondenominational education work in the poor areas of the city. The American urban missionary movement partook of the character of the British movement upon which it was modelled. It aimed primarily to spread "devout contentment" among the poor, and it shared the "social fad aspect" that made voluntary teaching in poor areas popular among the middle class.[29] A critic of American Sunday schools contended in 1832 that ministers merely indulged the amateur reformers "in a harmless employment for which they have a whimsical predilection." Charles Foster attributes the decline of the nondenominational Sunday schools to the resentment of ministers receiving increasing requests for financial assistance, to second thoughts about the efficacy of missionary work, and to the general deflation of optimism following the Panic of 1837.[30] To these causes should be added the changing relationship of the Sunday schools to the public schools as well as to the churches, plus the general and inherent difficulty, to the nineteenth-century mind, of giving moral training in a nonsectarian manner. The solution to both these problems had pushed the Sunday schools toward a more doctrinal emphasis before 1837.

In the years 1825 to 1830 the free day schools had been redirected toward a comprehensive public school ideal and had shown that they were a permanent network. Both of these developments affected the Sunday schools. Although they had intended originally to provide elementary instruction for children who could not attend school during the week, the Sunday schools came more and more

28. John Stanford, *Address . . . to the Children of the Union Sunday Schools* (New York, 1817), pp. 2–4; Carlos Martin, *William E. Dodge: the Christian Merchant* (New York, 1890), pp. 85–86.

29. Charles I. Foster, "The Urban Missionary Movement, 1814–1827," *Pennsylvania Magazine of History and Biography* 75 (1951), 49–51.

30. Savage, *Presbyterian Church*, p. 63; Foster, "Urban Missionary Movement," pp. 64–65.

to rely on the expanding public schools to teach reading and writing while they concentrated on religion. National magazines for Sunday schools emphasized this shift in the 1830's.[31] The facts of duplicate enrollment are not clear, but despite the intentions of the founders to carry on the work of the weekday schools with different children, it seems that those who would not attend during the week also failed to go to Sunday school. A school census of 1829 estimated that only 600 children who attended Sunday schools were not included in either public or private weekday schools.[32]

Public school instruction in fundamentals allowed the Sunday schools to shift to more religious instruction. This development spurred opponents of the pan-Protestant approach to establish separate denominational Sunday school organizations, the Episcopalians in 1817 and the Methodists in 1827, although some of the more evangelical churches of those denominations kept their Sunday schools in the union movement.[33] Defending the splinter movement in 1827 the Methodist Episcopal Union explained that free schools had shifted the prime object of Sunday schools from elementary education to religious instruction, and "on this account, however humiliating the fact, a general union of all parties becomes the more difficult . . . Whatever may be the intention, each teacher of religion will more or less inculcate his own view of Christianity . . . The managers are of the opinion that the most likely way for the several denominations to live and labor in peace, is for each to conduct its own affairs."[34]

A second change of emphasis then reenforced the denominational trend. The public schools' shift away from exclusive emphasis on the poor was paralleled by the Sunday schools. About 1830 a few Sunday school leaders decided to broaden the class mixture in Sunday schools by pressing for attendance by church members' children, and the shift was endorsed by a national convention in 1832.[35]

---

31. Clifton H. Brewer, *Early Episcopal Sunday Schools, 1814–1865* (Milwaukee, 1933) pp. 49, 96.

32. Foster, "Urban Missionary Movement," p. 56; Bourne, *PSS*, p. 111.

33. Rice, *Sunday School Movement*, p. 133; Henry Anstice, *History of St. George's Church . . . 1752–1911* (New York, Harper and Brothers, 1911), p. 89.

34. Addie G. Wardle, *History of the Sunday School Movement in the Methodist Episcopal Church* (New York, The Methodist Book Concern, 1918), p. 64.

35. Savage, *Presbyterian Church*, p. 64.

Now that the congregations were being urged to send their own children to Sunday school, many more people agreed with the Methodists about the difficulty of cooperation. The emphasis on religious training made interdenominational work all the more difficult, especially when the much criticized fad of Scripture memorization gave way to question-and-answer lessons and stories, which, however preferable pedagogically, verged closer toward denominational catechism.

Thus, the movement to draw a more comprehensive student body into the Sunday schools, as the public schools were doing, led to denominationalism. As the church members began sending their children to Sunday school, each school became more oriented toward a particular congregation rather than toward a particular poor area. In 1843 the Brick Presbyterian Church Sunday school had 114 students, 100 of whom were from church families. Their pastor, Gardiner Spring, wrote for the annual Presbyterian General Assembly in 1843 that "Sunday schools have been conducted in a more spiritual manner than formerly, with more direct efforts to indoctrinate the young in our distinctive principles."[36] The Sunday schools had adopted the public schools' policy of including children of all economic classes; at the same time, they differentiated their function from that of the public schools. They had begun around 1815 with the intention of serving the same purposes as public schools, but with different clients. By 1840 they served the same clients but a different purpose. They therefore illustrate a general phenomenon connected with urban growth: the increasing specialization of service institutions. In this case the differentiation was generated by a particular problem: the contradiction involved in the prevalent notions that religion and morals were inseparable, that the public schools could serve all faiths, and that the schools' primary function was the moral education of youth. For Protestants who were willing to have doctrine on Sunday and application the rest of the week, this institutional differentiation solved, or at least softened, that contradiction.

The Sunday schools were not the creatures of the public schools, nor did a single group of men sit down to plan the differentiation of functions as a deliberate solution to a problem. There were several pressures on the day schools to become more secular and other

36. *Ibid.*, pp. 64, 65.

pressures on the Sunday schools to become more denominational. Nevertheless, schoolmen saw the Sunday schools as an adjunct which would allow them to neutralize religious instruction and, hopefully, to make the public schools more inclusive, while Sunday school promoters noted that the expanding public day schools relieved them of the responsibility for elementary instruction in reading.

The process illumines another meaning of the word "common" in the historical development of common schools. In order to preserve their commonality the public schools avoided an area of substantial pluralism of belief. The effort failed with respect to the Catholic clergy and a large part of the Catholic laity, yet it worked for most of the city's Protestants, and it illustrates the general tendency of the public schools to assert commonality and avoid pluralism.[37]

The development of the public schools and Sunday schools illustrates another general process that accompanied urbanization, the institutionalization of solutions to community problems. School, work houses, and reformatories became the characteristic solutions to morality, idleness, and crime in the city. Ethnic and cultural heterogeneity became too great to rely on informal acculturation in the family, the neighborhood, or the job, and the numbers of unassimilated and unpersuaded were too great for the native establishment to deal with on a personal, ad hoc basis. The missionary work of cultural conversion became a full-time job requiring organization. Institutions mediated between the anxious dominant population and the poor or the newcomer.

AGENCIES OF MORAL EDUCATION:
SUPPLEMENTARY ORGANIZATIONS

The poor and the newcomer, however, often avoided voluntary institutions. Reformers had two different solutions to this persistent problem. One approach was to try to bolster the old informal educational process by visiting homes, distributing Bibles and tracts. The purpose was to "seek the sinner in his lurking place," and

37. The Jewish community, to a large extent, acquiesced in the same arrangement. See Alexander M. Dushkin, *Jewish Education in New York City* (New York, The Bureau of Jewish Education, 1918), p. 21; and David and Tamar de Sola Pool, *An Old Faith in the New World: Portrait of Shearith Israel, 1654–1954* (New York, Columbia University Press, 1955), p. 223. Catholics are discussed in Chap. Five below.

eventually to draw him out into the more formal church and school institutions.[38] This approach attempted to get at adults as well as children and to reassert the old tripartite responsibility for moral education in the home, the church, and the school. It flourished in the 1820's and 1830's.

In the 1840's, however, as crime rates, immigration, and poverty continued to mount, more and more reformers became disillusioned with missionary efforts in the home. Some, seeing that the public schools were excluding unkempt and undisciplined poor children, organized special schools in the slums, such as St. George's "ragged school." Charles Loring Brace, a Yale Divinity School graduate whose work as an urban chaplain made him despair of a solution which depended upon the reformation of adults, founded the Children's Aid Society in 1853, which aimed to provide Sunday meetings, night schools, reading rooms, industrial schools, and lodging houses for the youth of the slums. The Society opened a lodging house for homeless street children in 1854, and in 1855 began opening industrial schools, which by 1857 numbered six and, through the efforts of paid agents, enrolled 1176 students.[39]

Brace was an imaginative reformer and a strong environmentalist. He was convinced of the crucial role of the family and yet feared that the reformation of urban family life was hopeless under the physical conditions of the slum. He therefore settled on the evacuation of children from the city as the ultimate solution. This program became the most publicized and controversial activity of the Children's Aid Society in the late 1850's. It had precedent in the policy of indenturing almshouse children to rural masters, a practice which had increased between 1800 and 1850. Now Brace decided to apply this solution to a wide variety of delinquent and homeless children. To some extent he was simply expressing the romantic glorification of the countryside that accompanied all urban reform movements, but his main emphasis was on restoring the urban slum child to a healthy family life. He tried to find foster homes in the city where possible, but the places were few, and the prospect of sending children in large groups to towns in the West seemed to offer more hope of accommodating the city's seem-

38. Miller, *People are the City,* pp. 40, 46, 56.
39. Miller, *People are the City,* pp. 61–62; Charles L. Brace, *The Children's Aid Society: Its History, Plan and Results* (New York, 1893), pp. 3–4; Charles L. Brace, *Address upon the Industrial School Movement* . . . (New York, 1857), p. 13.

ingly endless supply of vagrant boys and girls. Brace opposed institutionalization wherever possible. The problem, he said, was how to
treat the child as an individual when there were so many. In
Massachusetts, he noted, institutions like the reformatory tried to
imitate the family, but through emigration children could be placed
in actual families in a normal, healthy environment. "The family
is God's Reformatory," said Brace, and there was no substitute for
the real thing. Between 1854 and 1860 the Society relocated 5000
children to small towns in upstate New York and in the West.
Brace estimated that fewer than 10 percent ever committed any
crimes in their new towns. Away from the city the child experienced
personal attention, whether he liked it or not. Communal responsibility for the individual child was possible. One boy was passed
around to seven different families before he settled down successfully. A minister in upstate New York wrote Brace that his community was too "Puritan" to let any of the children turn out
badly.[40]

Brace's Society continued to send about 3000 children a year
into the countryside; in addition, both Horace Greeley and Robert
Hartley urged poor families to move out of the cities and "Go
West." Although evacuation may have greatly improved the
environment and life chances of many children, however, it did
not change the urban conditions which produced delinquency. It
was a nostalgic solution. As America became more urban, the western states experienced their own delinquency problems, and
resistance to the Society's "placing-out" system developed. The
Children's Aid Society discontinued the system in 1890, by which
time most juvenile reform groups had turned to other solutions.[41]

40. Charles L. Brace, *The Best Method of Disposing of our Pauper and
Vagrant Children* (New York, 1859), pp. 4, 6–11, 14–16, 35–36; Robert
H. Bremner, *From the Depths; the Discovery of Poverty in the United States*
(New York, New York University Press, 1956), pp. 39–41; Miriam Z. Langsam,
*Children's West: A History of the Placing Out System of the New York
Children's Aid Society, 1853–1890* (Madison, The State Historical Society
of Wisconsin, 1964), p. 27. William C. Osborn, *The Crusade for Children:
A Review of Child Life in New York During 75 Years* (New York, 1928),
pp. 10–13, describes the journey of the first trainload of "New York boys"
to Michigan. On Brace, see R. Richard Wohl, "The 'Country Boy' Myth
and its Place in American Urban Culture: The Nineteenth-Century Contribution," *Perspectives in American History* III (1969), 91–95, 107–121.

41. Norman Ware, *Industrial Worker, 1840–1860* (Boston, Houghton Mifflin
Company, 1924), p. xx; Bremner, *From the Depths*, p. 38; see Langsam,
Children's West, passim.

Brace's emphasis on the importance of family and environment was shared by the Ladies Home Missionary Society. True to their name, they went into the slums and directly attacked the conditions that bred vice and disease. In 1852 they bought a converted brewery that had been housing about 1000 people in squalor at Five Points, the city's worst slum. Anticipating the work of later settlement workers, they built on that site a mission house where about twenty families could live in temperance, and they started a Sunday school and a day school for the neighborhood.[42]

Although the Children's Aid Society and the Ladies Home Missionary Society, like most other city reform groups, attributed poverty and crime to moral failings, they both attempted to do something about the family environment rather than just instruct people about their duties. Brace's evacuation plan, however, changed the child's environment rather than the city's, and the Five Points Mission and similar efforts were only tiny outposts in a desert of hopeless slum dwellers. These supplementary efforts, therefore, did not provide a sufficient solution to assimilating or disciplining the children whom the public and Sunday schools were not reaching. Missions, industrial schools, and evacuation were voluntary. Society still had to protect itself from the most recalcitrant, who resisted reformation, and to care for the most destitute, who were unable to provide themselves with the barest essentials. A fourth group of agencies for moral improvement dealt with these children.

AGENCIES OF MORAL EDUCATION:
INVOLUNTARY RESIDENTIAL INSTITUTIONS

In several ways, the Almshouse, orphan asylums, House of Refuge, and other institutions to which children were committed resembled the schools. They were founded to deal with the same

42. *The Old Brewery, and the New Mission House at the Points, by the Ladies of the Mission* (New York, 1854), pp. 49–50, 76, and *passim;* Miller, *People are the City,* p. 68. Other missionary work in the area is described, with many anecdotes, in *Five Points Monthly Record. The New Charitable Monthly,* or *"What is Done for the Poor,"* First Series (New York, 1854), and *ibid.,* Second Series (New York, 1855). See also, Carroll S. Rosenberg, "Protestants and Five Pointers: The Five Points House of Industry, 1850–1870," NYHS *Quarterly* 48 (October 1964), 327–347.

problems, and they shared many of the same assumptions about moral reform. But they were different in two important ways: admission was, in most cases, involuntary, and these institutions had custody of children twenty-four hours a day. They supervised the child's entire life: not only schooling but food, dress, lodging, work, and recreation. They served the dual purpose of immediate removal and possible reformation.

At the beginning of the nineteenth century the only custodial institutions in New York were the Almshouse and the prison. In prison youthful offenders were treated as adults, but in the Almshouse there was a carefully regulated program for children, including common education, religious instruction, and separate quarters. Both girls and boys were put out to service sometime between the ages of ten and fourteen, and the commissioners not only selected the masters but heard grievances and protected the "children of the public" after they left the custody of the Almshouse.[43] As the nineteenth century progressed, and poverty increased, the commissioners found it more and more difficult to supervise personally the apprenticeship of pauper children. Also, the Almshouse capacity did not keep pace with the rising population, much less with the disproportionate rise of destitute people in the city. Other institutions arose to deal with the city's surplus of pauper children. The Society for the Relief of Poor Widows with Small Children founded New York's first orphanage in 1806. Their inmates numbered 54 by 1809, rose to 120 in 1831 and 159 in 1850.[44]

The function of the Orphan Asylum, as of the Almshouse, was to shelter, teach, and bind out their particular group of dependent children. The purpose of the teaching was moral, and the justification was social, not personal. The orphanage operated a Lancasterian school and joined in the Scripture memorization craze. When the children could read and write, they were bound out as servants, and the boys were later bound again to a trade. The *Annual Reports* of the Orphan Asylum emphasize that almost none of their

43. *M.C.C.*, II, 661–673; New York City Almshouse Commissioners Minutes, 1791–1797, NYPL, *passim;* David M. Schneider, *The History of Public Welfare in New York State, 1609–1866* (Chicago, University of Chicago Press, 1938), pp. 186–187.
44. Mrs. Jonathan Odell et al., comps., *Origin and History of the Orphan Asylum Society in the City of New York, 1806–1896* (New York, n.d.), I, 31, 159, 301.

inmates were later convicted of crimes. Requesting city funds in 1837, they argued that they had saved lives and prevented crime.[45]

Other residential institutions were established for the moral training and occupational placement of dependent children, and the trend toward specialization was evident in the clientele each served. Among these were the Half Orphan Asylum, the Colored Orphan Asylum, the Roman Catholic Orphan Asylum, and the Institution for the Blind. No organization could cope with the entire problem, so each defined a particular group to work with. These institutions absorbed some of the increase of indigent children which the Almshouse could not take. Many other destitute children, however, simply lived out their brief lives in the slums, out of sight and out of mind of respectable New York, without moral training or material assistance.

The trend toward specialization is part of the general tendency to institutionalize solutions to social problems, but the institutionalization of juvenile delinquents is a special case. Unlike the asylums for dependent children, which could not keep pace with the problem, the institutionalization of delinquent children during this period illustrates the reverse: youths were increasingly put in custodial institutions who earlier would have remained at large.[46]

In the first quarter of the century youthful convicts had been sent to the penitentiary with adults. Their separation was a major goal of the general penal reform movement of the early national period. In 1819 Mayor Cadwallader Colden inspected the New York Penitentiary and made a report to the Common Council. As a result of a recent reform, boys under sixteen were separated at night, and they were taught reading and moral lessons by the Rev. John Stanford. But during most of the day they mingled with the other convicts. "While this is the case," Colden said, "it is in vain to expect that a Sentence condemning a child to the Penitentiary will have any beneficial effect, in his morals; on the con-

45. Odell, *Orphan Asylum,* pp. 31, 126, 166, 270; Petition of the Orphan Asylum Society to the Common Council, October 20, 1837, MS, Box 2774, NYMA.

46. A similar point of view is expressed in Anthony M. Platt, *The Child Savers: The Invention of Delinquency* (Chicago, University of Chicago Press, 1969), which describes the rise of penology for delinquents in the period 1870 to 1900. The history of New York City, and in particular of the House of Refuge, anticipates many of the developments of the period that Platt describes.

trary, it is probable that his vicious inclinations will be strengthened by association with experienced Villains."[47] As a result of this problem, reported District Attorney Hugh Maxwell in 1825, juries were reluctant to convict youthful petty thieves, even if they had been arrested four or five times. This leniency could not be relied upon, however. John Griscom's Society for the Prevention of Pauperism reported in 1821 that some boys were sent to the Penitentiary as vagrants merely because they had no parents and no job.[48]

The Society for the Prevention of Pauperism decided to turn its entire effort toward the problem of juvenile delinquency. This problem, after all, represented a direct challenge to the establishment mores by slum children, and it was here that moral reformation, as well as simple custody, could most materially and immediately benefit society. In 1823 the Society changed its name to the Society for the Reformation of Juvenile Delinquents.[49] Griscom, Eddy, Stanford, Maxwell, Colden and other penal reformers, influenced by developments in England and by efforts in Massachusetts to separate juvenile offenders, urged the establishment of a separate institution for juveniles. This would not be simply preferable to prison but more desirable than the street life vagrants led. Colden had made this important point in his 1818 report. If juveniles were secluded from others and well instructed, he said, "there would be room to hope that imprisonment would sometimes produce reformation. In that case a confinement of some length might be considered as a less punishment than a shorter one. It would often be a service to the Young Vagabonds who prowl our streets in idleness and ignorance, to place them where they would be for some time rescued from both."[50] Griscom based his public appeals on the old metaphor that penitentiaries were "schools and colleges of crime," and the new mayor, Stephen Allen, joined in

47. *M.C.C.*, X, 467–468.

48. James Hardie, *The Description of the City of New York* (New York, 1827), pp. 198–199; John H. Griscom, *Memoir of John Griscom* (New York, 1859), pp. 168–169.

49. Robert S. Pickett, *House of Refuge: Origins of Juvenile Reform in New York State, 1815–1857* (Syracuse, Syracuse University Press, 1969), p. 49.

50. *M.C.C.*, X, 467–468; the earliest agitation for an asylum for vagrants was by the Reverend John Stanford; see his Memorial to the Mayor, January 21, 1812, in Stanford MSS. vol. 4, pp. 19–28, NYHS. On English influence, see Peter Bedford to John Griscom, London, February 24, 1824, Griscom Papers, NYPL.

TABLE 18. "Habits of Children Previous to Commitment,"
New York House of Refuge, 1858.

| | White | | Colored | | |
Description	Boys	Girls	Boys	Girls	Total
Unfortunate	147	66	6	1	220
Pilfering	104	10	3	0	117
Vagrants	77	7	2	0	86
Bad	143	43	8	2	196
Beggars	8	28	0	0	36
Truants	20	0	1	0	21
Temporary commitments, as witnesses	1	0	0	0	1
Total	500	154	20	3	677

Source: Samuel Halliday, *The Lost and Found, or Life Among the Poor* (New York, 1859), p. 352.

the crusade to save the street children. Their plans materialized in 1825 when the House of Refuge opened its doors and the police delivered seven inmates. By fall the institution housed sixty-nine youths, of whom most were guilty of theft but some were simply vagrants.[51]

Significantly, the law of incorporation, passed unanimously by the legislature, included vagrancy as grounds for commitment, and it transferred parental authority to the institution. It also granted the managers power over the youths for an indeterminate period. This authority was successfully challenged by parents, who on a few occasions gained the release of their children, but in practice the House of Refuge made a substantial incursion on the liberties of juveniles.[52] The confusion between commitments for crime and merely undesirable circumstances is evident in the enumeration of the "Habits of Children previous to Commitment" in 1858 (Table 18).[53]

51. Pickett, *House of Refuge,* pp. 47, 50, 68, 80.
52. *Ibid.,* pp. 58–59, 76–77.
53. Similarly, in Massachusetts, boys could be incarcerated for "stubbornness," Michael B. Katz, *The Irony of Early School Reform: Educational Innovation in Mid-Nineteenth Century Massachusetts* (Cambridge, Harvard University Press, 1968), p. 178.

The purpose of the House of Refuge was not only incarceration but, if possible, reformation. The goals of its educational program, as stated by the first superintendent, Joseph Curtis, were very similar to those of schools in general: "the poor, misguided, and neglected youth should be taught to wash his face, comb his hair, tie his shoe, sit erect, keep out of dirt, learn his book, bridle his tongue, and do as he is told."[54] Many street children did not acquiesce in this program of institutionalized moral reform. Those who were well schooled in the contraculture resisted and avoided institutions of moral instruction.[55] Charles Brace discovered that street children "had a peculiar dread of Sunday Schools and religious exhortations, partly because of the general creed of their older associates, but more for fear that these exercises were a 'pious dodge' for trapping them into some place of detention." Brace attempted not to attack the boys' values too abruptly. His newsboys' lodging houses emphasized a square meal, and he organized informal "Boys' Meetings" for vagrants who would not attend Sunday school or church.[56]

The boys had good reason to fear incarceration. Samuel Halliday, a missionary for the Female Guardian Society, described the fate of one vagrant boy in his book, *The Lost and Found*.[57] Willie, the son of a poor widow, disliked school and became a truant with his friends. Then he began staying out all night. His mother, fearing that he would be arrested for vagrancy or, worse, become a thief, took him to the voluntary Home for the Friendless, from which he immediately ran away. She then had him committed to the Juvenile Asylum, an institution like the House of Refuge but less secure. Willie broke an arm and some ribs escaping from a second-story room. After months of street life, sleeping in alleys and

54. Pickett, *House of Refuge*, p. 61.

55. The term contraculture is used here to mean a set of values and beliefs which was not simply different but opposed to the established culture of respectable Protestant New York, or was perceived as opposed. See J. Milton Yinger, "Contraculture and Subculture," *American Sociological Review* 25 (1960), 625–635. Membership in the two groups was not distinct or absolute, but the differences were real enough, and they were dramatized in the confrontation between reformers and their clients. The values of the contraculture were not opposed in such stark terms as was supposed by members of the establishment, but the attribution of completely contrary values, such as idleness against industry, or vice against virtue, heightened the sense of difference, and thus the sense of group identity, in both cultures.

56. Brace, *Children's Aid*, pp. 6, 14.

57. Halliday, *Lost and Found*, pp. 133–142.

cemeteries, his mother found him again, tied him up with a clothesline, and chained him to a chair. She sent for Halliday, who said that he then "carried out what I had in view from the first, namely, committed him to the House of Refuge." When Halliday wrote the anecdote, Willie had been in the Refuge for fifteen months, making shoes, which says more for the missionary's vindictiveness than the youth's willfulness. "He is now nearly eleven years old, and is exceedingly desirous of coming away from the Refuge, which we strenuously oppose, for it is very evident to us that he is far from being weaned, and that he would surely fall into his old habits. He is always glad to see me, but seems dejected, and I think I have never seen him smile. His mother visits him frequently, and is anxious to obtain his release, in which I hope she may not succeed at least for some years to come."[58]

At mid-century Charles Brace advised gradual tactics in confronting the contraculture of street boys; he wanted to meet them on their own terms, in their own territory, and persuade them to change. The House of Refuge, however, was based on an opposite philosophy. Fear of incarceration would inhibit juvenile delinquency, claimed Hugh Maxwell. Boys who remained unpersuaded would receive the radical cure that little Willie got.[59] It is thus perilous to make generalizations dating the shifting attitudes of reformers in New York City in this period. The Children's Aid Society and the House of Refuge represent different attitudes which co-existed at mid-century, one emphasizing the child's individuality, the other an uncompromising standard. Despite this complexity of attitudes—the normal situation in human affairs—the pressure of increasing numbers in cities pushed institutions in the general direction of more impersonal and arbitrary procedures.

When a child arrived at the House of Refuge, he was first scrubbed, given a close haircut and a suit of clothes.[60] He was then

---

58. *Ibid.*, p. 142.
59. Brace, *Children's Aid*, p. 14; Hardie, *Description*, p. 199; Hugh Maxwell to John Griscom, October 21, 1825, Griscom Papers, NYPL.
60. This ritual is common to most involuntary residential institutions and serves the symbolic purpose of stripping away the inmate's previous identity. This and other forms of "personal defacement" are described in Erving Goffman, *Asylums: Essays on the Social Situation of Mental Patients and other Inmates* (Garden City, N.Y., Doubleday, 1961), pp. 16–21. The New York House of Refuge shared several of the characteristics of "total institutions" described by Goffman.

taken before the superintendent, told the rules, and given a badge with a "No. 1" on his sleeve. If he broke any rules, he received a badge labelled No. 2, then No. 3, and finally 4. Rank 3 meant no play time; rank 4, no Sunday dinner. Solitary confinement with bread and water were also employed. The managers thought that Curtis, the first superintendent, was too lenient. They pressured him into resigning in 1826 and appointed Nathaniel Hart, who believed in more corporal punishment.[61] Escapes were a constant problem at the House of Refuge, even though the boys were whipped and put in solitary when caught.[62]

By mid-century critics were describing the House of Refuge in the same terms the founders had described the Penitentiary. A disgruntled assistant superintendent said it was "a high school where mere vagrants are inducted into all the mysteries of crime." The penitentiary superintendent believed that the Refuge increased crime. "It is as regular a succession as the classes in a college, from the house of refuge to the penitentiary and from the penitentiary to the State Prison."[63] The Association for Improving the Condition of the Poor founded the Juvenile Asylum in 1851 for noncriminal dependent children in reaction to the penitentiary-like discipline of the House of Refuge. Just as the founders had wanted to separate youthful offenders from adults, later reformers wished to correct the indiscriminate mixing of convicted delinquents and the merely homeless destitute. Thus the process of specialization added another institution to the array of agencies for moral reformation.[64]

Although the public schools had custody of their children only six hours a day, on a voluntary basis, they shared some of the characteristics of the total institutions. They were engaged in the same moral crusade, and they viewed their clients' culture in the same antagonistic terms. Second, they shared some institutional features, such as regimented activity and corporal punishment. Finally, though both types of institution attempted to reform their inmates, they also looked upon custody per se as useful to society.

The total institutions began incarcerating some children who

61. Pickett, *House of Refuge,* pp. 142–145.
62. *Ibid.,* pp. 73, 83, 160; Gordon, *Gazeteer,* p. 322.
63. Pickett, *House of Refuge,* pp. 159–160.
64. *Ibid.,* pp. 102, 176.

would have been left free in an earlier period, and schoolmen increasingly looked to coercive school attendance as the necessary solution to the problems of the city's youth. There were, however, strong feelings against such a final abrogation of parental initiative among citizens in general and employers of child labor in particular. Also, the few mild laws that were passed in the second half of the nineteenth century were beyond the city's meagre means of enforcement. Nevertheless, the importance of the mere custodial function of the schools is suggested by the fact that the first state law concerning attendance was a truancy law, passed in 1853, which required children under fourteen to attend school only if their parents did not "keep them employed." This law and the schooling and child labor laws of the 1870's were widely ignored, yet they indicate that the reformers' general response to increasing cultural diversity and moral problems was in the direction of coercive institutionalization.[65]

Street boys and delinquents created a visible problem that aroused public pressure. The problem could be attacked by both the custodial and instructional function of schools; Sunday schools performed primarily an instructional function, total institutions primarily a custodial function. Public day schools were capable of doing both, but they could not reform a child unless they could get custody of him on a regular basis. Faced with growing delinquency, they pressed after 1850 for coercive attendance regulations. The importance of street children as a theme of both the critics and the supporters of the schools gave their rhetoric a harsh, correctional tone. The cultural confrontation between the school and its client was generally presumed to be hostile. Moral education was a battle between industry and idleness, cleanliness and filth, quiet obedience and unruly independence.

---

65. Boese, *Public Education,* pp. 126–127; Isaac S. Hartley, ed., *Memorial of Robert Milham Hartley* (Utica, 1882), p. 359; see also Halliday, *Lost and Found,* p. 347; Osborn, *Crusade for Children,* p. 25, and Adna Weber, *Labor Legislation in New York* (Albany, 1904), pp. 7–8.

CHAPTER FIVE

Schooling and
Cultural Diversity

Reformers of the early nineteenth century associated crime and vice with lack of education almost by definition; education was designed first and foremost to inhibit those moral failings. The question of whether degraded character caused poverty or poverty caused degraded character was seldom debated. Reformers did not question the causal relationship; moral education was the remedy aimed at both. The A.I.C.P. confidently stated that "economic derangements" could be corrected by changing attitudes. "Idleness and improvidence are the sure harbingers of poverty and suffering, while industry and forethought seldom fail to confer upon their possessor comfort and respectability. Many would be prudent and saving, if they knew how to be . . . In every thing, indeed, pertaining to their economic condition, many need to be instructed."[1] But crime, poverty, and vice were also associated with ethnic differences, especially after the massive increase in immigration which began in the 1830's.[2] By 1845, 35 percent of the city's population was

1. A.I.C.P., *Third Annual Report* (New York, 1846), p. 17.
2. Maldwyn Jones estimates immigration to the United States at about 10,000 a year at the turn of the eighteenth century. This figure declined during the Napoleonic Wars to perhaps 3000 annually, and immigration virtually ceased during the War of 1812. Substantial immigration, then, began around 1815. In the 1820's, 151,000 immigrants entered the U.S., and the figures after 1830 rose markedly: 1830's: 599,000; 1840's: 1,713,000; 1850's: 2,314,000. Maldwyn Jones, *American Immigration* (Chicago, University of Chicago Press, 1960), pp. 65, 93. New York City received by far the greatest number of these immigrants. From 1820 to 1860, when 5,437,914 immigrants entered the U.S., 3,742,532 landed at New York. Robert G. Albion, *Rise of the New York Port, 1815–1860* (New York, C. Scribner's Sons, 1939), p. 418.

foreign-born, and ten years later the figure had passed 50 percent.[3] Immigration provided a disproportionate number of the poor, and the poor provided a disproportionate number of criminals. New Yorkers often remarked at the correlation of foreign birth with social ills, and ethnicity became a major theme of reformers.

EDUCATION AND ETHNIC DIVERSITY

In the 1820's the Almshouse had reported that about one-third of the inmates were of foreign birth; by 1850, the proportion had risen to three-fourths. Prison officials reported similar proportions: 15,522 of the 21,299 committed to the New York prison in 1850 were foreign-born. Anti-immigration literature stressed these statistics. Deviance of all kinds was attributed to foreigners; the Lunatic Asylum admitted 391 persons in 1850, of whom 199, over half, were Irish; only 97 were native-born.[4]

Despite the faulty inferences native New Yorkers drew from such statistics, it was true that the port city became the home of the poorest immigrants while many of those with sufficient resources wisely moved inland. Unfortunately, many of those who had some savings when they arrived lost them in the first few hours. Newly arrived immigrants were shamefully fleeced by porters, agents, employers, and lodging house proprietors.[5] With such an introduction to the city, it is no wonder that many immigrants came to see dishonesty and theft as acceptable tactics in the new environment.[6]

Lack of funds was not the only reason for staying in New York City, however. The bewildered newcomer could find in New York

3. Kenneth Miller, *The People are the City* . . . (New York, Macmillan, 1962), p. 56; Albion, *Rise of the New York Port,* p. 419; *Census of the State of New York for 1855* . . . (Albany, 1857), pp. 8, 175.

4. In 1825–26, 32.6 percent of the 1468 Almshouse inmates were of foreign birth and, in 1850, 76.8 percent of 2355 inmates. *Annual Report of the Superintendent of the Almshouse* . . . (New York, 1826); *Second Annual Report of the Governors of the Almshouse* (New York, 1851). The prison and lunatic asylum figures are found in *ibid.,* pp. 50, 91.

5. The findings of an 1847 legislative investigation into frauds against immigrants are reported in Friedrich Kapp, *Immigration and the Commissioners of Emigration* . . . (New York, 1870), chap. IV.

6. Caroline Ware, "Cultural Groups in the United States," in Ware, ed., *The Cultural Approach to History* (New York, Columbia University Press, 1940), pp. 62–73, discusses the plight of nondominant cultural groups trying to understand the native culture, faced with contradictory attitudes.

solace in the sheer numbers of fellow immigrants. He could find some security and maintain a sense of identity in the immigrant community, with its segregated neighborhoods and ethnic social organizations.[7] Contemporary native opinion, however, did not generally view the immigrant community as a constructive force. Having relegated foreigners to the lowest jobs and worst housing, and having excluded them from native social organizations, nativists criticized the newcomer for his clannishness. Some saw it as a deliberate resistance to Americanization. Others asserted that it perpetuated the immigrant's natural inclination to crime and vice.[8] The New York Assembly investigating committee on tenements observed in 1857 that as the "foreign element" arrives in the city "we place at its disposal districts, localities, neighborhoods and dwellings, specially, as it were, adapted to the habits and associations of the most degraded of foreign paupers, enabling them at once to renew their familiarity with squalor, misery and vicious practices."[9] Whatever the other consequences of the immigrant community, it intensified the residential segregation that already existed between the rich and the poor, and it added ethnic and religious identity to the cultural differences already at issue between schoolmen and their scholars. By 1855 the sixth ward, the crime center of the city, was 42 percent Irish, and the lower east side, Wards 2, 4, and 7, were also heavily Irish. North of the Irish section lay Kleindeutschland, where over 60,000 Germans crowded into Wards 10, 11, and 13. Here there were German businesses and German churches, and here especially there were German beer halls by the hundreds, open and thriving on Sundays.[10] Sabbath breaking became an important issue in the 1840's because it combined the religious issue with social customs of the immigrants, like Sunday drinking and games. The Irish as well as the Germans scandalized Sabbatarians. Lydia Child overheard a Protestant lady rebuking

7. See Robert Ernst, *Immigrant Life in New York City, 1825–1863* (New York, King's Crown Press, 1949), chap. XI, and Douglass T. Miller, *Jacksonian Aristocracy* . . . (New York, Oxford University Press, 1967), p. 171.

8. Jones, *Immigration*, p. 156; John Webb Pratt, *Religion, Politics and Diversity: the Church-State Theme in New York History* (Ithaca, Cornell University Press, 1967), p. 171.

9. *Report of the select committee appointed to examine into the condition of the tenement houses of New York and Brooklyn, March 9, 1857,* New York State Assembly, Doc. 205, 1857, pp. 48–49.

10. Ernst, *Immigrant Life,* p. 40; Jones, *Immigration,* p. 135.

an Irish woman selling apples on Sunday. "This will soon be put down," she said. "You Catholics won't be allowed to desecrate the Sabbath in this way much longer." Mike Walsh, always ready to thumb his nose at the establishment, argued in the *Subterranean* that Sabbath breaking was protected by the Constitution. Walsh said that "bigotted fanatics" were organizing to enforce Sabbath observance. He responded: "What Sabbath? Some portion of our citizens keep it one day, some another, and the great mass of the people spend the first day of the week in amusing themselves, which is the only proper and rational manner."[11]

Most native leaders, however, did not think the cultural differences were legitimate. "A government, to be homogeneous, must preserve the homogeneity of its citizens," wrote the nativist Samuel Busey in 1856. Because they associated foreigners with crime and poverty, and because they feared and suspected the influence of the Catholic Church, to which so many immigrants belonged, they saw immigration as a generally negative and threatening cultural phenomenon. The frequently recurring metaphor of purification emphasizes this attitude. An Assembly report warned, "Like the vast Atlantic, we must decompose and cleanse the impurities which rush into our midst, or like the inland lake, we shall receive their poison into our whole national system." *Putnam's Monthly* used the same metaphor and indicated the solution to the pollution problem: "Our readers will agree with us that for the effectual defecation of the stream of life in a great city, there is but one rectifying agent—one infallible filter—the SCHOOL."[12]

The burden on the school was all the greater, and its job all the more difficult, because of various forms of nativist exclusion practiced in the city, not only from social organizations but from jobs as well.[13] This underlying contradiction—the admonition to assimilate, but the actual exclusion from native preserves—must have made the school rhetoric seem hypocritical to many immigrant children. If "no Irish need apply," why should they sit through

11. L. Maria Child, *Letters from New York*, sec. ser. (New York, 1845), p. 166; *The Subterranean*, vol. II, No. 3 (January 27, 1844), p. 299.

12. Samuel Busey, *Immigration: Its Evils and Consequences* (New York, 1856), p. 9; New York State Assembly, *Report . . . Tenement Houses*, p. 49; *Putnam's Monthly*, vol. II, No. 7 (July 1853), p. 2.

13. See Ernst, *Immigrant Life*, pp. 66–67; William Gowans to James Gowans, February 17, 1826, NYHS; Francis Wyse, *America, Its Realities and Resources* (London, 1846), III, 31–40.

years of school? This reemphasizes the theme of Chapter Three, that the school could do little to change slum conditions or alter the economic standing of the child. Most schoolmen were probably not averse to the success of limited numbers of the poor through education, but the schools' mission—and most promoters were quite frank about it—was to inculcate cooperative attitudes among the city's children whatever the vicissitudes of urban life might bring them. Acculturation is thus a more accurate term for the school's intention than assimilation, although the terms are sometimes used synonymously. The schools reflected the attitude of the general native public, who wished to Americanize the habits, not the status, of the immigrant.[14]

Outright nativist mob action had a long history in New York City. Although nativism often focused specifically on the Catholic Church, the competition between foreign and native labor usually caused economic overtones. This was true as early as 1806 when a native mob attacked St. Peter's Church on Christmas Eve and killed a man.[15] Immigration became a hot political issue between the Tammany Democrats and nativist New Yorkers in the 1830's, when immigration rates quadrupled and the depression of the late thirties exacerbated economic nativism. In 1835 native-Irish antagonisms caused the "Five Points Riot," and in 1837 the nativist Whigs succeeded in ousting Tammany from the mayor's office.[16]

It was during these tense times that the Public School Society was experimenting with programs to attract and acculturate the new waves of immigrants. The greatest barrier to success in this venture, especially with the Irish immigrants, was the dispute between Protestants and Catholics over the nature of moral education, and the geniune religious and legal issues should not be ignored. However, the public schools' brief experiment with foreign language

---

14. Milton Gordon makes the same distinction when he differentiates "behavioral assimilation" from "structural assimilation." Milton M. Gordon, *Assimilation in American Life: The Role of Race, Religion and National Origins* (New York, Oxford University Press, 1964), pp. 66–67.

15. Richard J. Purcell, "Immigration to the Canal Era," in Alexander C. Flick, ed., *History of the State of New York* (New York, Columbia University Press, 1933–1937), VII, 41.

16. Ernst, *Immigrant Life,* chap. IX; James G. Wilson, ed., *The Memorial History of the City of New York* (New York, 1893), III, 344, 378–379; Mary P. Carthy, *Old St. Patrick's: New York's First Cathedral* (New York, 1927), pp. 60–63.

instruction shows that conformism outweighed pluralism on cultural as well as on religious grounds.[17]

The Irish immigrants spoke English, but in the Kleindeutschland German was in constant use. The public schools thus had to break down the language barrier before anything else could be accomplished. Too many German children were going either to private German language schools or not attending at all. In December 1837, a committee of the Public School Society recommended that two schools be established with teachers who understood German. They were to be conducted in English, however, and attendance at these special schools, open to any child aged four to sixteen, was to be limited to twelve months' time, "the object of which is simply to prepare the children to pursue their education in the existing public schools and thus to become identified with our native population."[18] One such school, Primary School No. 16, opened the next spring, and after a year in operation the Primary School Committee inspected it. They found that 380 children had been admitted, of whom 233 remained on register in July 1839. They examined the 8 students in the fifth, or highest, class and found that they were "sufficiently advanced for transfer to other Primaries or to Public Schools, but no such transfer had been made since the opening of the school, owing, it was stated, to great reluctance on the part of the children to being removed from No. 16."

Obviously, the school was succeeding too well in appealing to German children. The teacher was subverting the original intention of the school, which was only to teach children to "converse a little" in English. Contrary to primary school rules, many of the children were writing in copybooks rather than on slates, and other procedures had been altered. The teacher, Mr. Ruby, argued that these changes were necessary because "the children could not be prevailed

17. See Vincent P. Lannie, *Public Money and Parochial Education; Bishop Hughes, Governor Seward, and the New York School Controversy* (Cleveland, Case Western Reserve University Press, 1968), p. 101. Lannie criticizes Catholic historians who have blamed nativism for the Catholics' failure to receive public money: "nativist hostility alone did not defeat the Catholic petition; for if Catholics enrolled under the banner of conscience, it must be remembered that non-Catholic Americans also had consciences and were guided by them." The distinction is not clear; nativism could be conscientious and still be hostile. The important point is that for most New Yorkers the religious issues were inseparable from the social issues. The present discussion attempts to show the effect of this concatenation of issues.

18. PSS, Executive Committee Minutes, December 7, 1837.

on to attend the other schools on account of dissimilarity of language, dress, manners etc and if turned from No. 16 would leave school entirely." The Committee's reaction to this argument for cultural compromise was ambivalent: "There may be some force in this reasoning, but the Committee are so fully impressed with the importance of making these children, though German by birth—Americans by education, & that this can be best accomplished by their attending the common schools & mingling with our children, they feel unwilling to adopt the teacher's proposition in full." They agreed to continue the school if it could be strictly limited to primary instruction.[19]

This compromise lasted throughout the 1840's, but it was clear that the Society didn't like compromises on language and culture. Although reluctant to abolish the German school over the objections of the community, they rejected a request for a school designed especially for Italian children. The German school had shown that children took longer to learn English in a special language school, they said. "When foreigners are in the habit of congregating together they retain their national customs, prejudices and feelings" and consequently "are not as good members of society as they would otherwise be." National customs and manners fell in the same negative category as national prejudices, and all had to go. Children who attended the German school, "as is well known, retain their national costume, manners and feelings, while those German children who mingle promiscuously in other schools lose all trace of nationality."[20]

It is no great surprise, then, that in 1850 the Society announced the abolition of the German school. Because German children in regular English schools learned English faster, and, "there being no other good reason for such separation," there was no point in continuing the school. The Board was confident that immigrants, "who come to this country to be Americans, and not foreigners," would appreciate their point of view.[21]

Cancelling the German school program was not a momentous turning point in the development of New York's public schools.

19. PSS, Executive Committee Minutes, July 1, 1839.
20. PSS, Executive Committee Minutes, July 6, 1843.
21. PSS, Annual Report, 1850, in *Report of Superintendent of Common Schools, 1852,* p. 109.

It may be, as the Public School Society said, that German children learned English faster in the regular English schools, and perhaps most of "the more intelligent class of Italians" and "the better class of Germans" did not want such schools.[22] Nevertheless, such decisions reduced the school system's flexibility. Standardization was not simply a bureaucratic phenomenon; it was part of the moral crusade. In order to assert one set of values, the schools had to negate others.

EDUCATION AND RELIGIOUS DIVERSITY

In order to save the immigrant children from delinquency the public school system had to get custody of them. For those who were Catholic, however, their clergy had other ideas. Stubborn and bitter differences between Protestants and Catholics over the nature of moral education frustrated the schoolmen's goal of providing moral education in an all-inclusive common school.

The Catholic population rose from only about 1300 in 1800 to 100,000 in 1850 (See Table 19), largely because of Irish immigration, although about half of the German immigrants were also Catholic.[23] Catholics thus increased from about 2 percent to about 19 percent of the total population during the period. The first Catholic church in New York, St. Peter's, was built in 1785, and in 1801 the trustees established a day school. In 1806 this school began to receive aid from the state school funds along with other denominational free schools.[24] By 1810, when the Catholic population had risen to over 15,000, St. Peter's school was able to provide free education for about one of every six Catholic children of school age (Table 19). The others attended private schools, or those of the new Free School Society, or did not receive any school instruction. The Church had neither the resources nor the inclination to develop a system of Catholic schools. The old informal mode of schooling persisted in the early nineteenth century; it left the initiative for day schooling to the parents, and it encouraged diversity by granting state funds to the free schools of any denominational

---

22. PSS, Executive Committee Minutes, July 6, 1843.
23. Purcell, "Immigration," p. 43.
24. M. H. Lucey, "The Founding of New York's First Parish School," *Catholic World* 93 (June 1911), 370.

Evolution of an Urban School System

TABLE 19.   Growth of Roman Catholic Population and Schools,
New York City, 1800–1855.

Year	Total population	Estimated Catholic population	Estimated Catholic school children, 5–15 (20 percent)	Estimated enrollment in Catholic schools	Number of Catholic schools (approx.)
1800	60,489	1,300	260	0	0
1802	—	4,462	892	—	1
1805	—	—	—	500	1
1808	—	14,000	2,800	—	1
1810	96,373	15,500	3,100	500	1
1814	95,519	—	—	486	1
1816	—	16,000	3,200	516	1
1817	—	—	—	587	2
1820	123,706	—	—	—	4
1822	—	20,000	4,000	692+	4
1825	166,086	—	—	—	—
1827	—	27,000	5,400	—	4
1830	197,112	35,000	7,000	—	5
1835	268,089	—	—	—	—
1840	312,710	60,000–80,000	12,000–16,000	3,000 free	8 free
				4,000–5,000 total	—
1841	—	—	—	5,000 free	—
1845	371,223	—	—	—	—
1850	515,547	100,000	20,000	—	16
1854	—	—	—	10,061	28
1855	629,810	—	—	—	—

Sources: Richard J. Purcell, "Immigration to the Canal Era," in Alexander Flick, ed., *History of the State of New York* (New York, 1933–1937), VII, 10, 44; J. A. Burns, *The Catholic School System in the United States: Its Principles, Origin, and Establishment* (New York, 1908), pp. 170, 267, 271; Robert Ernst, *Immigrant Life in New York City, 1825–1863* (New York, King's Crown Press, 1949), p. 135; Mary P. Carty, *Old St. Patrick's; New York's First Cathedral* (New York, 1947), p. 59; Charles J. Mahoney, *The Relation of the State to Religious Education in Early New York, 1633–1825* (Washington, 1941), pp. 118–119; Lawrence Kehoe, ed., *Complete Works of . . . John Hughes . . .* (New York, 1866), I, 107; Vincent P. Lannie, *Public Money and Parochial Education: Bishop Hughes, Governor Seward, and the New York School Controversy* (Cleveland, 1968), pp. 31, 256; E. M. Connors, *Church-State Relationships in Education in the State of New York* (Washington, 1951), pp. 5n, 46; Austin Flynn, The School Controversy in New York, 1840–1842 . . . , unpub. diss., Notre Dame, 1962, p. 171; Edwin R. Van Vleeck, The Development of Free Common Schools in New York State . . . , unpub. diss., Yale, 1937, p. 178; *Census of the State of New York for 1855* (Albany, 1857), p. xxiv.

group in the city. In 1815 another Catholic school, attached to St. Patrick's Church, opened its doors and applied for aid from the school fund, which it received in 1816. The rise of the nondenominational Free School Society, however, threatened this pluralistic arrangement. As described in Chapter Three above, when the Free School Society became alarmed over the expansion of the Bethel Baptist Church charity schools, they campaigned in Albany for the withdrawal of all funds for religious charity schools, arguing that such schools perpetuated prejudices and misused state funds. The legislature delegated its authority to the New York City Common Council, which decided in favor of the Free School Society, excluding all denominational schools from the school fund.[25]

The Bethel decision proved to have a more far-reaching effect on New York's Catholic Church than on the Baptists. It crystallized a new, unequivocal approval of nondenominational Protestant schooling and made the Free School Society—renamed the Public School Society—its main agent. Most Protestants eventually acquiesced in this new concept, partly because the moral instruction in the public schools was Protestant in text and orientation, partly because the Sunday schools provided a doctrinal supplement to their children's moral education, and partly because an adequate parochial school system was beyond the means of any denomination.[26]

Only the last of these considerations applied to the Catholics; their financial straits were probably more serious than any denomination's because their membership came predominantly from poor immigrants. Yet the Catholic clergy objected to the Protestant public schools both on doctrinal and cultural grounds. Moral education apart from sectarian religion was a Protestant delusion, they maintained, and the public schools taught biased views of Catholic history and culture as well. Despite meagre resources, therefore, the Catholic leaders continued to establish parish schools as new churches were founded. Using church basements at first, and the free services of Catholic teaching orders when possible, Catholics opened schools at St. Mary's in 1827, St. Joseph's and St. James's in 1833, St. Nicholas's in 1834, St. Paul's in 1835, and St. John's in 1840.[27]

25. Charles J. Mahoney, *The Relation of the State to Religious Education in Early New York, 1633–1825* (Washington, Catholic University of America Press, 1941), pp. 129–201, and Chap. Three above.

26. See Robert W. Lynn, *Protestant Strategies in Education* (New York, 1964), pp. 14–22, and Timothy Smith, "Protestant Schooling and American Nationality, 1800–1850," *Journal of American History* 53 (1967), 679–695. The efforts of various Protestant groups to establish parochial systems of education, and their decline, are reported in Francis X. Curran, *The Churches and the Schools: American Protestantism and Popular Elementary Education* (Chicago, Loyola University Press, 1954); see also, Lewis J. Sherrill, *Presbyterian Parochial Schools, 1846–1870* (New Haven, Yale University Press, 1932).

27. M. J. Considine, *A Brief Chronological Account of the Catholic Educational Institutions of the Archdiocese of New York* (New York, 1894), p. 13; J. A. Burns, *The Catholic School System in the United States: Its Principles, Origin, and Establishment* (New York, 1908), p. 222; E. M. Connors, *Church-State Relationships in Education in the State of New York* (Washington, Catholic University of America Press, 1951), p. 5.

By 1840 there were eight free schools, plus several Catholic pay schools, enrolling about 5000 children, perhaps one-fourth to one-third of the Catholic children of school age (Table 19). Although most Catholics were poor, many supported the parish schools as best they could because, like other immigrant institutions, the schools allowed them their cultural integrity. Alienated by the increasing nativism of the late 1830's, aware of their own growing political power as the main prop of the Democratic party, and encouraged by the sympathetic attitude of the Whig governor, William Seward, Catholics reopened the question of state aid to parochial schools. In 1840 they petitioned the legislature for funds. The ensuing controversy generated an avalanche of publicity on both sides. It produced serious internal divisions both within the Whig party and within the Catholic Church. It involved two years of complex politicking and debate and has inspired historians to lengthy and value-laden accounts from that day to this.[28] The following account attempts to relate the religious dispute to the moral mission of the public schools, to illustrate the cultural dimension of the controversy, and to assess, from the scant evidence available, the attitude of the Catholic laity toward the public schools. First, however, the highlights of the action are set forth.

BISHOP HUGHES AND THE SCHOOL QUESTION

In his 1840 message to the legislature Governor Seward urged the establishment of schools taught by teachers who shared the immigrants' language and religion. In February of that year Catholic school trustees submitted petitions for funds to the Common Council, which controlled their distribution. The Public School Society immediately presented a lengthy counterpetition. The Common Council decided against the Catholics. They held several further meetings and requested a public hearing, which was granted in October.[29] In a famous confrontation Bishop John Hughes aired the Catholic grievances at length and was rebutted by Hiram

28. William O. Bourne, *History of the Public School Society of the City of New York* (New York, 1870), gives the documents, with a Protestant slant; Lawrence Kehoe, ed., *Complete Works of . . . John Hughes . . .* (New York, 1866), vol. I, provides the Catholic viewpoint in equal detail. For recent debate, consult Lannie, *Public Money,* Bibliography.

29. Bourne, *PSS,* pp. 178, 186, 189–202.

Ketchum, a leading nativist, and Theodore Sedgwick, both representing the Public School Society, plus a variety of Protestant ministers.[30]

The Common Council attempted to effect a compromise based primarily on the expurgation of offensive passages from textbooks used by the public schools, but the gesture failed to satisfy the Catholics, who organized ward committees to get up petitions to the legislature. Seward, somewhat chastened in his enthusiasm for the immigrant's culture by a narrow election victory, left it to the legislature to find a solution. The Secretary of State, John Spencer, in his dual capacity as Superintendent of Common Schools, recommended in April 1841, a decentralized district plan which would break the monopoly of the Public School Society and create, he thought, healthy competition among schools. Further furious controversy followed. The motion to act upon the report was killed in the Senate by a vote of eleven to ten. The summer of 1841 saw more debate and some violence. The Catholics entered politics directly, nominating at Carroll Hall a slate of legislative candidates which excluded all Democrats who would not staunchly support educational reform in their favor. A Democratic landslide in November 1841, in which the only New York City Democrats to lose were those rejected at Carroll Hall, led to favorable action in the winter session.[31] The Maclay bill, with Seward's support, passed in April 1842. It was based on John Spencer's earlier report. It ended the expansion of the Public School Society and placed it under the general authority of elected officials. Ward commissioners were to establish and supervise all new schools. Hastily appended amendments, however, provided for a central Board of Education over the ward commissioners and prohibited sectarian teaching in the schools.

On the night that Seward signed the bill nativists fought Catholics in the city streets, and Hughes's house was stoned. But it was a victory for the Catholics only in the sense that the hated Public School Society was defeated, which, as Hughes said, was a "partial redress."[32] Hughes had set out to obtain public grants

30. *Ibid.,* pp. 202–323.
31. *Ibid.,* pp. 350, 355–372, 426; Lannie, *Public Money,* chaps. VII, VIII, IX.
32. Lannie, *Public Money,* pp. 241–242; Connors, *Church-State Relationships,* p. 43.

to Catholic parish schools, and he had failed. The Catholics could only hope to exert majority influence in a few wards, and besides, as the *New York Tribune* pointed out, "the Catholic claim must rest on Rights of Conscience and Equity—on the rights of individuals and not masses—of minorities and not majorities."[33]

The amended Maclay bill did not change the majoritarian ethic that guided the moral mission of the schools; it just transferred its operation to the ward level. Nor did it end the public school monopoly as John Spencer had hoped; it just transferred it from a private board to an elective board. It was not a compromise, at least not a successful one; it was a new institutional arrangement unsatisfactory to both protagonists, the Public School Society and the Catholic clergy. The Maclay bill has often been considered a milestone in the history of public education in New York because it extended the operation of local district control, which had been in force upstate, to the city, and because it curbed the growth of the "private" Public School Society and established elective officials to govern the schools. However, district control was qualified by the amendment providing a central Board of Education. It resulted in relatively trivial educational differences, except in symbolic terms, from ward to ward, and it was temporary, becoming, in turn, the object of a centralization reform in 1896 (Manhattan) and 1898 (four boroughs). Similarly, the demise of the Public School Society is more important in the political than in the social history of education, because the Society had consolidated and systematized the city's schooling services, and this important development was not significantly affected by the change in management. Also, the Public School Society had accurately reflected the views of the Protestant majority. The first city superintendent, William Stone, was a nativist as avid as the School Society's Hiram Ketchum, and he immediately set out to enforce Bible readings "without note or comment" on a citywide basis.[34] The substitution of some sort of public control for the Public School Society was inevitable in the long run, although under a centralized system with an appointive board— the system which prevailed in the twentieth century until recently—public control is extremely indirect and weak. At any rate, the advantages which accrue to the schoolchild from public control

33. Lannie, *Public Money*, p. 214.
34. *Ibid.*, p. 252.

of large urban educational systems are not as self-evident as earlier historians seem to have believed. The judgment of Max Weber applies to the Maclay bill: "It does not matter for the character of bureaucracy whether its authority is called 'private' or 'public.' "[35]

CATHOLIC OBJECTIONS TO THE PUBLIC SCHOOLS

The Public School Society's woes are trivial in historical terms, for its mission and its tactics were resumed by the Board of Education. But the dissatisfaction of John Hughes reflected more than personal defeat; he was a spokesman, albeit a militant one, for the grievances of Catholic immigrants, who were the objects of a prejudice that defined them as part of a contraculture. The bitterness of the debate and the impossibility of gaining public funds for Catholic moral instruction had persuaded Hughes as early as 1840 that the Catholics would have to finance a system of their own. He described the fight in 1840 as an effort "to detach the children of our holy Faith from the dangerous connection and influence of the public schools."[36] Still, Hughes fought on, defending the Catholic claims to public money. The arguments on both sides were repetitive and generally unsophisticated, but the dilemma was very real, and it was deeply rooted in cultural as well as religious differences. The three main objections of the Catholic clergy to the public schools may be summarized as textual, catechetical, and cultural. The textual issue was simply which Bible to use, the King James or the Douay version. If it had not been for the other issues, this problem might have been negotiated, but as a symbolic issue it put things in black and white terms and thus remained a prominent grievance. Under the Maclay bill, with more local option, some schools introduced the Douay Bible, or alternated between the Protestant and Catholic texts.[37]

35. H. H. Gerth and C. Wright Mills, trans. and eds., *From Max Weber: Essays in Sociology* (New York, Oxford University Press, 1946), p. 197.
36. Bishop Hughes to Bishop Blanc of New Orleans, August 27, 1840, in Austin Flynn, The School Controversy in New York, 1840–1842, unpub. diss., Notre Dame, 1962, p. 65, with whose kind permission I draw upon and quote from his unpublished material; see also, Connors, *Church-State Relationships*, p. 47.
37. New York City Board of Education, *Report of the Select Committee . . . on Different Charges of Abuse Made by the County Superintendent . . .* (New York, 1845).

The catechetical issue was at the heart of the religious controversy. Protestants had maintained from the time of the Reformation that the individual was capable of interpreting the Bible without the mediation of a priesthood, and therefore, although Protestants still employed rote catechism in instruction, Bible reading per se played a large role in religious instruction. The Catholic Church, in contrast, maintained that specific explication must accompany Bible reading. The Protestants claimed, with some reason, that reading the Bible in schools "without note or comment" avoided doctrinal interpretation and therefore was nonsectarian. The Catholics replied with equal correctness, that the practice was based on a distinctly Protestant concept and was therefore sectarian. Neither side budged an inch from these positions. The Protestants doggedly reasserted a solution that had worked among Protestant denominations because they all agreed more or less on the premise that individuals could interpret the Bible for themselves. The Board also announced an attempt to define and incorporate "nonsectarian religious fundamentals" into the curriculum. Catholics, however, believed that "all Christian morals are founded on dogmas, and have no adequate basis to support them without dogmas."[38] Nevertheless, they did not propose a means by which children of different religions could go to school together, probably because Hughes did not think it possible. Thus, not only the beliefs but the aims of the two sides were opposed. The Public School Society wanted an inclusive school system; Hughes wanted state funds for separate religious schools. He never attempted to negotiate a reconciliation, as his predecessor Dubois had in the 1830's, and he found irrelevant the efforts of his subordinate Father Varela to have the public schools expurgate anti-Catholic passages from their books. That would not solve the moral training problem; only Catholic schools could do that.[39]

The textual and catechetical objections probably worried the

38. PSS, Executive Committee Minutes, October 24, 1838; *Truth Teller,* September 14, 1839, in Flynn, School Controversy, p. 55.
39. On Varela and the schoolbook expurgation campaign, see Connors, *Church-State Relationships,* pp. 22–23; Bourne, *PSS,* chap. XI; Lannie, *Public Money,* chap. V. On the general issue, see Marie Fell, *The Foundations of Nativism in American Textbooks, 1783–1860* (Washington, Catholic University of America Press, 1941); and Ruth M. Elson, *Guardians of Tradition: American Schoolbooks of the Nineteenth Century* (Lincoln, Nebraska, University of Nebraska Press, 1964), pp. 47–54.

religious leaders more than the parents or the school children. The cultural objections, however—the negative historical and sociological image of Catholics projected by the public schools—affected the child's self-image, his pride, and his expectations.

The best exposition of the Protestant bias of the schools is found in a series of speeches Hughes gave at meetings in the basement of St. James's Church from July to October of 1840, which have been recorded in paraphrase. The meetings were designed to alert Catholics to the insidious dangers of the public schools, the Bishop said.[40] He found abundant material in public school texts. The "Character of Martin Luther," written by a Presbyterian, called him one of the greatest men in history. "Now, no doubt Martin Luther had a character," quipped Hughes, "but people draw it very differently . . . Catholics, thanks to the education which they gave him, may think very highly of his talents, but they have not much admiration of his virtues." There was no balance, he complained. Why not have something on brave Sir Thomas More, by a Catholic writer, he asked.[41] Nowhere in the public school texts, said Hughes, would a Catholic child learn that there had been "some respectable Catholic writers" in such fields as history, literature, and law. Nowhere would he learn of Catholic toleration in Maryland in the midst of persecution in the Protestant colonies. Nowhere would he learn that great inventors, explorers, and poets had been Catholics.[42] Hughes concluded that the School Society wanted to teach children "that Catholics are necessarily, morally, intellectually, infallibly, a stupid race."[43]

To this negative view of Catholic culture and history were added slurs against Irish immigrants. Hughes found a schoolbook in which Irish immigration was described as an "oppressive influx," which, if continued, would make America "the common sewer of Ireland." Immigrants were "in many cases drunken and depraved." This stemmed from their religion. Intemperance was "probably . . . a part of the papal system." An Irish character in a story went to confession and "returned quite invigorated for the perpetuation of new offences."[44] Hughes's speeches laid out in great detail the condi-

40. Flynn, School Controversy, p. 58.
41. Kehoe, *Hughes,* p. 51.
42. *Ibid.,* pp. 107, 115–117.
43. *Ibid.,* p. 116.
44. *Ibid.,* p. 62.

tions which caused the American hierarchy to declare in their pastoral letter of 1840, that Catholics who attended public schools were in great danger of "the fatal influence of the false shame which generally arises from the mockery or the superciliousness of those who undervalue their creed."[45]

One could expurgate books, but not minds; the schools were permeated with a missionary Protestantism that their proprietors associated with general morality. If books were expurgated, the incidental, hidden curriculum would come out in the attitudes of teachers and peers. When the school succeeded in winning the Catholic immigrant child's credence and allegiance, as it often did, it created a generational conflict between the child and his immigrant parents. This conflict was very likely to occur with or without the public school, of course, yet it was implicit in the school's aims to hasten the process. Hughes complained in a petition that Catholic children who went to the public schools "become intractable, disobedient, and even contemptuous towards their parents." Thomas McGee wrote in 1855 of Irish children who "go to the public school. They are called 'Paddies' . . . They come home, and they want explanations; and here is, precisely where the second generation breaks off from the first . . . If . . . the family tie is snapt . . . our children become our opponents."[46] Someone has said of New York City that it was not a melting pot but a pressure cooker. Acculturation was not an easy educational process; it was a bruising, inevitably insulting process, and because the fruits of becoming "Americanized" were not readily visible, many immigrants resisted the process.

Many resisted, but some did not. Some New York Catholics sent their children to the public schools despite fears for their religion and customs. In the early years of the century the clergy did not enjoin their parishoners from attending Protestant schools, and some must have gone simply because the Catholic schools were full. It is impossible to determine how many. When the Free School Society instituted Tuesday afternoon denominational catechism for all their children in 1813, they reported only 9 Catholic children

45. Flynn, School Controversy, p. 26.
46. Kehoe, *Hughes,* p. 103; Ernst, *Immigrant Life,* p. 180; see also Oscar Handlin, *Boston's Immigrants, 1790–1880* (New York, enlarged edition, Atheneum, 1959), p. 135.

out of 798 students, a figure cited by the Catholic historians, J. A. Burns and E. M. Connors.[47] The next year, however, they reported that 57 children out of 933 were catechized by Roman Catholic representatives, a figure cited by the Protestant historian A. Emerson Palmer.[48] Figures from the 1840's are also fragmentary. Hughes said that 4000 to 5000 children were educated in Catholic schools, and that only a "few hundred" Catholics attended public schools, while thousands received "only such education as is afforded in the streets of New York."[49] Such claims could not mask the fact, however, that many Catholics were attending the public schools. Despite Hughes's declaration that parents who sent their children to public school were "sinning against God," Catholics were divided on the issue.[50]

Some went to public schools because conditions in the Catholic parish schools were bad. Hughes himself wanted to get state aid so that "we could bring our children out of the damp basements of our churches into the pure air of better localities." Some were not willing to wait loyally for Hughes to succeed. Father Cummings, of St. Stephens's Church, complained that the basement parish school was inferior to the neighborhood public school, and he marched the students off in a group and enrolled them there.[51] In some schools the teachers' competence was also criticized.[52]

Other Catholics had more positive reasons. They agreed with the public schools' goal of Americanizing the immigrant child. They wanted their children to join the dominant culture, whatever it took. These were the people whom Hughes most wanted to dissuade. They were the New York counterparts of Orestes Brownson, who argued in Boston in the 1850's, much to Hughes's dismay, that "common school education is the order of the day," and that

47. FSS, *Annual Report* (New York, 1814); Burns, *Catholic School System,* p. 171; Connors, *Church-State Relationships,* p. 3.

48. FSS, *Annual Report* (New York, 1815); A. Emerson Palmer, *The New York Public School: Being a History of Free Education in the City of New York* (New York, The Macmillan Company, 1905), p. 36. The program was discontinued in 1815.

49. Kehoe, *Hughes,* p. 79.

50. Connors, *Church-State Relationships,* p. 39.

51. *Address of the Roman Catholics to their Fellow Citizens . . .* Board of Aldermen, Doc. 20, August 10, 1840 (New York, 1840), p. 322; Flynn, School Controversy, p. 180.

52. Michael Lucey, "Administration of the Parish Schools," *Catholic World* 94 (March 1912), 60; Connors, *Church-State Relationships,* p. 13.

Catholic opposition to them would only perpetuate the immigrants' status as a "foreign colony" in America. In New York the Catholic newspaper *Truth Teller* supported the public school system in the 1840's. They opposed foreign languages in the schools and argued for advancement through common schooling.[53]

Many Catholics preferred the public schools to none at all, but substantial numbers preferred Catholic schools to public schools. This impression is supported by figures from the suburb of Manhattanville in 1847. The Free School trustees there noted that "the following report, showing the comparative attendance since the establishment of the Catholic Schools, was received . . .

February, 1847

On register		Attendance	
Boys	Girls	Boys	Girls
110	94	93	54
Total:	204	Total:	148

February, 1848

On register		Attendance	
Boys	Girls	Boys	Girls
50	29	36	19
Total:	79	Total:	55

The figures suggest that many Catholics were in the public school, but that many transferred to the Catholic schools when they opened.[54]

Despite the pragmatic attitude of some Catholic laymen, compromise between the Protestant public school system and the Catholic clergy had failed. John Hughes and Hiram Ketchum were not the best men to send to a bargaining table, but personality was not the important factor in the controversy. The public school system was committed to reformation, not accommodation, and the Catholic hierarchy was committed to specifically Catholic education. It was not just a question of gradualism versus immediatism in acculturation, but rather of how much diversity was ultimately desirable or even tolerable. In his 1842 message Governor Seward

53. Connors, *Church-State Relationships,* p. 49; Lannie, *Public Money,* p. 41.
54. Manhattanville Free School, Minutes, 1838–1850, NYHS, November 1847.

criticized the notion that "society must conform itself to the public schools, instead of the public schools adapting themselves to the exigencies of society." John Spencer's report, which went even further than Seward's messages, said that the Public School Society had created an "educational establishment" something like the religious establishments of Europe. There was, he said, "the idea prevalent among the people, that an attempt is made to *coerce* them, directly or indirectly, to do something which others take a great interest in having done." People were not left "to act *spontaneously*—to *originate* anything . . . It is not a *voluntary* system."[55]

The cultural situation in the city was such that a decision in favor of a "spontaneous" and "voluntary" system of schooling would have been most unlikely. A version of the Spencer idea made it through the legislature as the Maclay bill of 1842, but it was safely hemmed in to avoid any significant loss of control to nonconforming groups. The Catholic Church was heir to historical enmity and suspicion by Protestants, and nativism grew apace with immigration. Immigrants and the poor were regarded in general as the prime danger to law and virtue in the city. The school was moral reform institutionalized. Equality was proclaimed for all, but the meeting ground was not neutral. Some people were more equal than others, and the difference was moral.

William Seward and John Spencer, in their desire to bring everyone into an American community without coercive conformity, and Charles Brace, in his aversion to institutionalization and his understanding of alienation, have affinities to certain modern critics of the establishment and its schools, and, like them, their critique of standardized institutions in the mass urban society had an element of nostalgia for the way things used to be, when men in the city could interact in ways more personal, spontaneous, informal, and independent. But the schoolmen who forged the Public School Society, the penologists who devised the House of Refuse, and the legislators who held the line against minority sectarian teaching in the common schools were more modern in the sense that their reactions to early urban diversity and disruption were an accurate

55. Connors, *Church-State Relationships,* p. 40; Kehoe, *Hughes,* p. 370.

prediction of the trend ever since. The task of constructive socialization was increasingly assigned to institutions when the informal environment and the values of a large part of the population came to be regarded as antagonistic to the aims and the security of the rest. In return, many people, especially immigrants, who were part of the contraculture by definition, saw the schools as a threat to their family life and their freedom. Schools were the main institutions charged with the responsibility of homogenization. It was not their exclusive purpose, but it dominated the thinking of schoolmen. Because poverty, social deviance, and religious differences were seen in highly charged moral terms, the schoolmen did not conceive of homogenization as a process which would produce a stable mixture of the original ingredients, but rather as a sort of social alchemy, in which some undesirable members of society would be transformed into useful members.

CHAPTER SIX

The Systematization
of Schooling

William Seward's secretary of state, John Spencer, had envisaged
a system of diverse, competing, independent schools in New York
City which would receive state funds. His solution ignored the
nativist hostility and suspicion of the 1840's, and it denied the valid-
ity of the connections that missionary schoolmen had made between
Catholicism, immigration, poverty, vice, and alien customs. Thus
his solution did not survive. Reinforcing these cultural reasons,
moreover, the internal bureaucratic structure and procedures of
the school system militated against such diversity. Between 1805,
when the Free School Society was founded, and 1853, when they
turned over their schools to the Board of Education, schooling services in New York were consolidated, coordinated, and standardized
in a process that one is tempted to call a bureaucratic revolution.[1]
This process did not significantly change the percentage of students
who received a common education, but it provided a means of
keeping pace with the great increase in absolute numbers of children
in the city. Similarly, the systematization of the schools did not increase the mixture of socioeconomic backgrounds in the school,
which had been broad in the 1790's, but rather was a means of
coping with the great increase of impoverished and socially

1. On the bureaucratization of schools see David Tyack, "Bureaucracy and
the Common School: The Example of Portland, Oregon, 1851–1913," *American
Quarterly* 19 (1967), 475–498, and Michael B. Katz, "The Emergence of
Bureaucracy in Urban Education: The Boston Case, 1850–1884," *History
of Education Quarterly* 8 (1968), 155–188, 319–357.

alienated people in the city. It was the result of an attempt to hold together an increasingly fractionalized population.

The main events in the unification of the city's public schools can be reiterated briefly. The Free School Society was founded in 1805 to provide schooling for the churchless poor. Almost immediately, however, the members changed their charter (1808) to accept any poor children, since the charity schools of the various denominations were not sufficient. The free schools and all the charity schools received state funds beginning in 1815, in proportion to their enrollments. In 1824, when the Bethel Baptist Church had three schools, the Free School Society, fearing that their growing organization of six schools would face competition for students and funds, waged a successful campaign to eliminate all denominational schools from public money. This gave the Society a virtual monopoly on government aid. At the same time the Society changed its name and its rules to promote the ideal of public schools for all the city's children. By 1835 the Public School Society had fifteen schools. They established primary departments, adopted the schools of other groups, and in general became accepted as the central provider of elementary education in New York. Meanwhile, pay schools became fewer, relative to population, and more expensive. Most churches turned their energies to Sunday schools for their congregations, having shed the responsibility they had long felt for the secular education of the poor. The Catholic clergy resisted the trend and reopened the question of state aid to their schools in 1840. The result, the Maclay bill of 1842, established an elective Board of Education and forebade the further expansion of the Public School Society. While the Board of Education began establishing ward schools, the Public School Society maintained its eighteen upper departments and fifty-six primaries, but the trustees did not get along well with the new board to which they had been subordinated. The Society was no longer necessary, and it could no longer grow. In 1853, sadly, and with a tinge of bitterness, the Society turned over its schools to the city, thus unifying a system which, despite some features of district control, linked 235 boys', girls', and primary departments in a coordinated system.

The Public School Society had been the main agent of this systematization, which involved the expansion and consolidation of schools, the extension of curriculum and age groups, articulation between levels, and, in theory at least, the standardization of students' treatment and teachers' performance. But the Society had not foreseen the "perfect system" of the 1850's when they began in 1805, and they had not created it by themselves. Bureaucracy was not their brain-child; it was the city's way of doing things, the product of all the problems and pressures and reform efforts of the inhabitants of America's preeminent metropolis. There were protests against the consolidation of the schooling system, but beneath these splashes of controversy ran a strong current of cooperation and approval from many groups in the city. The scale of social problems increased so rapidly that piecemeal educational efforts could not keep pace. Year after year, common sense led to the consolidation of schools for economy and efficiency, and the pressure of numbers led to standardization. It was the impact of these mundane forces as much as of the highly normative motives discussed in Chapters Four and Five that accounts for the development of the system. The bureaucratic ethic and the moral mission of the schoolmen arose from the same problem—the rapid expansion and diversification of the population—and they tended toward the same result—a vigorously conformist system. However, the bureaucractic values of efficiency and impartiality should be recognized, along with the effort to acculturate, as separate factors in the systematization of the schools.

THE CONCEPT OF SYSTEM:
MODELS FOR NEW YORK CITY

At the turn of the eighteenth century the word "system," in reference to schooling, was in a state of flux, as was the use of the term "public." In its older usage it denoted a pedagogical method or a plan for organizing a single school. However, Americans watched with interest during the early years of their republic while Condorcet in France and Frederick the Great in Prussia developed national systems of education. At the national level in America these plans generated only a flurry of admiring essays calling for the general provision of schooling. At the state level, two key elements of the continental systems, the regulation of curriculum and the articulation between different levels of schooling, evolved very slowly or not al all. Educational "systems" in the new American states generally meant the legislative provision for schooling rather than its actual regulation. In New York State, Governor George Clinton referred to the 1795 legislation as a "system for the encouragement of common schools."[2] Articulation between elementary and secondary levels was particularly slow in New York because the state Regents controlled aid to academies and colleges, while a separate state superintendent supervised aid to common schools. Even within each sphere regulation was minimal in the period 1800 to 1850.[3] Americans had too strong a tradition of local control in the first half of the century to accept a regulatory concept of system even at the state level.

Strangely enough, then, the only analogues of the continental European systems to develop in America in the early nineteenth century were at the city level. In urban New York, there were enough problems and enough children to provide the raw materials for such a system within the local control tradition. Bishop John Hughes made the connection when he charged in 1840 that the city school system was Prussian in origin. Hughes was right about the similarity but wrong in thinking that Prussian schools were a direct model for the city's system. Although various American educators, notably Horace Mann and John Griscom, wrote accounts praising some aspects of German schools, the New Yorkers, including Griscom, developed their city's system almost exclusively on English or Scottish models. The Sunday school, the monitorial school, the infant school, the high school—all were explicitly based on British institutions.

New Yorkers looked to England rather than France or Germany because they knew it best and because they were concerned with urban, not national, solutions. Thomas Eddy, Divie and Joanna Bethune, John Griscom, and others looked to their English friends for advice because England's cities, especially London, had already experienced the problems New York was beginning to face. The

2. Charles Z. Lincoln, ed., *State of New York, Messages from the Governors* . . . (Albany, J. B. Lyon Company, 1909), II, 512.
3. Frank C. Abbott, *Government Policy and Higher Education: A Study of the Regents of the University of the State of New York, 1784–1949* (Ithaca, Cornell University Press, 1958), pp. 15, 25–28, 39–41; Elsie G. Hobson, *Educational Legislation and Administration in the State of New York, 1777–1850* (Chicago, University of Chicago Press, 1918), chaps. III and IV; Sidney Sherwood, *The University of the State of New York* . . . (Washington, United States Bureau of Education, 1900), pp. 92–99.

colonial rejection of a corrupt England, which had always been tempered by an element of provincial insecurity, gave way when America's first genuine citydwellers saw their own city becoming corrupted. They sought advice from those with experience.

This strong orientation toward England accounts somewhat for the rather strange lack of interest in New England educational systems among New York City educators early in the century. They were seeking urban models, so it was more logical to look in London than in Boston, their smaller neighbor. New Yorkers, especially the Quakers and the Anglicans, felt a special cultural tie to London, and a certain historical antipathy toward the Calvinists to the east. Also, New England emigrants did not play as big a role in educational reform in the city as they did upstate, where their numbers were much greater and many whole communities were settled by New Englanders.[4] Jedediah Peck in the 1790's and Gideon Hawley in the 1820's, major leaders in the development of common schools in the state, were both Connecticut expatriates. When the New York City Common Council was faced with Peck's 1795 law for common schools, however, they did not know quite what to do about it. As explained in Chapter Two, they rather halfheartedly committed themselves to creating "public" schools on the New England model, like upstate communities, but they did not follow through. Instead they called their church schools "free schools" and gave them the money. Eventually they gave it all to the Free School Society, an interdenominational but "private" monopoly.

State superintendents like Hawley, in turn, did not know quite what to do about the city's system. They did not wish to force a mode of school financing on the city if its leaders were happy with what they already had. As long as the city's system was working, the state left it alone. Urban and rural conditions were not the same. Almost all educational legislation in New York State from 1795 to 1850 included separate clauses for New York City as a special case.[5] Thus, historians who have described New York City as an errant part of the state system, finally brought into line with upstate practice in 1842 by the introduction of district control and elective boards, have missed the full significance of early urban

---

4. See Lois K. Mathews, *The Expansion of New England* (Boston, Houghton Mifflin Company, 1909), pp. 153–169.

5. Hobson, *Legislation, passim.*

school development. In the city, "system" came to mean detailed, centralized regulation and controlled promotion between levels long before these elements were introduced into the state system. The features of the state system introduced into the city in 1842, ward control and elective boards, were short-lived; the indigenous bureaucratic features of control and uniformity were not. The history of the city's school system is different from that of the state and should be seen as separate, in inspiration and in organization.

LANCASTERIAN SCHOOLS AND THE CONCEPT OF SYSTEM

In the early years of the nineteenth century, when Thomas Eddy was eagerly corresponding with Patrick Colquhoun about the promise of monitorial instruction, they used the word "system" in the sense of a pedagogical method or a way of organizing a single school. Because Joseph Lancaster's system was both of these, but also promised a general panacea, the Lancasterian movement in New York City was instrumental in bringing about a new concept of system as a way of regulating a whole group of schools. The Free School Society had only one school when they adopted the "system" in 1806, but even then DeWitt Clinton had prophesied that Lancaster's method would create "a new era in education." Although by "system" he still meant a method of organizing a given school, Clinton boasted that the New York Free School had become a "parent seminary," and Lancasterian schools had "sprung from its bosum" owing to visits from two Philadelphia school societies.[6] When the same propagation began in New York City, the potential for an interschool system was established. At first different groups established Lancasterian schools; gradually they were unified under one group.

The Lancasterian system of instruction was efficient, both pedagogically and economically, and it demanded highly disciplined procedures. These qualities made the school into a kind of machine, and schoolmen emphasized the similarity. Governor Clinton told the Legislature in 1818 that the "system operates with the same

6. DeWitt Clinton, Speech at the Opening of the New York Free School, 1808, in William O. Bourne, *History of the Public School Society of the City of New York* (New York, 1870), p. 19; *ibid.,* pp. 22, 23.

efficiency in education as labor-saving machinery does in the useful arts."[7] Machinery had a positive symbolic connotation to these reformers. They thought of the technological advantages of automation, not the dehumanizing effect on the worker or the sad economic plight that befell factory workers.[8] Early in the century, when the Lancasterian plan was introduced, the factory suggested only the intriguing possibilities of labor-saving inventions, and schoolmen found it an appropriate analogy for their efforts in school organization. It remained a recurrent theme in their rhetoric.

The efficiency of the Lancasterian system meant more to its advocates than mere economy. It was not simply a cheap way to teach thousands of poor children, as was charged by critics then and since; it was also considered a more effective way to teach. Many poor children stayed in school only a short time, and in the Lancasterian system, its proponents believed, they would learn faster. Clinton pictured the children in New York's Free School "marching, with unexampled rapidity and with perfect discipline, to the goal of knowledge." John Griscom considered the system a good example of "the *science* of education," the goal of which was "*simplifying* and *accelerating* the acquisition of knowledge." Content was broken down into small steps, and promotion in one subject was independent of promotion in another, a procedure for individual progress that was lost with the introduction of graded schools after 1850. Every pupil was busy all the time, which was considered a pedagogical improvement and a good lesson in industriousness.[9]

The regimentation of the students in the Lancasterian system was symbolically and psychologically appropriate to the moral mission of the schools. Any standardized school organization would have had some appeal in terms of teaching discipline and order,

7. A. Emerson Palmer, *The New York Public School* (New York, The Macmillan Company, 1905), p. 27.

8. On the positive image of the factory in nineteenth-century America, see Leo Marx, *The Machine in the Garden: Technology and the Pastoral Ideal in America* (New York, Oxford University Press, 1964), pp. 180–181, and *passim*.

9. Bourne, *PSS,* p. 19; John F. Reigart, *The Lancasterian System of Instruction in the Schools of New York City* (New York, Teachers College, Columbia University, Contributions to Education, No. 81, 1916), p. 53; Carl F. Kaestle, ed., *Joseph Lancaster and the Monitorial School Movement: A Documentary History* (New York, Teachers College Press, forthcoming), Introduction.

but the Lancasterian organization was particularly strong on these qualities. By bringing the pupils into an obedient subordination, the school imposed order on chaos. The school was a model for society. A committee investigating tenements in the 1850's stated the theory behind the emphasis on systematization in social reform:

> It is a law of nature, applicable to society as to physics, that continued disorder must result in ultimate destruction. In the social as the human system, symmetry is essential of health . . . It is because our social structures too often lack the essential laws of proportion and assimilation . . . the adaptedness of parts to each other and to the whole—it is, in effect, because society would escape from obedience to the order which governs nature and individual man—that the political economist encounters such startling problems.[10]

This philosophy of order developed in the period 1800 to 1850 in response to urban problems. Order in society and the systematization of schools went hand in hand; the latter was an attempt to promote the former.

The systematization of schools would also solve the problem of scale. Once the system was established, it was recursive. No matter how many new children appeared, poor or rich, immigrant or native, the system would simply provide more identical schools and train more identical teachers. This would be fair, and it would be efficient. One board of trustees could make decisions rather than dozens of groups which ran one or two schools. The Lancasterian system, with its detailed procedures, prescribed content, authoritarian pedagogy, and hierarchical teaching structure, offered a vehicle for the creation of such an interschool system. New York experienced the problems of population expansion, rising poverty, crime, ethnic diversity, and economic stratification both earlier and more severely than other American cities. Not having the long-standing involvement with free education that New England had, New York leaders were attracted by the detailed plans of Lancaster, which could be infinitely duplicated. New York became the American Mecca for monitorial school enthusiasts.

---

10. *Report of the Select Committee . . . Tenement Houses of New York and Brooklyn* (Albany, New York State Assembly Documents, No. 205, 1857), pp. 8–9. On systematization as a general function of the industrial revolution, see Jacques Ellul, *The Technological Society,* trans. John Wilkinson (New York, Alfred Knopf, 1964), p. 43.

EXPANSION AND CONSOLIDATION

Expertise was an important element in the successful growth of the Free School Society. One of the original trustees had visited Lancaster's schools and had corresponded with him. In the early years the Society followed Lancaster's *Improvements in Education* as a guide, but in 1818, when they had established three schools, they produced a manual of their own to standardize their system of instruction and to publicize their efforts. In the same year the Society engaged Charles Picton, a teacher trained in monitorial schools in England, to take charge of the fourth school and to further perfect their monitorial procedures.[11] The Society allowed their new resident expert to contract with St. Peter's Catholic Church to reorganize its free school on the Lancasterian model.[12] By that date several other schools had shifted to monitorial instruction, including the charity schools of the Episcopal, Dutch, Presbyterian, and Methodist churches, the Manumission Society school, and the Economical School, a French organization of which Clinton was a trustee.[13]

Some groups in New York, rather than imitate the Society's Lancasterian schools and hire teachers trained by the Society, decided that it would be easier simply to get their schooling directly from the Society. Thus in 1809 the Masons arranged with the Free School Society to educate fifty orphaned or poor children of their members, and the Fire Department later made a similar arrangement.[14] In 1816 the Presbyterians discontinued their charity school and sent their poor children to Free School No. 1, paying to the Society their portion of the state school fund. In this way the Society gained students; in other cases they gained whole schools. In 1823, at the city's request, the Almshouse school became Public School

11. Bourne, *PSS*, pp. 31–32.

12. J. A. Burns, *The Catholic School System in the United States: Its Principles, Origin, and Establishment* (New York, 1908), p. 269; Thomas Boese, *Public Education in the City of New York: Its History, Condition and Statistics* (New York, 1869), p. 223.

13. Edward A. Fitzpatrick, *The Educational Views and Influence of DeWitt Clinton* (New York, Teachers College, Columbia University, Contributions to Education, No. 44, 1911), pp. 103, 114.

14. William W. Cutler, Philosophy, Philanthropy, and Public Education: A Social History of the New York Public School Society, 1805–1853, unpub. diss., Cornell University, 1968, p. 64; Boese, *Public Education,* p. 224.

No. 6.[15] When state funds were withdrawn from denominational schools in 1825, St. Michael's Episcopal Church in Bloomingdale found that they could no longer maintain their charity school. In 1826 they petitioned the Public School Society to take over the school, and the Society agreed. St. Michael's School became Public School No. 9.[16]

By the 1820's, the trustees of the Free School Society, with considerable encouragement from the community, were committed to operating a coordinated system of schools, rather than merely promoting the Lancasterian idea. In 1822, when the Baptists began expanding, the trustees resolved to try to keep anyone "from interfering with the liberal and extensive views of the Free School Society in the education of all the poor children of this Metropolis." The bureaucratic arguments for a unitary system became explicit in the controversy with the Bethel Baptist Church. In 1825, they argued that "by being divided and distributed through so many channels," the school fund was used less economically than if it were to be spent "by a single society having but the alone object in view of general education."[17] Turning their attention from the city's charity schools to its independent pay schools, the Society remarked that the "great variety of plans pursued in the different schools, and the various and dissimilar school-books used in them, retards the progress of, and increases the expense to, children removed from one to another." The Society vowed to create a "uniform system in all the elementary schools of the city," which was especially important to the lower classes, who moved frequently.[18] They further argued the advantages of close supervision in a centralized system. Supporting the Society's concept, the Common Council told the legislature, "The happy effects of such visitations and examinations have been fully exemplified in the schools of the Free-School Society."[19]

15. Shepherd Knapp, *A History of the Brick Presbyterian Church in the City of New York* (New York, 1909), p. 207; Palmer, *Public School,* p. 57.
16. Bourne, *PSS,* pp. 699–700; Public School Society Minutes, February 5, 1830.
17. Charles J. Mahoney, *The Relation of the State to Religious Education in Early New York, 1633–1825* (Washington, Catholic University of America Press, 1941), pp. 131–132; Palmer, *Public School,* p. 49.
18. Bourne, *PSS,* pp. 86, 82.
19. *Ibid.,* p. 66.

Having discovered the virtues of uniformity and supervision, the Public School Society continued its consolidation policy. With the Common Council's support, their budget rose dramatically after 1825, and the number of students attending schools in the system rose too, especially after the tuition experiment was abandoned in 1832.[20] Specialized schooling organizations yielded to the superior resources and abilities of the Society. When the trustees became convinced in 1832 that the experiment of the Infant School Society, begun in 1827, was worthwhile, they adopted their schools as primary schools and began establishing more. In 1834 the Manumission Society followed suit, turning over its seven schools to the central system and terminating a philanthropic enterprise that had begun in 1785.[21] This consolidation resulted at first in reduced attendance by Negro children because of the insensitivity of the Public School Society. In 1836 a committee reported that because the trustees had introduced new books and procedures, replaced some teachers who had long experience in the Manumission Society schools, and reduced the status of all but one of the schools to the primary level, "strong prejudices had grown up against the Public School Society." The employment of a black agent somewhat placated this resentment.[22] As with individual students, however, the Society yielded little to the needs of a school being assimilated, while the school yielded a lot.

To the trustees of individual schools and separate societies, incorporation into the Public School Society brought financial security and experience in training and supervising teachers. The Society had succeeded in creating a permanent and uniform system. Their ultimate goal, however, to include all the children of the city in their system, eluded them. They received a monopoly of all the public funds, but they could not claim to be educating all the children. In the controversy over the Catholics' request for funds Governor Seward raised this point against them: "no system is perfect which does not accomplish what it proposes; . . . our system, therefore, is deficient in comprehensiveness in the exact proportion of the children that it leaves uneducated."[23]

20. *Ibid.*, p. xxxii.
21. *Ibid.*, pp. 659–664; 674–676.
22. Boese, *Public Education*, p. 227; Bourne, *PSS*, pp. 678–679.
23. Governor William Seward, Annual Message, 1841, in Bourne, *PSS*, p. 355.

The solution that the legislature devised, however, demonstrated
how thoroughly the concept of a unitary system had been accepted,
for they did not break down the system and give money to independent schools, as had been the practice from 1800 to 1825 and
as the Catholics now requested, but instead they legitimized the
unitary system by making school officers elective. The provisions
allowing the Public School Society to operate intact under the new
board were only a recognition of their contribution, a politically
necessary gesture; it was incongruous because it compromised the
very concept the Society had worked so long to popularize. The
Public School Society trustees and the new Board of Education
disagreed on matters of money, building construction, preparation
for the Free Academy, the value of monitorial instruction, and other
issues in the uncomfortable decade of their coexistence.[24]

In 1853, at the suggestion of the Board of Education, negotiations
were successfully held to dissolve the Public School Society and
transfer their schools to the ward system. Hiram Ketchum, who
had been with the Society since the Bethel Baptist Church controversy of the 1820's, published a defensive speech in 1853 called
Winding-Up of the Public School Society, in which he said, almost
redundantly, that the two systems had failed to work harmoni-
ously.[25] Each group claimed that the other was inefficient, the most
appropriate charge for one bureaucracy to level at another. Competition between systems was against the whole bureaucratic ethic
that had developed, and, because the public board had more legal
power, they absorbed the Society, as the Society had absorbed so
many other schools, some willingly and some reluctantly.

The legacy the Public School Society left to the unified system
was one of clearly defined hierarchy and standardization. Although
these bureaucratic values were somewhat modified by ward control
in the second half of the century, they still guided the outlook and
expectations of schoolmen on the central board, who gradually reasserted central control. The New York City school system entered
the twentieth century as a recentralized bureaucracy that would
have made Divie Bethune's heart warm: it had 488 schools, en-

24. PSS, Executive Committee Minutes, February 3, 1848, February 6,
and July 3, 1851.

25. Hiram Ketchum, *Winding-Up of the Public School Society* . . . (New
York, 1853), pp. 10–11.

rolling 398,000 students in four boroughs, and under the revised charter of 1901 a central board held all significant powers of policy, personnel, and the purse.[26] However, most of the features associated with centralized urban school bureaucracies did not first develop in the early twentieth century, but in the early nineteenth century.

HIERARCHY

The expansion of the school system occurred in two dimensions. The multiplication of identical common schools under central direction may be thought of as horizontal expansion. At the same time, the developing concept of system also came to mean the consolidation of different levels of schools, and the articulation of the relationships between them, which may be termed the vertical expansion of the system. This development is important in the history of pedagogy because it curbed the Public School Society's single-minded defense of rote monitorial instruction, which, they found, was not as appropriate to either infant or high school levels as to the common school curriculum. Vertical expansion was also important in the history of educational opportunity, for only when the levels became connected and, finally, when they all became tuition free, could the talented but resourceless boy expect to make the difficult climb to the top. Thus the Board of Education appropriately lauded the Free Academy, opened in 1849, as the "keystone in the arch of our system of popular education." The impact of the Free Academy on the lower and lower middle classes may not have been great in actual numbers, but when it opened, the hierarchical system finally existed in fact as well as in theory.[27]

The process of expansion upward and downward began in the 1820's, after the Public School Society had successfully established itself as the chief provider of common schooling in the city. When it first began, the Society had admitted children over six years old; later the limit was five.[28] The program of each school was the same, and each school included the whole age range of pupils. There

26. Palmer, *Public School,* pp. 144–146, 152, 155–156, 163–164, 185–189, 272–274, 293, 298–302.
27. Board of Education Annual Report, 1851, in *Annual Report of the Superintendent of Common Schools of the State of New York . . . 1852* (Albany, 1852), p. 94.
28. Bourne, *PSS,* pp. 39, 111, 121.

were nine basic classes, determined according to reading ability, but some other subjects had more or fewer levels. Promotion was going on constantly on an individual basis; it depended on whether the child had mastered a particular skill or learned a certain set of facts. There were, therefore, no grades as the term was later used. A child entered school, stayed as long as he wanted to, and progressed as far as he could. When he left, if he had gone to the top class in every subject, he would presumably be ready for a grammar school, but whether he went or not was for him and his parents to decide, and whether he was ready or not was for the grammar school master to decide. The school system did not certify students or promote them beyond the common level.

Some schoolmen had recognized a need for more accessible high school facilities in the 1820's. Again, as in the case of the Sunday schools and the Lancasterian schools, inspiration came from across the Atlantic. In 1818, John Griscom, a central figure in New York reform efforts as well as a prosperous schoolmaster and a noted lecturer in chemistry, journeyed to Europe, where he met such famed Europeans as LaFayette, Scott, and Wordsworth, visited schools, and spoke with educators. The success of the Free School Society in New York had led him to wonder about the applicability of monitorial instruction to the high school level. In his journal he wrote: "On visiting the High School of Edinburgh, and becoming acquainted with its gifted principal, now Professor Pillans, my doubts of the possibility of applying the system to classical education with entire success, were fully removed."[29] The Edinburgh High School was "eminent almost to a proverb," Griscom said, even though each master taught about 150 boys with the help of monitors, and there were nearly 900 boys in all.[30]

Griscom corresponded with James Pillans on his return, getting advice on the establishment of a similar school in New York. He founded a share-holding society for the purpose, built a large brick building, engaged a successful private classics teacher as coprincipal, and in 1825 opened the New York High School. It soon filled

29. John H. Griscom, *Memoir of John Griscom* (New York, 1859), pp. 201–202.
30. *Ibid.,* p. 202; John Griscom, *Monitorial Instruction . . . an Address . . . at the Opening of the New York High-School* (New York, 1859), p. 100.

up with 650 boys whose parents were eager to pay the low tuition rates. The neighboring private schools were deprived of some of their pupils, and private masters in general were against the application of the monitorial system to higher subjects. They promptly expelled Griscom and his colleague from the Teachers Society.[31] Despite this opposition and the initial chaos of organizing 650 pupils on a new plan, the school prospered. The trustees began a girls' school on the same plan, and the teachers organized a society to discuss policy and pedagogy. However, Griscom's associate was killed in a stagecoach accident, the girls' school declined, never having been as successfully organized as the boys', and Griscom found the management very tiring. When the Mechanics' Society offered him a tidy profit for the building in 1831, he sold it, settled with the trustees, and closed the school.[32] The constant criticism of the private masters probably worried Griscom more than he admitted. John Pintard wrote his daughter in 1833: "I regret to say that the High Schools in our neighborhood have gone down. They could not it seems stand private competition . . . It pained me to read the notice on the wall. Sic transit. It was a good effort."[33]

Many people, however, thought that the monitorial system was not suitable to secondary education. Thus, the first effort to provide a quasi-public high school in New York failed. Had it continued, it might have been integrated into the expanding system, but at this time there was more demand for public attention to the poorer, younger children than for the aspiring grammar scholar. The public system extended downward before it extended upward because that is where the social problems lay. Even while Griscom was running the New York High School, he wrote a friend in Bristol, "Any publication thou canst lay hands upon, on infant schools, will be interesting to me, for education now absorbs nearly all my time and attention."[34] Meanwhile, Joanna Bethune, an indefatigable ex-

31. See James Pillans to John Griscom, Edinburgh, October 27, 1821, Griscom Papers, NYPL. The Teachers' Society had been revived in 1819 but disbanded again in 1825. George Batchelor, *History of all the Teachers' Associations ever established in the City of New York . . .* (New York, 1861), p. 6.

32. Griscom, *Memoir*, pp. 211–214; New York High Schools, Minutes of the Teachers, 1829, NYHS.

33. John Pintard to his daughter, March 1, 1833 in *Letters from John Pintard*, vol. IV (New York, NYHS *Collections*, 1940), p. 130.

34. Griscom, *Memoir*, p. 210.

perimenter, was also studying the infant school movement in England. In 1827 Governor Clinton suggested that she and her friends form an association to introduce this innovation in New York.

With Clinton as their patron, the ladies organized the Infant School Society and opened a school for children from eighteen months to six years old in the basement of a church. The governor implied that infant schools should become a part of the system when he praised them in his 1828 annual message as "the pedestal to the pyramid."[35] The Public School Society agreed, and they assigned a committee to study the question. The two "foundation axioms" of the committee's positive report were "that the inculcation of moral, ideal, and literal knowledge cannot be commenced at too early a period after the faculty of speech is developed" and that the Society should provide "a place in which the younger children of the poor may pass the day comfortably . . . instead of wandering the streets, exposed to the contamination of vice." The first axiom, based on Lockean psychology, was reinforced by the Society's growing mistrust of the family's influence on its most worrisome clients. The second axiom affirmed and extended the custodial responsibility of the school in a city with problems of working mothers and vagrant children.

Having decided that "it is expedient that infant schools be gradually established throughout the city," the committee concluded that it would be more efficient and convenient for the Society itself to operate the infant schools, a foregone conclusion at this stage in the system's development. If something was needed in quantity, the Society could do it best.[36] In a series of moves between 1829 and 1832 the Society took over the operation of the schools, with the ladies of the Infant School Society as advisors. In 1832 a committee appointed to visit the Boston schools spurred the Society's efforts by reporting that in that city facilities for younger children had helped reduce the vagrancy problem. The trustees proceeded to hire women teachers and eliminate the monitorial procedures

35. Bourne, *PSS,* p. 659. See DeWitt Clinton to Joanna Bethune, June 9, 1827, and October 1, 1827, DeWitt Clinton Papers, CU, vol. 23, pp. 141, 194.
36. Bourne, *PSS,* pp. 660–661.

for their youngest charges, being persuaded by the Infant School
Society ladies that small children required the attention and love
of an adult woman, not drill and repetition by an older student.
Eventually they assigned the first four (later five) reading classes
to these schools and regularized promotion requirements from one
level to the next. The primary schools became an articulated part
of the system.[37]

Meanwhile the Public School Society had discussed the need for
a central high school as early as 1826, and in an *Address to the
Public* in 1829 they again emphasized that a complete system would
need both classical and English high school facilities, as Boston had,
plus a school for teachers. But infant schools and common schools
were the basis of the system "and until its foundations are firmly
and amply laid, we would not proceed another step." Again in
1832 they recorded, "As part of a perfect system, the Committee
looks towards the establishment of a high school, or seminary for
the higher branches of an English education," but again they said
it would have to await further development of the lower schools.[38]

They did, however, add some higher subjects like astronomy and
algebra in their existing schools, and they appointed assistant teachers to replace student monitors for these higher branches.[39] Again,
vertical extension of the system modified the use of monitors. While
the extension upward increased the curricular hierarchy through
which the student could pass, the use of assistant teachers introduced another level into the system's hierarchy of personnel. One
could now be promoted from student to monitor, then monitor general, assistant teacher, teacher, principal, and, by mid-century, assistant superintendent, and superintendent. This creation of career
patterns within the system reinforced the bureaucracy. It produced
lifelong employees instead of transients, people committed to the
system instead of competing innovators. The hierarchy gave the
system's employees something to look forward to, and it provided

37. *Ibid.*, pp. 663–664; Boese, *Public Education*, p. 121; PSS, Primary
School Committee Minutes, July 1, 1846; *A Manual of the System of Discipline
and Instruction for the Schools of the Public School Society of New York*
(New York, 1850), p. 17.

38. Bourne, *PSS*, pp. 107, 116; Public School Society Minutes, December,
1832.

39. Boese, *Public Education*, p. 226; Batchelor, *Teachers Associations*, p. 9.

the system with a means of reward. This sense of security and common enterprise, bought at the price of subordination within the system, constituted a basic change in the teaching profession.

The Society's desire to perfect their system with a grammar school level was deferred longer than they expected and was finally taken out of their hands altogether. The depression of the late 1830's and the intense Catholic controversy of 1840–1842 prevented any action in those years, and the Maclay bill prohibited the Public School Society from expanding its facilities. It was left to the Board of Education, the new heirs of the system, to launch the Free Academy, the "splendid crown of our Common School system."[40] Summing up its place in the system, a speaker told the New York Historical Society in 1857 that the Academy "gives completeness to the system of public instruction, and is an integrant branch of the whole system for the enlightenment of the people."[41]

By 1850, then, the vertical extension of the system was complete. The hierarchy was continuous; students passed through it according to explicit, standard rules, in theory, at least. From age three or four until receiving the bachelor's degree a child could receive tuition-free instruction in the unified system. It was a Jeffersonian accomplishment, but it was not achieved because someone had conceived of such a hierarchy of free schooling back in 1787. It developed through a seemingly inexorable process of consolidation, extension, and articulation of school programs in response to the schooling needs, primarily moral and social, of New York's burgeoning population.

The sense of accomplishment that schoolmen enthusiastically exhibited suggests a symbolic and psychological function of the systematization process. Schoolmen were beset with problems; the public and the schoolmen themselves increasingly looked to the schools to solve social ills that they could at best only alleviate. They could not, after all, harmonize the city's economic or ethnic groups or end vagrancy and crime. These jobs would never be finished; in the meantime, the creation of a system served as an attainable goal. It could be completed. One could diagram it and point to the buildings. There was a sense of finality to the metaphors about the key-

40. *Putnam's Monthly,* vol. II, No. 7 (July 1853), p. 9.
41. John W. Francis, *Old New York: 50 Years Reminiscences, 1804–1857* (New York, 1858), p. 188.

stone of the arch and the pedestal of the pyramid which was more gratifying than the reality: the transience of the students, the conflict with the Catholics, and the continuing vagrancy and crime.[42]

Pride in the system, independent of its success in solving the problems that generated it, can also be seen in the imposing buildings the system built. There was a complete change between 1800 and 1850 in the architectural identity of the school. In the eighteenth century a "school" was essentially a person, one who held classes in an upstairs apartment or at most in a schoolhouse which looked much like other houses. But the builders of the public school system, anxious to escape the stigma of their charity school beginnings and to bring their schoolchildren out of the damp church basements where many of them had started, developed an urge to create grand public buildings which would be permanent and prominent. The Lancasterian plan, by demanding especially large spaces, encouraged this development. Reports of the Board of Education in the 1840's and 1850's increasingly emphasized floor plans and illustrations of public schools. The principal result of impressive school buildings, of course, was improved facilities for education. The secondary effect, however, was to further differentiate the school from the rest of the society. The architectural trend mirrored institutional development. The buildings, no matter how useful, were also ornaments to the success and permanence of the system. They were objects of civic pride, but that made them monuments in, rather than parts of, the city where the people lived.

STANDARDIZATION AND THE VALUES OF THE SYSTEM

By 1850 the hierarchical development of the system was complete. The proprietorship of a unified system gave the schoolmen an opportunity to put their theories of efficiency to work. The horizontal development of the system, in which a majority of the city's common schools were consolidated, made it possible to offer the same curriculum under the same rules to all the students in the system. The arguments of the Public School Society in favor of standardized curriculum and method were, basically, that different

42. On goal displacement as a general feature of bureaucracy, see Robert K. Merton, "Bureaucratic Structure and Personality," in Merton et al., eds., *Reader in Bureaucracy* (New York, Free Press, 1952), pp. 365–366.

books and procedures made transfers difficult and comparisons between schools impossible. Independent schools were, in a word, inefficient. But other values than just efficiency urged the schoolmen
to develop standardized control of the schools: the desire to be
fair to all those who would accept the rules of the system, and
the desire to raise the quality of teaching. The dilemma of standardized impartiality and quality control through systematization
is that the decision-making processes are taken out of the hands
of the person who deals directly with the system's clients—the children—and therefore tends to depersonalize the relationship. The
teacher becomes more a part of the apparatus and less able to be
flexible. Also, to the extent that the system intentionally masks the
identity of the student to ensure impartiality, the student loses part
of his individuality. Formalized impartiality leads to anonymity.

Depersonalization in the schools came from other sources as well.
The scale of operations in the city's schools, which had necessitated
the systematization, also increased the anonymity of the student.
A boy who went to James Liddell's school in 1796 with 60 other
children might have gone to Free School No. 3 in 1820, with 600
other children. The problem of numbers was, of course, common
to all collective enterprises in the city, so the experience of getting
lost in the crowd was not unique to the schoolchild. But again,
it should be emphasized, the moral mission of the schools reinforced
the bureaucratic trend toward standardization. The schools became
institutions set apart from, and in some respects, opposed to, the
rest of the students' world. In the case of the indigent, the immigrant, the irreligious, or simply the impish child, the school told
him to put off part of his personality when he crossed the doorstep.
The effort to harmonize the population meant, inevitably, a further
depersonalization.

Schoolmen were not ogres; at least, as a group they included
no more than their share of ogres. The standardization of teacher
and student behavior was not designed to stifle creativity or healthy
latitude, whether it did or not. The schoolmen attacked "traces
of nationality" in German immigrant children because they associated them with personal traits that they believed were destructive
for the child as well as the society. Nor did they establish rigid
procedures for teachers in order to destroy the teachers' personal
strengths, but to enforce general policies they believed in, some of

which were very humane. Nevertheless, without making a value judgment on particular policies, one can conclude that the process of standardization made the relationship of the governors to the teachers, and by extension, of the teachers to the students, a primarily negative one. The main function of the downward relationship was to discover infractions and eliminate deviation. The examples which follow will illustrate the ways in which the governors of the system sought to do that.

THE WAYS OF THE BUREAUCRACY

When the Free School Society began in 1805, the trustees did not have to worry much about regulating a system. They had their Lancasterian tracts as a guide, and they were even willing, in the spirit of their new enterprise, to innovate a little. Clinton, the Society's president, said in 1808 that the first teacher had "generally followed the prescribed plan. Wherever he has deviated, he has improved."[43] By 1825, however, when the Society had six schools, they were prepared to argue that differences between schools were bad. After they won their battle with Bethel, they set out to prove their point. Standardization, they found, required more than just printed manuals. In 1828, they hired Samuel Seton, first as a visitor to recruit students, but soon after as a supervisor, the first full-time, system-level professional in the city's history.[44] Seton investigated charges of infractions, conducted examinations of students' progress, reported to the board, and carried out their decisions. He was an "agent" of the trustees, not a superintendent with executive powers, but the distinction was probably slight in practice since Seton was himself a trustee.

Examinations, as is often the case with standardized testing, were used as a measure of the teachers' success as well as the students'. When a whole school was substandard in achievement, the trustees held the teachers responsible. In 1831 a committee was assigned "to reexamine Boys' Departments Nos. 2, 4, 8, and 9, with power to invite the principals thereof—one or all—to resign." Three were fired as a result.[45] The trustees made such comparisons regularly,

43. Bourne, *PSS,* p. 20.
44. Boese, *Public Education,* pp. 255–256.
45. *Ibid.,* p. 226.

"to ascertain the relative standing of the several schools to each other." The most common reason for firing teachers was continuous substandard examination results.[46]

The trustees hoped that by firing the teachers whose students had not progressed that they would raise the quality of instruction. To this negative inducement, however, they did attempt to add a more positive approach. In 1848 the Primary School Committee appointed one of their teachers, Lucey Whitney, to be a system-wide supervisor. The manual should be her guide, they said, and uniformity the aim. But since primary divisions had not been regulated quite so strictly as the upper divisions, there would be some differences. "As a model or pattern school, you are at liberty to take your own (No. 19), the Committee not having found one that meets their views better . . . You are advised to communicate to this Committee for approval any particular plan or practice in other schools which may be considered better than your own. All teachers should be learners."[47] Miss Whitney tried to help teachers improve their pedagogy, and her reports on the orderliness and efficiency of the different schools provided a further basis on which the trustees could rate teachers.

Concerning a more specific practice, corporal punishment, the trustees also found that negative sanctions were not sufficient. Lancaster had vociferously opposed physical punishments; although he dreamed up some rather bizarre substitutes to shame or ridicule misbehaving students, his basic mechanism for motivation was competition. He and his followers strove continuously to eliminate corporal punishment, but it was an uphill fight, for caning was an almost universal practice in nineteenth-century schools, both public and private. The New York Free School Society trustees were committed Lancasterian advocates, and they attempted to abolish corporal punishment by executive order. In January 1823, they ordered that punishment with the rod cease, and only after "every other persuasion has failed, a small leathern strap map be applied to the palm of the hand." The teachers protested that they would not be able to keep order, and the trustees relented, first extending

46. PSS, Executive Committee Minutes, September 2, 1841, December 4, 1851.
47. Instructions to Miss Whitney, September, 1848, loose MS in vol. 58, PSS Records, NYHS.

the permission for strapping to the whole hand, and finally, in June, repealing the original order. They then advised a limited use of the rod, never on the head. The trustees called the teachers together again in 1825 to urge "mild moral government" and condemn severe corporal punishment.[48] They continued to make further rulings, for example, that only full teachers, not assistants, could punish children, but negative regulations seemed to do little good.

In 1838 a special committee on corporal punishment turned to more positive inducements. They decided to offer a premium of $100 to any teacher who could "first show that the school can be conducted successfully without the infliction of the common daily corporal punishment." Apparently, no teacher was able, or perhaps inclined, to demonstrate the possibility, for the award was not given, and in 1840 the Executive Committee received complaints from the neighbors of School No. 15 that the teachers were punishing the students too harshly.[49] Soon, however, the trustees' persistence paid off. By 1845 Seton was able to announce that the girls' division of No. 5 had been three years with no form of corporal punishment and six schools had not used the rod. The next year the agent reported again that "one school had been conducted twelve months without any corporal punishment and in many schools the amount of that kind of punishment has lessened." The teachers of these schools were given certificates of merit.[50] The trustees also instructed Miss Whitney, the new supervisor, to lay particular stress on discipline without corporal punishment. It is well to note their use of centralized control to encourage humane policies because the discussion above has often emphasized the negative effects of systematization.

By mid-century the governors of the system regulated many aspects of school conduct that the eighteenth-century schoolmaster had decided for himself. In addition to prescribing curriculum, classroom procedures, hours, and examinations, the Public School Society investigated and prohibited unauthorized use of their schoolrooms, especially by their own teachers, many of whom were giving private lessons in French or music after hours. They investigated and eliminated unauthorized books donated to the school libraries.

48. Boese, *Public Education,* p. 224; Palmer, *Public School,* pp. 58–59.
49. PSS, Executive Committee Minutes, April 5, 1838, February 6, 1840.
50. PSS, Executive Committee Minutes, December 21, 1845, May 7, 1846.

They sent their agent to find out why some schools had omitted
public exhibitions, armed with a directive that "compliance with
the bye-law in relation to Public Exhibitions is expected and insisted
upon." They sent him out again to discover why some teachers
were planning vacations for a different week than the schedule
called for, and to prevent them from doing so.[51] In order to make
the school inspections more fair the Public School Society resolved
"to withhold from the teachers information of the day on which
their schools are to be examined," and in order to make entrance
examinations to the Free Academy more fair the Board of Education resolved to withhold the names of the candidates from the
examining professors.[52] The Public School Society gradually standardized teachers' pay scales, and, as one might expect, the teachers
responded by petitioning collectively for raises.[53] Standardization
thus changed the life of both teachers and students.

When the Public School Society turned over its schools to the
Board of Education in 1853, nearly all of the features associated
with modern urban school bureaucracies were already evident. The
degree of functional change after 1853, of course, should not be
minimized. At the end of the nineteenth century, with a much
larger high school population and the advent of differentiated cur-
ricula, the schools became much more involved in career choice
and training. Nevertheless, the organizational structure of the school
system had been established in New York City in the antebellum
period. The system applied collective decisions to a large mass of
people; it promulgated detailed procedures and then attempted to
ensure quality by eliminating deviation from those procedures. The
system's governors employed supervision, inspection, punishments,
and rewards to encourage uniform performance, and they made
explicit the relationships between levels in the authoritative hierarchy for teachers and the curriculum hierarchy for students.

One of the problems in trying to encourage fairness and high

51. PSS, Executive Committee Minutes, July 6 and August 3, 1837. The
quotation is from August 3.
52. PSS, Executive Committee Minutes, September 6, 1838; Robert Kelly,
*Addresses Delivered upon the occasion of the Opening of the Free Academy,
June 27, 1849* (New York, 1849), p. 11.
53. PSS, Executive Committee Minutes, December 1, 1836; March 2, May
18, and July 6, 1837, December 2, 1852.

quality through standardization is that people are not, in fact, machines, and they cannot be relied upon, fortunately or unfortunately, to be where a diagram says they should be or perform the way a manual says they should. When the supervisor, Miss Whitney, went around the system assessing efficiency, she found that one of the main problems was teacher absence. In several schools the teacher-monitor-pupil hierarchy was nonexistent because of frequent teacher absence, and the monitors had all they could do to keep order.[54] When teachers were present, they did not, of course, always apply the rules impartially. James Steers entered a Public School in the late 1830's, and he was placed in the Junior Sixth, or lowest class in the upper division. The teacher did not like Steers, and in five years the boy was promoted only to the Junior Seventh class. Although other boys said his writing was better than theirs, he was never promoted from slate to copybook as they were. When the Board of Education built a ward school nearby, he transferred there, and, he said, "to my astonishment I was immediately put into the highest class in the school."[55] No system could entirely standardize people's feelings, any more than it could eliminate crime or erase a child's ethnic identity.

It could not do any of those things entirely, but it could do all of them partially. In a city of diversity, rancor, and chaos, the school system offered a promise of symmetry, harmony, and orderly progress. How effectively the schools contributed to those goals in the larger society is impossible to assess, although its contribution was surely gradual and imperfect. Within the system, however, despite personal prejudices and constant minor infractions, the regimentation worked, partly because its main participants—the children—were more malleable than adults, and partly because the schools could expel dissenters. Finally, at an even further remove from the social realities of education, the system provided a symbolic gratification, a sense of getting control of the problem, and, in the middle of the nineteenth century, a sense of closure, of having finished something. That something was a school system, solid and

54. Miss Whitney's Report, June 27, 1849, loose MS in PSS Records, vol. 58, NYHS, pp. 4, 7, 20.
55. Philip J. Mosenthal and Charles F. Horne, eds., *The City College: Memories of Sixty Years* (New York, G. P. Putnam's Sons, 1907), pp. 160, 164; there were four classes, numbered Six through Nine, with junior and senior divisions in each.

permanent. It had been started in 1805 by a group of philanthropic men who hoped to usher in "a new era in education." They did not foresee nor plan the highly centralized bureaucracy that was to grow up from their "parent seminary," but by 1850 it was established, and its characteristics are present in urban school bureaucracies today.

Conclusion

RECAPITULATION

By 1850 New York City's schools had shifted from private to public control and had shifted predominantly from pay to free tuition. Although these developments were important, nominal public control and free tuition did not change the actual schooling of children in the city as much as some earlier histories have implied. These changes did not, for example, substantially alter the percentage or socioeconomic complexion of children attending school. The available evidence suggests that over 50 percent of the city's school-age children attended school annually in the 1790's, when the unregulated schooling practices of the colonial period still prevailed, and that between 50 and 75 percent attended school in the middle of the nineteenth century.[1] Children from a wide socioeconomic range attended the pay schools of the 1790's; although

1. The computation for the 1790's estimate is found in Table 10 above. To be strictly comparable, 1850 figures would have to be total enrollment, not average attendance, but the 1796 figures were based on actual student lists and therefore eliminated duplicates (children who attended more than one school in the year), which is impossible for nineteenth century summary figures (see Table 12 above). The rate given there for 1829 (58 percent), is based on total enrollment, not average attendance, slightly inflated because of a computation problem. The 1850 Census figure cited there, which resulted in an estimated enrollment rate of about 55 percent, is ambiguous. It says "number of pupils," which implies total enrollment, but does not give the source and is much lower than Board of Education reports of "Whole Number Taught" (see Table 13 above for reports of over 100 percent). Figures for 1796 and 1850 are also not strictly comparable because of the change of organization in the schools. In 1850 the schools were active recruiters attempting to increase their

many of the city's poor in the 1790's may have been left out of these schools and the charity schools, the free schools of nineteenth-century New York also excluded many poor children who had to work or were unacceptable in appearance or behavior. The most significant changes in this period were rather in the organization and purpose of the schools.

In colonial New York the initiative for schooling was on the individual. Schools were not the critical agencies of literarcy, job training, cultural assimilation, or moral education, although schools of various kinds supplemented the family, apprenticeship, and the churches in those functions. Many children learned their three R's in the city's numerous and inexpensive pay schools or charity schools, but in other respects schooling was supplementary. Predetermined patterns of educational activities for children were therefore vague.

New Yorkers of the late colonial period found this unorganized mode of schooling adequate; indeed, it was peculiarly well suited to the city's social condition. New York's cosmopolitan history—her commercial prominence and her amalgamated Dutch-English population—left the city with an unusual cultural makeup in the eighteenth century. Although there was a general trend toward the use of the English language, the non-English cultural groups maintained their integrity, and no single set of religious ideas or social mores predominated. Ethnic and religious differences were not correlated with social disruption or immoral conduct. When cultural tension did arise, as in the King's College controversy, it was ultimately neutralized because the factions were roughly equal. Conflict suspended at the leadership level had very little effect on the operation of schooling in late colonial New York.

New immigration upset this delicate balance between harmony and diversity. Irish and French immigration in the 1790's foreshadowed the cultural and economic problems of nineteenth-century immigration: the newcomers were predominantly poor and predominantly Catholic. At first, the numbers of immigrants were

---

enrollment and liable to overestimation in order to receive more state funds. The upper limit of 75 percent suggested above is based on the census report of "Number Attending School During the Year, As Returned by Families" (*U.S. Census, 1850,* Table 8), which, one would suspect, is an overestimate since many parents might have feared disapproval or some official action if they reported their children not in school.

small enough to be assimilated or ignored. The unregulated and diverse schools of the colonial period prevailed in the 1790's. Soon, however, in response to increasing poverty and crime in the city, New York's leaders turned to schooling as a deliberate instrument for acculturation of those whom the colonial arrangements were leaving out.

Despite the coincidence of an active teachers' organization and a state law for school support, the city failed to systematize its common schools in the 1790's. The city's leaders were unwilling to systematize schooling through any sweeping subsidization of the independent schoolmasters. The colonial mode of schooling, unable to accommodate the great influx of resourceless newcomers, atrophied in the nineteenth century, and the independent schools became restricted more and more to the wealthy minority. Meanwhile, the city's public school system arose from the charity schools, which had played a traditional but numerically slight role in the colonial period.

The balance of New York's cultural diversity had kept the city government from becoming involved in common schooling, and independent schools had sufficed. Also, the inherited concept of public education emphasized training the elite for leadership, and providing a modicum of charity schooling for the poor. Thus the first nineteenth-century effort to respond to urban problems was under private auspices, not governmental, and it sought to expand charity schooling, not to subsidize schools for those who could pay. Beginning in 1805 with this traditional approach but a significant nondenominational emphasis, the New York Free School Society gradually became the main provider of common schooling in the city, with the blessing of the city's government and most of its citizens. Although the problem of religion in the Society's schools was more serious to some Protestant groups in the city than it was to the Quakers who dominated the early Society, the city's native Protestants gradually acquiesced in the development of a system of nondenominational schools which would teach basic social morality with a Protestant bias, in addition to providing rudimentary literary training. They were spurred toward this goal by the threatening alienation between respectable native New Yorkers and the city's working class, especially the immigrants, who were mostly poor and Catholic.

Residential segregation, economic stratification, and cultural diversity combined to estrange the group that founded the schools and the group they hoped would attend them. The schools became the principal setting for the confrontation of two cultures, which made schooling a very different process than in the late colonial period. Although the schoolmen had difficulty in attracting and holding in the schools those children they most wanted to reform, they persisted because they associated crime, vagrancy, and immorality with cultural traits, because they believed that poverty resulted primarily from moral failings, and because they thought that all of these problems could be attacked through schooling.

The city's population multiplied tenfold from 1800 to 1850, and the tremendous increase in the scale of problems, combined with the alienation and segregation of the well-to-do from the poor, increased people's reliance on institutional solutions to social problems. Reformers tried to rationalize charity, standardize schools, and incarcerate vagrants. These were symptoms of a general effort to impose systematic solutions on chaotic urban conditions. The frequency of personal contacts across class lines, the possibility of ad hoc decisions, and the relevance of individual circumstances in making judgments declined as the population soared.

In education these developments led to uniform interschool regulation and an explicitly hierarchical promotion structure. Examinations, curriculum, salaries, and pedagogical routines were standardized. Uniformity became the most essential value of the system, not only because the schools were a primary agent of moral conformism but also because schoolmen wanted to raise minimum standards and encourage rewards based on merit, both for teachers and students. While the "perfected" system may not have brought common education to any greater proportion of the poor than the old colonial schools had, it was a way of coping with a problem of much greater scale, and, by 1850, it provided explicit avenues of advancement to free higher education for some lucky workingmen's sons who had the talent and could stay in the system.

The rapid growth of the city between 1800 and 1850 had fostered the development of a coordinated school system, and that process of systematization transformed not only the organization of schools but their purpose in the city. The schools became active recruiters and pressed for coercive authority to bring all wayward children into the system. Schools became the agents of a majoritarian ethic; as the main institutions for acculturation, the schools were explicitly opposed to the informal learning environment of many of the city's children. It is somewhat ironic that the schools became more conformist as the population became more diverse, although it is also logical; the latter caused the former. It is more ironic that the very effort to create a single, unified school system caused a crisis for the city's Catholics and led to the development of a separate new system of schools. Despite their failure to attract the children of the very poor, the very wealthy, and the very Catholic, however, the public schools as a coordinated system were transformed into an engine of great potential influence, for they were now amenable to uniform policy decisions. The potential importance of schooling in resolving social problems was thus greatly magnified; schools were seen in a wholly different way than in the colonial period.

EPILOGUE: FURTHER REFLECTIONS

The systematization of the schools allowed general policies to influence all schools uniformly and thus transformed both the means and the ends of schooling in New York City. But the bureaucracy which resulted from this systematization has, in the years since this transformation, often proved unwieldy and ineffective, and its effects have been, in large measure, illiberal and stifling. Educational reformers in New York and elsewhere have often sought, and still seek, to rehumanize the school bureaucracy, to encourage more value pluralism in the schools, and place more emphasis on personal development than on preparation for a role in society. The difficulty of that task lies in the fact that the school system reflects larger social trends, some of which seem irreversible, such as the anonymity of relations in mass society. Also, the school system performs social functions like occupational preparation and the granting of credentials that are desired not just by school bureaucrats but by the great majority of people in the society. Other functions, such as behavioral assimilation and moral training, have resulted from a broad consensus among community leaders and parents. Given New York's exploding population and cultural diversity, plus the growing belief in the efficacy of a common school experience, it seems implausible that schoolmen of the early nineteenth century could have chosen any alternative to the creation of a unitary system.

If there is to be a new diversification in schooling today—if the creation of a more just society demands more genuine value pluralism in the schools, and I believe it does—it will require great imagination and the will to alter some basic functions of school systems. The standardization of the schools is bound up in the process of increasing complexity in society. The roots of educational systematization are not found simply in the ill will of individuals, in the recurring vogues of efficiency jargon in schools, or in the inward turning and sterility of periodic humanist reforms, although all of these illumine the more basic development generated by economic and cultural needs. The roots are in the economic system, in ethnic problems, and in the very demography to which urban school systems must respond.

There is also a philosophical tension between individualized treatment and impartiality. Standardization has not only the negative value basis of conformity but the positive value basis of impartiality. Standardization and conformism in the schools may tend to stifle creativity, alienate those whose culture it attacks, and blunt students' motivation to learn by dispensing standardized units of instruction. But standardization also represents an effort to hold in check the personal prejudices and whimsical judgments of individuals by enforcing collective decisions about fair play and opportunity. Thus, those who wish to reshape the system in ways that will liberate individuals will also have to attend to the problem of ensuring fairness, however imperfectly the present rule-governed system may do it.

In large organizations the balance between individual freedom and group conformism is at best delicate. Historically, the pressure of numbers has constantly tipped that balance further toward conformism. Social disruption, caused by inequitable distribution of income and housing, and by ethnic and racial diversity, has intensified the demographic pressure in cities. These forces have shaped the urban school system from its earliest stages to the present. Its present form was not inevitable, and it is not impervious to change;

but, in view of the deeply rooted causes of systematization, more widespread and fundamental effort than is now apparent will be needed to change the bureaucratic functions and procedures of schools. The present school system is a reflection of the city's persistent institutional approach to urban problems, one which has aimed ideally to uplift, hopefully to reconcile, and minimally to control, its turbulent population.

BIBLIOGRAPHICAL NOTE   INDEX

Bibliographical Note

Although this study focuses on the creation of a unitary school system, it has attempted to trace the social as well as the institutional history of schooling in New York City. The sources of evidence are therefore widely varied. A thorough bibliography is available in the doctoral dissertation, The Origins of an Urban School System: New York, 1750–1850 (Harvard University, 1970), of which this book is a revision. The following note suggests the types of primary sources used and reviews the most relevant secondary works.

The holdings of the New York Municipal Archives, chiefly the Filed Papers of the City Clerk, are useful in studying the city's social and governmental history, but because they are not indexed beyond 1800, work in these files is difficult and time-consuming. The papers from the period before 1800 are indexed and proved a gold mine for the analysis of schooling in 1796 presented in Chapter Two. The principal archival source for the other chapters was the New-York Historical Society's rich collection of family and institutional papers, including seventy volumes of New York Public School Society records, as well as papers of John Pintard, John Stanford, Stephen Allen, and other men involved in the city's educational development. Relevant manuscript holdings of the New York Public Library were also consulted, such as the correspondence to John Griscom, the Methodist Church records, and the minutes of the New York Almshouse Commissioners. The Columbia University Library helps round out the city's educational history with Columbia (and King's) College records and the important DeWitt Clinton Papers. Other manuscript sources were scattered: wills and census returns in various city offices, baptisms and Sunday school records in the churches.

Published sources from the period studied were equally important. As the footnotes suggest, considerable reliance was placed on the traditional sources of the institutional historian, in this case the reports and promotional literature of organizations which dealt with children, such as the Public School Society, the Board of Education, the New York Association for Improving the Condition of the Poor, the Orphan Asylum Society, and the Children's Aid Society, supplemented by the published minutes of the Common Council and reports of the state legislature. I. N. Phelps Stokes, *Iconography of Manhattan Island,* 6 vols. (New York, R. H. Dodd, 1895–1928) is invaluable for studying the city's government and institutions.

It is very difficult to get at the students' view of education in this period except by inference. Some sense of education as a personal experience was gained from publications like Mark Van Doren, ed., *The Correspondence of Aaron Burr and his daughter Theodosia* (New York, Covici-Friede, 1929), Helen M. Morgan, ed., *A Season in New York, 1801: Letters of Harriet and Maria Trumbull* (Pittsburgh, University of Pittsburgh Press, 1969), and A. W. Moynihan, *Jack Winthrop of Old 15: A Story of School-Life in a New York City Public School* (New York, 1887). The activities and views of the leaders were traced in memoirs such as Samuel Halliday, *The Lost and Found, or Life Among the Poor* (New York, 1859), and Stephen W. Tyng, *Forty Years' Experience in Sunday Schools* (New York, 1860), and in published correspondence, such as Harry R. Warfel, ed., *Letters of Noah Webster* (New York, Library Publishers, 1953), Lawrence Kehoe, ed., *Complete Works of the Most Rev. John Hughes,* 2 vols. (New York, 1866), Samuel L. Knapp, ed., *The Life of Thomas Eddy* (London, 1836), and the *Letters from John Pintard,* 4 vols. (New York, NYHS, *Collections,* 1937–1940). The city's social condition, and men's reactions to it, are further revealed in such books as Kenneth and Anna M. Roberts, eds., *Moreau de St. Méry's American Journey, 1793–1798* (Garden City, N.Y., Doubleday, 1947), Ward Stafford, *New Missionary Field* (New York, 1817), James Hardie, *The Description of the City of New York* (New York, 1827), Philopedos [pseud.], *A Few Remarks About Sick Children in New York* (New York, 1852), and Samuel C. Busey, *Immigration, Its Evils and Consequences* (New York, 1856).

Numerous secondary works aided both narrative and interpretation. On the social history of America in general during this period, the most useful books were Jackson T. Main, *The Social Structure of Revolutionary America* (Princeton, Princeton University Press, 1965), Marvin Meyers, *The Jacksonian Persuasion: Politics and Belief* (Stanford, Stanford University Press, 1957), Robert H. Bremner, *From the Depths: The Discovery of Poverty in the United States* (New York, New York University Press, 1956), Carl Bridenbaugh, *Cities in Revolt: Urban Life in America, 1743–1776* (New York, Alfred Knopf, 1955), and Charles I. Foster, *An Errand of Mercy: The Evangelical United Front, 1790–1837* (Chapel Hill, University of North Carolina Press, 1960); on New York in particular, see Sidney

I. Pomerantz, *New York, an American City, 1783–1803; A Study of Urban Life* (New York, Columbia University Studies in History, Economics, and Public Law, No. 442, 1938), Raymond A. Mohl, *Poverty in New York, 1783–1825* (New York, Oxford University Press, 1971), Carroll S. Rosenberg, *Religion and the Rise of the American City: The New York City Mission Movement, 1812–1870* (Ithaca, Cornell University Press, 1971), and Douglas T. Miller, *Jacksonian Aristocracy: Class and Democracy in New York, 1830–1860* (New York, 1967).

The two premier works on education in colonial America are Bernard Bailyn, *Education in the Forming of American Society: Needs and Opportunities for Study* (Chapel Hill, University of North Carolina Press, 1960), and Lawrence A. Cremin, *American Education: The Colonial Experience, 1607–1783* (New York, Harper and Row, 1970). These two landmarks of scholarship may be supplemented for New York with William Kemp, *Support of Schools in Colonial New York by the Society for the Propagation of the Gospel in Foreign Parts* (New York, Teachers College Contributions to Education, No. 56, 1913), William H. Kilpatrick, *The Dutch Schools of New Netherland and Colonial New York* (Washington, United States Bureau of Education, Bulletin No. 12, 1912), and Henry W. Dunshee, *History of the School of the Reformed Protestant Dutch Church in New York, 1633–1883* (New York, 2nd ed., 1883). On New York's educational institutions in the nineteenth century, see William O. Bourne, *History of the Public School Society of the City of New York* (New York, 1870), Thomas Boese, *Public Education in the City of New York: Its History, Condition and Statistics* (New York, 1869), A. Emerson Palmer, *The New York Public School: Being a History of Free Education in the City of New York* (New York, The Macmillan Company, 1905), and John F. Reigart, *The Lancasterian System of Instruction in the Schools of New York City* (New York, Teachers College Contributions to Education, No. 81, 1916), all dated but useful, plus Edwin W. Rice, *The Sunday School Movement, 1780–1917, and the American Sunday School Union, 1817–1917* (Philadelphia, The American Sunday School Union, 1917), Robert S. Pickett, *House of Refuge: Origins of Juvenile Reform in New York State, 1815–1857* (Syracuse, Syracuse University Press, 1969), and Miriam Z. Langsam, *Children's West: A History of the Placing-Out System of the New York Children's Aid Society, 1853–1890* (Madison, The State Historical Society of Wisconsin, 1964). Histories of individual schools and churches are numerous but repay study, for example, Edward S. Moffat, *Trinity School, New York City, 1709–1959* (unpub. diss., Columbia University, 1963), and Shepherd Knapp, *A History of the Brick Presbyterian Church in the City of New York* (New York, 1909).

Although the relationship between education and jobs is largely uncharted historically, the standard works on apprenticeship and labor have been helpful: Marcus Jernegan, *Laboring and Dependent Classes in Colonial America, 1607–1783* (Chicago, University of Chicago Press, 1931), Richard B. Morris, *Government and Labor in Early America* (New York, Columbia University Press, 1946), Carl Bridenbaugh, *The Colonial Craftsman* (New York, New York University Press, 1950), Paul H. Douglass, *American Apprenticeship and Industrial Education* (New York, Columbia University Studies in History, Economics, and Public Law, vol. 45, No. 2, 1921), Samuel McKee, *Labor in Colonial New York, 1664–1776* (New York, Columbia University Studies in History, Economics and Public Law, No. 410, 1935), and Robert F. Seybolt, *Apprenticeship and Apprenticeship Education in Colonial New England and New York* (New York, Teachers College Contributions to Education, No. 85, 1917). More recent and more suggestive is Stephan Thernstrom, *Poverty and Progress: Social Mobility in a Nineteenth Century City* (Cambridge, Harvard University Press, 1964).

On immigration Oscar Handlin, *The Uprooted* (Boston, Little, Brown, and Company, 1951) is an influential overview, and Maldwyn A. Jones, *American Immigration* (Chicago, University of Chicago Press, 1960) provides additional background, but Robert Ernst's detailed and sturdy work, *Immigrant Life in New York City, 1825–1863* (New York, King's Crown Press, 1949), proved most helpful to the present study. On nativism, Ray A. Billington, *The Protestant Crusade, 1800–1860: A Study of the Origins of American Nativism* (New York, Macmillan Company, 1938), is a lively compendium about a dreary phenomenon. The social history of Catholic schooling, like that of public schooling, needs much more work. Older studies useful for institutional and ideological developments include J. A. Burns, *The Catholic School System in the United States: Its Principles, Origin, and Establishment* (New York, 1908), Charles J. Mahoney, *The Relation of the State to Religious Education in Early New York, 1633–1825* (Washington, Catholic University of America Press, 1941), and Edward M. Connors, *Church-State Relationships in Education in the State of New York* (Washington, Catholic University of America Press, 1951). Vincent P. Lannie, *Public Money and Parochial Education: Bishop Hughes, Governor Seward, and the New York School Controversy* (Cleveland, Case Western Reserve University Press, 1968) is a detailed political study on a limited topic, while Robert D. Cross, "Origins of the Catholic Parochial Schools in America," *American Benedictine Review* 16 (1965), 194–209, the best general analysis, concentrates on the late nineteenth century. The development of church-state separation in education is traced in John W. Pratt, *Religion, Politics and Diversity: the Church-State Theme in New York History* (Ithaca, Cornell University Press, 1967).

The interpretation of public schooling presented in the present study

is not entirely consonant with any previous educational history. However, historical works that were suggestive in interpretation include
Albert Fishlow, "The American Common School Revival: Fact or
Fancy," in Henry Rosovsky, ed., *Industrialization in Two Systems:
Essays in Honor of Alexander Gerschenkron* (New York, Wiley,
1966), pp. 40–67, which draws attention away from the famous common school reformers of the 1840's, Anthony M. Platt, *The Child
Savers: The Invention of Delinquency* (Chicago, University of Chi-
cago Press, 1969), which questions the benevolence of juvenile in-
carceration, Michael B. Katz, *The Irony of Early School Reform:
Educational Innovation in Mid-Nineteenth Century Massachusetts*
(Cambridge, Harvard University Press, 1968), which takes a new
critical look at the social class basis of public schooling, and two
ground-breaking essays on educational bureaucracy, David B. Tyack,
"Bureaucracy and the Common School: The Example of Portland,
Oregon, 1851–1913," *American Quarterly* 19 (1967), 475–498, and
Michael B. Katz, "The Emergence of Bureaucracy in Urban Education: the Boston Case, 1850–1884," *History of Education Quarterly*
8 (1968), 155–188, 319–357. Two important works appeared after
this study was written: Michael B. Katz, *Class, Bureaucracy, and
Schools: The Illusion of Educational Change in America* (New York,
Praeger Publishers, 1971), a brief and provocative book which asks
many similar questions and arrives at rather more radical conclusions,
and David J. Rothman, *The Discovery of the Asylum: Social Order
and Disorder in the New Republic* (Boston, Little, Brown and Company, 1971), which traces the institutionalization of deviants in Jacksonian America, a process similar to the one described here for schools.
The excellent doctoral dissertation of Stanley K. Schultz, The Education of Urban Americans: Boston, 1789–1860 (University of Chicago,
1969), which provides many parallels with New York's development,
also came to hand after this study was completed. Among nonhistorical
works pertinent to the themes of this book the most provocative were
Jacques Ellul, *The Technological Society,* John Wilkinson, trans.
(New York, Alfred Knopf, 1964), an intricate analysis of "technique,"
the implementation of standardized solutions, Milton M. Gordon, *Assimilation in American Life: The Role of Race, Religion, and National Origins* (New York, Oxford University Press, 1964), which
contains a lucid conceptual framework for the processes of acculturation and assimilation, and Erving Goffman, *Asylums: Essays on the
Social Situation of Mental Patients and Other Inmates* (Garden City,
Anchor Books, 1961), which describes and illustrates the functional
characteristics of "total" institutions. Although none of these generated
the analysis of this book, each helped reinforce it in some way.

Index